Persuasion
University of Oklahoma Edition

Charles U. Larson
Northern Illinois University, Emeritus

THOMSON
™
WADSWORTH

Australia · Canada · Mexico · Singapore · Spain · United Kingdom · United States

THOMSON

WADSWORTH

Persuasion
Larson

Executive Editors:
Michele Baird, Maureen Staudt &
Michael Stranz

Project Development Manager:
Linda de Stefano

Marketing Coordinators:
Lindsay Annett and Sara Mercurio

Production/Manufacturing Supervisor:
Donna M. Brown

Pre-Media Services Supervisor:
Dan Plofchan

Rights & Permissions Specialists:
Kalina Hintz and Bahman Naraghi

Cover Image
Getty Images*

The Adaptable Courseware Program
consists of products and additions to
existing Thomson products that are
produced from camera-ready copy.
Peer review, class testing, and
accuracy are primarily the responsibility
of the author(s).

Persuasion/ Larson
ISBN 0-495-31571-0

International Divisions List

Asia (Including India):
Thomson Learning
(a division of Thomson Asia Pte Ltd)
5 Shenton Way #01-01
UIC Building
Singapore 068808
Tel: (65) 6410-1200
Fax: (65) 6410-1208

Australia/New Zealand:
Thomson Learning Australia
102 Dodds Street
Southbank, Victoria 3006
Australia

Latin America:
Thomson Learning
Seneca 53
Colonia Polano
11560 Mexico, D.F., Mexico
Tel (525) 281-2906
Fax (525) 281-2656

Canada:
Thomson Nelson
1120 Birchmount Road
Toronto, Ontario
Canada M1K 5G4
Tel (416) 752-9100
Fax (416) 752-8102

UK/Europe/Middle East/Africa:
Thomson Learning
High Holborn House
50-51 Bedford Row
London, WC1R 4LS
United Kingdom
Tel 44 (020) 7067-2500
Fax 44 (020) 7067-2600

Spain (Includes Portugal):
Thomson Paraninfo
Calle Magallanes 25
28015 Madrid
España
Tel 34 (0)91 446-3350
Fax 34 (0)91 445-6218

Custom Contents

PART I

Theoretical Premises

Persuasion rocks. It rocks not only our individual worlds but the whole world around us. Persuasion both changes our world and represents a way that our world changes us. Persuasion is about choice. Understanding persuasion helps us make better choices and is essential to live in our ever-changing world. It is clear that persuasion can make the world a better place just as Martin Luther King, Jr., made it clear through persuasion that society could be a better place.

Unfortunately, persuasion also has a dark side. We live in a period of reconstruction in the United States. We now face a different kind of enemy—and, perhaps, a different kind of *influence*, one that previously was unknown in this country. And persuasion is much larger than the United States and the Western world—today it is global. The more difficult task of reconstruction remains the restoration of trust in our major institutions. Trust in business leadership has also been shaken. Wall Street used persuasion to cover up years of corporate deceit, aided by one of the nation's elite accounting firms, and Enron was only the tip of the iceberg of what was to become a cascade of accounting scandals and insider trading. Trust in religious institutions was destroyed after repeated revelations of sexual improprieties by priests with minors. Ethical violations have even touched Martha Stewart and her homemaking enterprises.

Another challenge to our understanding of persuasion involves the introduction and rapid adoption of new, high-impact technologies such as personal computers and the digitization of many older technologies. And we have the ongoing development of virtual realities of all sorts. Easy and instant global communication affects us as never before. Traditional ways of doing business, conducting national and international politics, interacting with others, and even building cultures became obsolete following the globalization of virtually every aspect of human endeavor. Examples include the ability to buy, sell, trade, and bid online and to communicate continuously with a host of entities like the stock and commodities markets, airlines, friends, relatives, strangers, and even entire governments across the globe. And we do this twenty-four hours a day, seven days a week.

Underlying all of this change, however, is a constant—persuasion from all sides. In fact, persuasion has been the great common denominator in the arenas of economics, politics, religion, business, and interpersonal relations ever since humans began to interact. Never before, however, has persuasion had such potential as a tool for affecting our daily lives, as a means to many ends—both good and bad—and as a presence in every moment of our waking lives. The world we face rests on the power of persuasion.

We need to approach this profusion of persuasion in our everyday lives with an awareness that, at its core, persuasion is a symbolic act for both persuaders and receivers. We use symbols—usually words or images—in commercial interactions, interpersonal relations, family life, political endeavors, and international relations. Persuasion basically represents a democratic and humanistic attempt to influence others, to convince them to take certain actions—purchasing, voting, cooperating with one another—instead of forcing or coercing them to do so. For the most part, persuasion uses either logical or emotional means to accomplish desired ends, instead of force. Recent research and theory suggest that we process logical persuasion carefully and critically, but we process most emotional persuasion far less critically. In either case, the logical or emotional persuasion seeks to give us "good reasons" for acting. These good reasons must be delivered to the receivers via an appropriate medium, whether "one-to-one" interpersonal communication or "one-to-many" forms of communication, such as contemporary media. And the good reasons must be acceptable in terms of the norms and values of culture and society.

As you read this book, I hope that you change in important ways. We live in a world in which persuasive messages of various types continually compete for our attention, our beliefs, and our actions. What's more, the exciting times in which we live depend heavily on successful persuasion, and we spend far more time receiving persuasion than sending persuasion. We are predominantly in the role of the persuadee, receiver, or consumer of persuasive messages. So the aim of this book and class is to make you a more critical and responsible consumer of persuasion.

In some ways, you are already a critical receiver, but you can improve your reception skills. You need to identify how critical a receiver you are at the outset. How easily are you persuaded? How does persuasion work on you? What tactics are most effective with you? With others? Which are least effective?

Part I investigates these questions and establishes a perspective. Throughout Parts I, II, and III of this book you will find several tools to help you understand the concepts and theories we consider. First is a list of **Learning Goals** that precede each chapter. Second is a list of **Key Terms** at the end of each chapter. To be a successful student of persuasion, you should be able to achieve the learning goals and identify and explain the key terms. To keep our eyes on the ethics crisis described in the preceding paragraphs, each chapter also has an **Application of Ethics** exercise that you can do individually or as a class. Additionally, each chapter contains one or more interactive **boxes** that direct you to become more aware of the increasing cultural diversity we face and the impact of the interactive media explosion we are facing.

In Chapter 1, we examine how persuasion dominates our lives. We look at several definitions of persuasion, ranging from those rooted in ancient Greece to those derived from the contemporary diverse and interactivity-mediated world. Our discussion also focuses on a useful model of persuasion suggested by Hugh Rank, a scholar of persuasion, advertising, and propaganda. The model grew out of his work with the National Council of Teachers of English (NCTE) and their concern with the increase in "doublespeak"—the attempt to use words to confuse and mislead—to miscommunicate. In Chapter 2, Richard L. Johannesen discusses a variety of approaches to the ethical issues that arise whenever persuasion occurs. Keep in mind that these approaches and issues involve both persuaders and persuadees—senders and receivers. In Joe Scudder's Chapter 3, we explore the traditional humanist roots of persuasion. It is remarkable how many of the principles articulated long ago remain as good practice today. We also see the importance of understanding how persuasion is grounded in human experience and society. Scudder's Chapter 4 focuses on social science methods and what they have revealed to us about persuasion. In Chapter 5, we examine human symbolic behavior, especially as it occurs in language and in images. Finally, Chapter 6 offers several alternative ways receivers can analyze, interpret, decode, and critique persuasive language. It is not important that you find one theory or approach that you prefer, but rather that you consider the various alternatives.

1

Persuasion in Today's Changing World

LEARNING GOALS

After reading this chapter, you should be able to:

1. Identify and use interactive media.

2. Identify and explain instances of doublespeak in contemporary persuasion.

3. Explain persuasion as it is defined here and give examples of it from your life.

4. Recognize our increasing cultural diversity and make attempts to interact with persons who are culturally different than you.

5. Explain common ground and seek it in your persuasive encounters with others.

6. Explain the SMCR model of communication and its dynamics.

7. Identify persuasive messages that are processed in the central and peripheral information-processing channels.

8. Identify instances of Rank's intensifying and down playing strategies in persuasion targeted at you.

9. Develop your abilities to engage in self-protection using the Rank model.

We are engulfed in a sea of information—more than we can ever hope to process. Much of it is useless, and we can safely ignore it, but some of it is essential. This essential information should influence us to make wise and educated decisions—some easy and some difficult. Several factors that can and do influence us are the environment, our social and cultural mores, interpersonal relations, persuasion, and other factors and/or people. Our focus here is on how **persuasion** as the central form of influence in our lives is used to prompt us to vote, to purchase, to believe, and to act. We live in the age of electronic media. Mass media have been with us for a long time—since the printing press—but in a media-rich and highly technological culture, persuasion gains new power. Consider but a few new media that play important roles in our lives: the Internet, cell phones, the iPod, email, handheld computers, podcasting, blogs, and many others. All these make it easier for individuals to influence others by having their say. A soldier fighting a war in a foreign land emails his family and friends about his experiences and what is *really* happening on the front, or a person who witnessed an armed robbery describes her experiences in her blog; thus, we ordinary people become "news reporters" in exciting and individual ways, and we are being faced with ethical decisions about what to report, how reliable our sources may be, whether our biases enter in, and so on.

One theme we'll pursue throughout this book is the degree to which new **interactive media** (i.e., media in which the receiver is able to actively participate in the communication process, such as a radio talk show) persuade the public at large and individuals in particular. While these media offer us the opportunity to participate in important decision-making processes like purchasing, voting, joining, or donating, they also

can "dehumanize" us. Because these media can track results (e.g., the number of "hits" on an Internet site and, in some cases, by whom) they can turn us into statistics—ratings numbers for advertisers, public opinion numbers for politicians, and return-on-investment numbers for businesses. Earlier media could track results to a certain degree (e.g., the Neilson television or Arbitron radio ratings). However, they were based on small samples and relied on viewer and listener self reports, which could be falsified. With interactive media, the "footprints" of users are recorded by actual phone calls to a given 1–800 number, hits on the Internet, the people meter combined with viewer logs, and in other ways. These new capabilities for receiver input are but a few of the challenges facing receivers (e.g., privacy issues and being invested with the power to become part of the persuasion going on). And these interactive media are not limited to cell phone or Internet uses. They include video games (which research shows can increase violent behavior), touch-sensitive screens, virtual reality, electronic payments at gas pumps that are also surrounded with persuasive ads, ATMs, and many more—all of which involve persuasion to some degree.

As the following activity box demonstrates, such interactivity can even involve physical activities such as hunting. You will be encountering such activity boxes throughout this book. They are intended to get you to do one or more of several things. First, you should consider the topics or issues being discussed and ask yourself how they relate to persuasion. Second, if there is a website mentioned, go to it and ask yourself the same question. If the issue involved interests you, go to InfoTrac® College Edition and explore it further. Finally, the boxes sometimes raise ethical questions or issues of how cultural diversity could be

---

B O X 1.1 The Age of Interactive Media: Imagine the Possibilities

One website called liveshot.com was recently developed by a Texas entrepreneur. It is an interactive hunt for big game—wild boar, antelope, deer, bear, and such. It allows persons from remote locations to interact with a robotic rifle and target the game by using a mouse that allows the "hunter" to manipulate a real rifle mounted in a real blind located in Texas where the hunt takes place. The hunter can visually inspect the hunting terrain, looking for targets using a webcam. When a target is found, the user can manipulate (i.e., aim) the robotic rifle and squeeze its trigger. One of liveshot's first users was a quadriplegic man in Indiana who hadn't hunted in 17 years and who did the aiming and shooting via a mouse operated by puffs of air he blew into a tube. By the way, he was wearing camouflage (*All Things Considered,* 2005).

Should he have had a hunting license? What other uses of this kind of interactivity can you imagine?

Imagine the implications of this level of interactive media for various persuasive attempts and how such interactions will involve receivers. The possibilities are mind-boggling, and they're on the way or are already here in competitive sports, shopping, dating, gaming, voting, and a host of other applications. For example, we have already witnessed stalking on the Internet, and in the United Kingdom sports fans can interactively tune in fan interviews and delete the commentator's interpretations. They can even manipulate camera angles, volume, and more on an individual basis, thus creating their own individualized "version" of the soccer match. What might that ability do to sports broadcasting in general?

---

involved. Try to grapple with these questions and issues and perhaps bring them up in class.

Another powerful change in our persuasion world is the degree to which our culture reflects increasing diversity. **Cultural diversity** (i.e., the increasing numbers of persons from other cultural backgrounds, races, ethnicities, sexual preferences, educations, etc.) calls for us to make adjustments in all forms of communication, including persuasion. Many times the communication results of cultural diversity are very positive. For example, in Gillette, Wyoming, the Prairie Winds organization regularly hosts a cultural festival with ethnic food, dancing, music, art, crafts, and demonstrations, and attendees can participate in them (*News Record,* 2005). Unfortunately, sometimes the results of miscommunication across diverse cultures are tragic. For example, in 2004, a Hmong deer hunter in Wisconsin killed five people because he misunderstood a persuasive attempt to convince him that the deer stand he was using belonged to someone else. He was found guilty of killing them and is now serving a life sentence without chance of parole.

As the child of Swedish immigrants, I can relate to such cultural differences in persuasion. My parents voted Democrat because their countrymen told them to; they believed in and joined certain causes, groups, churches, and bought certain brands because their fellow countrymen did; and they responded to persuasive appeals from advertisers, politicians, and ideologues for the same reasons. Today, new immigrants to America face the same kinds of appeals and respond from their own culturally diverse backgrounds, and undoubtedly they will join, vote, believe in, and donate as their countrymen do. This applies to existing subcultures as well (e.g., Latinos respond to persuasive appeals as their reference groups do, and the same applies to Blacks, Asians and Pacific Islanders, and others).

Consider the decisions you make while pursuing your degree: to enlist in ROTC, to move out and rent your own place, to vote for a certain candidate, or to join a cause. We all bring our own cultural values and psychological needs to these decisions and to others like them, and thus our decisions will be diverse. (Note: A box dealing with cultural diversity occurs in each chapter in this book. Get involved with those boxes in the same way you have been advised to get involved with the interactive media boxes.) Let's begin to explore how these various factors interact with persuasive tactics in the information age.

PERSUASION IN AN INFORMATION AGE

We live in an age in which more information is available than any person can hope to access and consider. Persuasion has changed a great deal since the days when one person could hope to reach only as many people as could assemble within reach of his or her voice. The arrival of the print medium permitted persuaders to reach many more people and allowed audiences to read and reread persuasive appeals, and even to compare them with a variety of other evidence. With radio persuaders expanded this "one-to-many" model, but the medium also brought us an enormous increase in advertising, political appeals, and increasingly sophisticated persuasive techniques. The medium also brought receivers a new kind of persuader—broadcast demagogues such as Father Coughlin and Huey Long, and more recently, Rush Limbaugh and others. Television brought us even more of these kinds of persuaders, such as Bill O'Reilly and others.

Interactive media will continue to alter the nature of persuading and the experience of being persuaded. In recent times, politicians, ideologues, and others have persuaded us to support various candidates and causes. In Minnesota, a professional wrestler named Jesse Ventura was elected governor for the most irrational and emotional reasons. His campaign's use of interactive Internet and email tactics helped Jesse "The Body" sweep away his quarrelsome opponents by convincing the public that voting for him was an individual way to protest the system. He went on to wage a running battle with the legislature and made numerous outrageous

claims. Ultimately the same interactive media that helped elect him also brought him down as chat groups, email, and Internet bulletin boards spread the news about the governor's blunders. Constant media persuasion has also convinced many of us that we need interactive items such as ATM cards, remote control devices, personal computers, home pages, the Internet, digital cameras, high-speed connectivity, cellular telephones, handheld devices like the Palm Pilot or the BlackBerry, and many others.

Do these brief examples of emotional, knee-jerk forms of persuasion mean that we need to automatically reject all the persuasive appeals coming at us from advertisers, politicians, and others? Absolutely not—in fact, it's essential that we consider many of the persuasive appeals simply to sort the wheat from the chaff. Whether as individuals, families, corporations, or governments, we need to be persuaded to do our part on a number of fronts. Take, for example, the need to preserve and restore our environment while moving toward energy independence. This means we need to decide whether to support drilling for oil in the Alaskan Wildlife Reserve or whether we should subsidize development of hydrogen energy. There are logical and emotional arguments on both sides. What are the potential costs, benefits, and alternatives?

For these and other reasons, it is more important than ever to train ourselves to become critical receivers of persuasion in an interactive information age, and providing this training is a central goal of this book and this class. As we move from chapter to chapter, you should be able to arm yourself with tools of analysis, perspectives, exercises, and examples that will allow you to become a truly critical receiver of persuasion.

Let's consider just a few of the reasons we need to become more selective receivers of persuasive messages. Researcher Jamie Beckett (1989) reported in the *San Francisco Examiner* that the average U.S. adult is exposed to 255 advertisements every day. *Advertising Age* magazine may be closer to the truth when it estimated that the average American sees, reads, or hears more than 5,000 persuasive advertising messages a day. And communications professor Arthur Asa Berger (2000) reports, "Some estimate that the total number of impressions one processes in one day is as high as 15,000" (p. 81). The 5,000 figure is probably closest to the true number of ads to which we are exposed on a daily basis. These persuasive messages appear in many formats. Take the familiar television spot advertisement, with its high-tech artistry, computer graphics, sophisticated special effects, computer animation, and digitally sweetened sound. Over 25 years ago, communications expert Neil Postman (1981) called attention to just one aspect of persuasion and its potency in shaping our values—the television commercial. By the time you're 20 years old, you're likely to have seen over a million commercials—about a thousand a week. What impressions do we get from them? Here is Postman's analysis:

> A commercial teaches a child three interesting things . . . first is that all problems are resolvable. Second that all problems are resolvable fast, . . . and third is that all problems are resolvable fast through the agency of some technology. It may be a drug. It may be a detergent. It may be an airplane or some piece of machinery. The essential message is that the problems that beset people are solvable if only we will allow ourselves to be ministered to by a technology (p. 4).

How often are we affected by this comforting belief? Did we buy a product because we subconsciously felt that it might make us more attractive, help us land a job, or impress a teacher? As these ads become more and more sophisticated, they become shorter, so the receiver must confront more of them each day, and this requires us to be alert to our need to evaluate them more critically. Instead of the staple 30-second spots of yesteryear, we now see 15- and even 10-second spots dominating TV advertising, and the 7 1/2-second spot is common in England. Product placement in television and film (e.g., a character in the story drinks a Coke) may only last a few seconds, but research shows that it persuades consumers to buy the product.

Other media also contain influential persuasive messages—newspaper and magazine advertisements, billboards and signs along the roadside, radio spots, t-shirts with product names, home pages, faxes, PR releases, and even signs in public restrooms. We find ourselves deluged with direct-marketing appeals such as catalogs, direct-mail offers, telemarketing, infomercials, Internet appeals, and more. And these persuasive appeals go beyond just building brand awareness to include persuasion that influences us in subtle ways, including messages of social and individual importance. For example, the Illinois Department of Public Health uses billboards to promote a website for people who want to quit smoking. Massive databases and sophisticated data filing and retrieval systems make it possible for persuaders to segment us into narrow groups that are vulnerable to persuasion. These examples serve to provide us with even more reasons to become critical receivers. Direct marketing uses the voluminous data about individuals that is available, and it hopes to soon be able to create market segments as small as one person. What are the implications of such deep market segmentation? How much information about ourselves should we give away? What about our right to privacy?

This is a good time for you to become familiar with your InfoTrac® College Edition subscription. Access the Web page at www.infotraccollege.com/ and type in your password. (If you don't have a password, go to the *Persuasion* book companion website at http://communication.wadsworth.com/larson11 for information about how to obtain one.) Type "persuasion" in the subject search engine and click enter. How many entries are listed? Examine one of the psychology entries and one of the rhetoric journal articles or "see also" items. (In later links, you can use the "Related Subjects" options.) Browse some interesting titles in both the academic and popular press to see the kinds of academic research being done in persuasion and see how the press approaches topics related to persuasion.

PERSUASION IN A TECHNOLOGICAL WORLD

Persuasion is essential in inducing people to try, accept, and finally adopt the many new ways of thinking, believing, and behaving that come with the global shift to a technological age. Students are urged to take more core subjects and courses in computer technology at college. Parents tell their children to reduce the volume of music systems to avoid hearing damage. The U.S. government tries to convince citizens to conserve energy by adopting energy efficient appliances or hybrid vehicles. Churches, schools, and community groups find it necessary to use sophisticated technologies (e.g., email "care lists" or "canned" fundraising direct marketing campaigns) to gain or maintain membership and financial support. Meanwhile, marketers use new technologies to convince consumers that a given product such as a cell phone camera will add excitement to their lives.

The title of this book suggests both its purpose and your job as a persuadee. *Persuasion: Reception and Responsibility* aims to make you aware of changes in the logical, emotional, and cultural persuasive appeals targeted directly at you. The book focuses on your job to engage in "**response-ability**," or your ability to wisely and critically respond to the persuasion you encounter and to make wise choices. Of course, persuasion is hardly a recent phenomenon, and it would have been good in past times for audiences to have response-ability. If they had, many tyrants might not have risen to power and wars might have been avoided. The National Council of Teachers of English (NCTE) recognized this need for people to engage their response-ability when it instituted its regular conferences on **doublespeak**, which it defined as deliberate miscommunication. The organization also announced an annual "doublespeak award" to be given to the persuader(s) whose language was most "grossly unfactual, deceptive, evasive, confusing, or self-contradictory." The award alerts persuadees to the often confusing and sometimes misleading use of words in persuasion.

DOUBLESPEAK IN A PERSUASION-FILLED WORLD

Even in a persuasion-riddled world such as ours, you would not need defensive training if all persuaders were open and honest. Too many, however, try to persuade by using doublespeak. Doublespeak comes in several guises: the half truth, the euphemism, hair-splitting, the trial balloon, bogus issues, jargon, and others. Consider the "peacekeeping" military missions engaged in around the world by our government or Bill Clinton's insistence that he had never "had sex with that woman" (referring to Monica Lewinsky). The term "ethnic cleansing" referred to mass murder in several parts of the world, and it camouflaged the existence of concentration camps and the mass slaughter of thousands by using words that sounded almost antiseptic.

If you find the words "ethnic cleansing" disturbing, access InfoTrac College Edition under the subject index option, and enter them in the search engine. You will find many articles that elaborate on the term and the genocide that followed. Which did you find most surprising?

Of course, doublespeak isn't confined to the world of politics. A real estate ad indicating that a house is "convenient to the interstate" probably means that you will hear cars whoosh by day and night. A "handyman's special" means lots of repairs. A "good work car" really means a "junker." CEOs at Enron, AIG, WorldCom, and others used doublespeak to confuse and bilk investors and employees by convincing them that "liabilities" were "assets" and that "spending" meant "earning."

For some good examples of doublespeak here and in other countries, access InfoTrac College Edition, and enter the words "euphemism" and "half truths" in the search engine. Which of the items is the most interesting? Start identifying examples of doublespeak as you encounter them. You'll be surprised how often persuaders try to miscommunicate.

B O X 1.2   Becoming an Advertising Medium—Ethical or Unethical?

 Viral advertising is a new form of interactive communication that turns the audience into a persuasive advertising channel, as each receiver spreads the message online like a (benign) virus. The technique resembles a chain letter. First the advertiser places an attractive or entertaining interactive message such as a game on the Web and begins to direct consumers to visit the website, which also contains a variety of advertising links from which to choose. One of these is "send this site to a friend." And the consumer does just that, because it is fun and easy to share things via the Internet. One such site at www.subservientchicken.com, is sponsored by Burger King and plays on the old "Have it Your Way!" slogan in promoting chicken offerings as opposed to the Whopper. The website features someone dressed in a chicken suit. The viewer can command the chicken to run, fly, hop, skip, and so on. There are several hundred actions programmed into the game, but If asked to perform a distasteful or obscene act, the "chicken" confronts the screen and shakes its finger at the "naughty" user. The technique persuades on at least two levels: the purchase of the product and the decision to forward the "fun" interactive site much as you might do with a chain letter. Can you think of other instances of persuasion in which this viral approach might be exploited? What about political campaigns? Religious appeals? Worthy causes? What are the ethical implications of partici- pating in viral marketing (e.g., using "fun" media to hook consumers or urging them to spread the message)?

DEFINING PERSUASION: FROM ARISTOTLE TO ELABORATION LIKELIHOOD

Definitions of Persuasion

The ancient Greeks were among the first to sys- tematize the use of persuasion, calling it "**rhetoric.**" They studied it in their schools, applied it in their legal proceedings, and used it to build the first democracies in their city-states. Aristotle was the primary rhetorical theorist in ancient Greece, authoring more than 1,000 books and categorizing all the knowledge types in the known world for his schoolmate Alexander the Great. He defined rhetoric as "the faculty of observing in any given case, the available means of persuasion." According to Aristotle, persuasion consists of artistic and inart- istic proofs. The persuader controls **artistic proof** such as the choice of evidence, the organization of the persuasion, style of delivery, and language choices. **Inartistic proof** includes things not con- trolled by the speaker, such as the occasion, the time allotted to the speaker, and the speaker's phy- sical appearance. According to Aristotle, persuasion

succeeds or fails based on a source's credibility, or **ethos**; the use of emotional appeals, or **pathos**; logical or rational appeals, or **logos**; or a combina- tion of all these (Roberts, 1924). Aristotle also thought that persuasion is most effective when based on the **common ground**, which is the shared beliefs, values, and interests existing between per- suaders and persuadees. This shared territory permits persuaders to make certain assumptions about the audience and its beliefs. Assuming these beliefs, persuaders use **enthymemes**—a form of argument in which the first or major premise in the proof remains unstated by the persuader and, instead, is supplied by the audience. A familiar example is "All men are mortal; Socrates is a man; therefore Socrates is mortal." The persuader needs to identify common ground or those major premises held by the audience and use them in enthymemes (see Figure 1.1).

Roman students of persuasion added specific advice on what a persuasive speech ought to include. Cicero identified five elements of persuasive speaking: (1) inventing or discovering evidence and arguments, (2) organizing them, (3) styling them artistically, (4) memorizing them, and (5) delivering them skillfully.

FIGURE 1.1 The Lincoln Financial Group establishes common ground in this advertisement between the company and any person of any race or ethnicity who is approaching retirement. Note the satisfied and happy looks on both of the faces and the healthy appearance of both persons. This resonates with the desire to have a happy, healthy retirement and helps build the common ground. Note also the examples referred to in the ad copy—"40 years building," "30 years paying off," and "20 years saving," each of which would probably resonate with any potential retiree, and the idea that "Now I want to LIVE." These words continue building common ground between the company and the potential customer.

SOURCE: Used by permission of the Lincoln Financial Group.

Both Aristotle's and Cicero's definitions focus on the sources of messages and on the persuader's skill and art in building a speech. In the communication discipline, we consider these "rhetorical" approaches to the study of persuasion because they grew out of the rhetorical traditions of the Greeks and Romans. They are still applied in current research on persuasion and its effects.

Later students of persuasion reflected the changes that accompanied the emergence of elec-tronic media and the social sciences following World War II. Over 50 years ago, communication scholars Winston Brembeck and William Howell (1952) broke new theoretical ground when they described persuasion as "the conscious attempt to modify thought and action by manipulating the motives of men toward predetermined ends" (p. 24). In their definition, we see a notable shift from logic in persuasion toward a focus on the more "emotional" means of persuasion—those that stimulate the internal motives of the audience. Twenty years later they defined persuasion as "communication intended to influence choice" (p. 19). Wallace Fotheringham (1966), another early persuasion theorist, defined persuasion as "that body of effects in receivers" caused by a persuader's message (p. 7). Here, even unintended messages could be persuasive if they caused changes in the receivers' attitudes, beliefs, or actions. Literary critic and language theorist, Kenneth Burke (1970) defined persuasion in an intriguing way. He said that persuasion was really the artful use of the "resources of ambiguity." Burke believed that if receivers feel they are being spoken to in their "own language" and hear references to their own beliefs and values, they will develop a sense of **identification** with the persuader, believing that the persuader is like them—a concept close to Aristotle's "common ground." In Burke's theory, when persuaders try to act, believe, and talk like the audience, they create a bond with listeners, who will identify with them and will follow their advice on issues.

Taking our cues from Aristotle, Burke, and others, persuasion is defined here as "the process of **co-creation** by sources and receivers of a state of identification through the use of verbal and/or visual symbols." This definition implies that persuasion requires intellectual and emotional participation between both persuader and persuadee that leads to shared meaning and co-created identification. Communication professor and researcher Herbert Simons (2001) agrees and calls this result "coactive persuasion." Notice that like our definition, coactive persuasion is receiver-oriented and situational, relying on similarities between persuaders and persuadees and appeals to things acceptable to the persuadee, thus inducing action (p. 75).

In one sense, all persuasion consists of **self-persuasion**. We rarely act in accordance with persuasion unless we participate or interact in the process logically and/or emotionally. The words "process," "co-created," and "identification" are central in this definition.

The **elaboration likelihood model** (ELM) serves as an organizational model of persuasion and resulted in significant changes in the way theorists view persuasion. It serves as a central model throughout this book. Social psychologists Richard Petty and John Cacioppo (1986) suggested the ELM as a cognitive model in which persuasion takes one of two routes. In the **central information processing route** the receiver consciously and directly focuses on the persuasive communication while mentally elaborating on the issues and actively seeking more information. This requires significant effort on the part of the receiver. The target of the persuasive message searches out the issues, supporting evidence, alternatives, respective costs and benefits, and other potential outcomes. It usually operates in making important decisions such as purchasing a new car. Here we probably read brochures, compare prices, or go online to discover the actual amount of a dealer's profit and how the vehicle is rated by various consumer publications. Sometimes persuasion requires only a momentary period of concentration on an issue. According to the ELM, this persuasion occurs in the **peripheral information processing route**. There information may be processed almost instantly or just by the senses, without direct focusing on or researching of the decision. We decide to buy Cracker Jacks at the ball park to get the "free" prize and because they are mentioned in the song "Take Me Out to the Ball Game" that is sung at the middle of the seventh inning. At any given moment, there are millions of pieces of such trivial information available, but we consciously attend to only a few of them. The peripheral route resembles a sponge. We soak up persuasive information and may act on it, but we remain unaware of or unfocused on it in any direct or effortful way. The peripheral route usually contains shortcuts for making decisions and often includes emotional appeals.

Persuasion and Other Forms of Influence

Most communication scholars agree that persuasion usually relies on communication that attempts to change another person in some way. Many suggest that the attempt must succeed to be

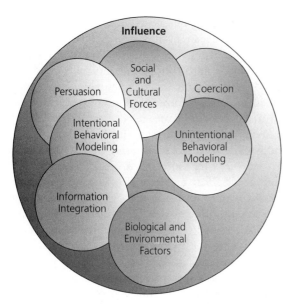

FIGURE 1.2   The relationship of persuasion to other forms of influence.

considered persuasion, and most agree that persuasion requires participation by a sender and a receiver. Persuasion usually succeeds when it adapts to the receiver's world—the situation, the context, the culture, and receivers' emotions and motivations. Figure 1.2 illustrates the relationships among various terms of influence that often confuse the new student of persuasion. The importance of each type of influence probably varies substantially from person to person and according to the context. The central point of this diagram is that many forces (including persuasion) bring change to our lives.

Those who study persuasion don't always distinguish among these forms of influence. In many discussions, "influence" and "persuasion" are interchangeable. We need to distinguish among several terms related to persuasion, including "influence," "coercion," "compliance-gaining," "acquiescence," "behavioral modeling," and "information integration."

Influence refers to a person's attitude or behavioral change. There are several ways that attitudes or behaviors may change. For example, many fans adopt the styles or behavior of their pop idols. This represents influence through behavior modeling. Similarly, many adults are embarrassed when their young child uses profanity in public—profanity that was overheard at home. This is an unintended outcome of behavioral modeling. In contrast, most parents consciously model more positive behaviors for their children, hoping to persuade them to emulate those behaviors. Persuasion always entails some degree of choice. In contrast, **coercion** uses some level of force—physical or psychological—to gain compliance, such as when peer pressure results in changes in attitude or behavior; you really don't want to go to the rock concert, but you choose to go because you know that it will please the person who invited you. So, persuasion and coercion represent two ends of a continuum ranging from free choice to forced choice. Although terrorism uses coercion, the co-creation of states of identification doesn't often result, but persuasion of a different sort can occur as an unexpected result. For example, acceptance of cultural diversity suffered after 9/11, and many people avoided air travel—especially if other passengers appeared to be of Middle Eastern extraction. Influence occurs when a person chooses a certain action in return for some future concession, as frequently happens in political favor swapping. Persuasion, as a kind of influence, occurred in making a political deal because some common ground was reached, but none of the people involved *really* changed their minds based on the merits of the actual issues. Information integration and analysis is another route to influence that doesn't involve persuasion. For example, a manager may change his or her inventory management behavior after learning that quarterly sales were up or down. Something overheard in conversation, read in the newspaper, or seen on the Internet may lead to changes in behavior, but this is not persuasion since no co-creation occurred. Co-creation is central to our definition of persuasion. Persuasive contexts extend beyond public-speaking situations but all involve some kind of co-creation. For instance, protest marches, decision-making get-togethers, staff meetings, sales presentations, and mass media events all involve the co-creation of identification between persuaders and receivers.

CRITERIA FOR RESPONSIBLE PERSUASION

How does cooperative and co-creative persuasion happen? What makes it work? Although persuasion occurs under various circumstances, three conditions seem to increase the chances that responsible receivers will make wise and knowledgeable decisions. First, responsible persuasion is most likely to occur if all parties have an equal opportunity to persuade and approximately equal access to the medium of communication. If one side imposes a gag rule on the proponents of the other side of an issue while advocates of the other side have freedom to persuade, then receivers get a one-sided and biased view of the issue. Although they are persuaded, the persuasion isn't exactly fair because of the gag rule.

Second, in an ideal world, persuaders reveal their agendas to the audience. They tell us their ultimate aims and goals and how they intend to achieve them. Unfortunately, this doesn't always happen. Political candidates need to tell us how they intend to improve the schools, how their tax proposal works, and so on. Auto manufacturers need to convince us that they are at work trying to build reliable, fuel-efficient cars. And ideologues need to warn their audience about possible negative outcomes if their ideology is implemented—the results of outlawing the "morning after" pill, for instance. Knowing the persuader's **hidden agenda** puts receivers on guard against their messages, and even just a hint of the real goals of a persuader makes us more likely to make informed choices.

Third, and most important, receivers must critically test the assertions and evidence presented to them. This means looking for information from all sides and withholding judgment until we have sufficient data. Critical receivers can still make responsible decisions even if the first two criteria for responsible persuasion are missing. In recent elections, many candidates used negative advertising and brief sound bites. As campaign critic and communication researcher Kathleen Hall Jamieson (1992) observed almost two decades ago, "All forms of campaign discourse were becoming alike. . . . assertion was substituted for argument and attack for engagement" (p. 212). In many interviews conducted since making that observation, Jamieson confirms the continuance of this assertion versus argument and attack versus engagement pattern. Critical receivers must go beyond these sound bites and do critical research before making a voting decision.

Access InfoTrac College Edition, and enter the words "negative political advertising" in the search engine. Explore some of the articles that are referenced. Observe yourself being persuaded and how persuasion happens to you. You will be more critical and therefore more effective in rejecting messages when appropriate—and in accepting others when that is wise.

THE SMCR MODEL OF PERSUASION

The simplest model of communication, and one of the oldest and most widely referenced, is Shannon and Weaver's (1949) **SMCR model** (see Figure 1.3). The model contains these essential elements:

- A source (S) (or persuader), who or which is the encoder of the message. The code can be verbal, nonverbal, visual, or musical, or in some other modality.

- A message (M), which is meant to convey the source's meaning through any of the codes.

- A channel (C), which carries the message and which might have distracting noise.

- A receiver (R) (or persuadee), who decodes the message, trying to sift out channel noise and adding his or her own interpretation.

Suppose you tell a friend that the words used in a TV ad for the new Toyota RAV emphasize how large the car seems when it really isn't. In this case, you help your friend to make or not make a choice by explaining a source-related aspect of

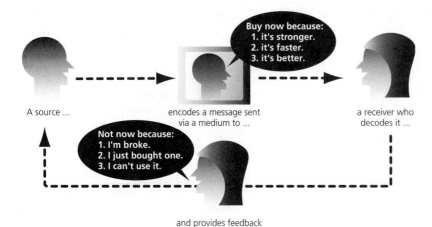

FIGURE 1.3 The SMCR model.

A source ...

encodes a message sent via a medium to ...

a receiver who decodes it ...

and provides feedback

persuasion—in this case word choice. Then you alert your friend to the doublespeak in the ad—the product "virtually guarantees" fun times. You ask what the word "virtually" means in this advertising claim and thus focus attention on the message itself. You also point out that skillful editing and the use of special effects make the vehicle seem large. Here, you focus on the persuasive impact of the channel carrying the persuasive information. Finally, you might ask your friend what internal or unstated reason he or she has for wanting to be popular, and how they think the RAV will result in fun times. Here you focus on the receiver element of the model. Because persuasion is a process, being a critical receiver means being prepared for all four elements—the motives of the source (obvious or disguised), message elements (verbal and visual symbolic meanings), the channel or medium used to send the message, and finally what the receiver brings to the source's argument(s). Try using several tools to determine a source's motives. For example, language choice often tips us off to the source's intent. The ideas that the source thinks are persuasive to the audience almost always appear expressed in the words and metaphors used. Are they questions or exclamations? Are they short and punchy or long and soothing? For example, when Schick introduced a "cosmetic" razor called the "Personal Touch," I wondered to whom the

product was targeted and asked myself questions about the language being used. What do the words "cosmetic," "personal," and "touch" tell you about Schick's view of its potential customers? Was it aiming at a "macho" man or at women who feel they deserve special attention? The language used tells us that the target is female and the motive is to make them feel special when considering the product. Analyzing the source's message provides the receiver with two benefits. First, it alerts us to the persuasion being aimed at us. Second, it tells us things about the source that can help us when the source becomes the target of our own persuasion. Other tools also help us to analyze the intent of the message. We will look at receivers' needs and emotions, and we'll also look at the evidence contained in messages and at how it relates to the persuasive goal.

Consider the layout, graphics, and wording of an ad placed across the country by the International Fund for Animal Welfare (IFAW), opposing the harvest of baby seals in Canada—a highly emotional issue as the young seals are clubbed to death (see Figure 1.4). The copy in the ad reads:

> Do you really know what can go into a simple fish sandwich? . . . Fish caught by Canadian Fishermen who also kill the baby seals. Your purchase of a McDonald's or Burger King Fish Sandwich could help buy

Do you really know what can go into a simple fish sandwich?

Fish caught by Canadian Fishermen who also kill the baby seals. Your purchase of a McDonald's or Burger King Fish Sandwich could help buy the boats, hard wooden clubs, and guns used by the seal hunters as they turn from fishing to the cruelty of killing adult and baby seals.

If you made a pledge today not to buy fish sandwiches from McDonald's or Burger King unless you were assured by the companies that no Canadian fish was used…your decision would save the seals. Canadian fishermen would have to stop sealing since they are totally dependent on their fish sales, with seal hunting a tiny sideline in comparison.

Canadian *Globe and Mail* of 13 March 1984, had this to say of IFAW's call for a worldwide boycott of Canadian fish: *"…But what really has the officials spooked is the U.S. market. (There) The International Fund for*

Animal Welfare (IFAW), which spearheads the anti-sealing protest worldwide, has started pressing U.S. purchasers not to take Canadian fish. The U.S. market is worth $1-billion a year to Canadian fishermen and the fast-food business in the United States is about a fifth of that market. Canada fears that, if one U.S. fast-food chain caves in to the protestors, all will surrender."

Over 15,000 seals, mostly babies just 2-4 weeks old, have been clubbed or shot over the last 28 days…and yet the Canadian Minister of Fisheries says there is no baby seal hunt.

You have it in your hands to save the baby seals today.

Please write or telephone one or both of the companies listed below and seek an assurance that they will not purchase Canadian fish until the Canadian Government passes a law banning the seal hunt forever.

Mr Fred L. Turner,
Chairman of the Board,
McDonald's Corporation,
McDonald's Plaza, Oak Brook, Illinois,
IL 60521
Tel. 312/887-3200

Mr J Jeffrey Campbell, Chairman,
Burger King Corporation,
7360 North Kendall Drive,
Miami,
Florida FL 33156
Tel: 305/596-7277

SAVE THE SEALS

NO TO CANADIAN FISH

To the International Fund for Animal Welfare

I'll put animals first … I'll do my part to help you fight the baby seal hunters.

Enclosed is my tax-exempt contribution to IFAW in the amount of:

☐ $10 ☐ $15 ☐ $25 ☐ $35 ☐ $50 ☐ $100 ☐ $500 Other $_____

We need hundreds of gifts this size to save the baby seals forever.

Name_____
(please print)
Address_____
_____
_____ Zip Code___

International Fund for Animal Welfare
169 Main Street, Yarmouth Port,
Massachusetts 02675 U.S.A.
Our financial statement is available to contributors.

IFAW

Our boycott campaign needs your support. We cannot succeed without your funds, to carry our boycott to every community in America.

A copy of the last financial report filed with the Department of State may be obtained by writing to: N.Y. State Department of State, Office of Charities Registration, Albany, N.Y. 12231 or IFAW.

FIGURE 1.4 Ad encouraging people to boycott fish sandwiches to stop the killing of harp seals.

SOURCE: Used by permission of IFAW.

the boats, hard wooden clubs, and guns used by the seal hunters as they turn from fishing to the cruelty of killing adult and baby seals.

The images and words such as "hard wooden clubs" alert you to the underlying emotional persuasion used and should prompt you to investigate more fully because emotional appeals are more likely to be biased, incomplete, or unethical. Research reveals that very few Canadian fishermen are also seal hunters; that clubbing the seals is

actually the least painful means of harvesting them; and that the furs of the seals are the object of the hunt not their flesh. It is not used in the fish sandwich as the visuals suggest. Looking carefully at the message prompts you to get the other side of the story. It also alerts you to the kinds of effects that the channel has on persuasion. An appeal on the same issue using radio would probably fail because radio lacks visual imagery. Imagine a TV ad documenting the harp seal slaughter. Would this make the message more or less effective? TV makes us more vulnerable to certain types of messages, such as humorous ones, demonstrations, exaggerations, comparisons, and before/after appeals. Video footage of the clubbing of the seals would certainly raise audience emotions.

Finally, the SMCR model suggests we need to look at ourselves to determine what kinds of motives, biases, and perspectives we bring to the persuasion. What fascinations, needs, and desires do we add in the co-creation? How do we interact with the message and the medium used? Does our cultural heritage shade the meaning of the message? Persuaders including politicians, ideologues, advertisers, propagandists, and even our coworkers, friends, and colleagues continuously seek answers to questions like these. Communication researcher Patricia Sullivan (1993) describes these steps (i.e., **tactics** flow from **strategies**, which in turn flow from overall **goals**) in her analysis of a keynote speech given by Reverend Jesse Jackson at a Democratic National Convention. Jackson's goal was to unite the party. He stressed the common ground shared among the various factions of the party; and he got the audience interacting with the message by entitling his speech "Common Ground and Common Sense," thus making the issue of unity central. He also employed a call–response (or interactive) format for parts of the speech by uttering a phrase or sentence that the audience then repeated, uniting them further.

RANK'S MODEL OF PERSUASION

Some years ago the National Council of Teachers of English (NCTE) asked for ways to teach students to become critical receivers of persuasion. Researcher Hugh Rank (1976), put the challenge this way: "These kids are growing up in a propaganda blitz unparalleled in human history.... Schools should shift their emphasis in order to train the larger segment of our population in a new kind of literacy so that more citizens can recognize the more sophisticated techniques and patterns of persuasion" (p. 5). Rank outlined a simple, easy-to-

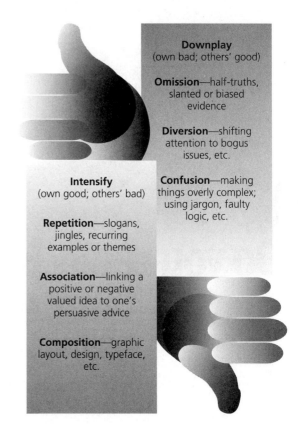

FIGURE 1.5 Rank's intensify/downplay schema.
SOURCE: Adapted by permission of Hugh Rank.

use but insightful model of persuasion, called the intensify/downplay model. It helps people to be critical receivers using a series of four strategies and six associated tactics. Rank maintains that persuaders employ these major strategies to achieve their goals. Persuaders either **intensify** certain aspects of their product, cause, or candidate, or they intensify some aspect of the competition. They also downplay certain aspects of their product or candidate, or they downplay positive aspects of the competition. Often, they do both. Figure 1.5 illustrates this model. Strategically, persuaders choose from four courses of action. They can:

1. Intensify their own good points
2. Intensify the weak points of the opposition

3. Downplay their own weak points

4. Downplay the good points of the opposition

Persuaders use tactics such as repetition, association, and composition to intensify their own good points or the bad points of the opposition, and they use omission, diversion, and confusion to downplay their own bad points or the good points of the opposition. Any one of these tactics can be used logically or emotionally using interactive or more traditional media.

Persuasive strategy, then, results from the overall step-by-step program for reaching some goal. Strategy dictates tactics or the specific kinds of arguments, evidence, or points the persuader makes. For example, a politician wants to persuade voters to support her candidacy (the goal), so she tries to make them feel good about her platform and character (the strategy of intensifying her own good). She accomplishes this by taking forthright stands on the issues. She also repeats her campaign slogan on yard signs, billboards, buttons, bumper stickers, electronic advertisements, and her website, and she uses the Capitol in the background of all her ads.

Intensification

All persuaders want to look good in the eyes of the audience—the voters, joiners, donors, or potential customers. Some tactics intensify the persuader's own good points ("He's always been a willing and honest servant for good causes."). Others intensify the bad points of the other guy, thus making the persuader look good by comparison ("He's a flim-flam man—I wouldn't trust him."). The tactics of repetition, association, and composition are all effective in implementing the strategy of intensification of our own good or others' bad points.

Repetition. One way to intensify good or bad points about a product, person, or candidate is to repeat them over and over again. That's why slogans, jingles, and logotypes work. For example, Energizer batteries "keep going and going" in TV spots, magazine ads, and even on their packages. The harp seal ad repeatedly intensifies the bad aspects of the hunt.

A fascinating discussion of repetition in advertising can be accessed on InfoTrac College Edition by entering the words "slogans" and "jingles" in the search engine. Would they be processed in the central or the peripheral route?

Association. Another tactic for intensification is association which (1) links a cause, product, or candidate (2) to something already liked or disliked (3) by the audience. Thus, the cause, product, or candidate becomes identified with the thing liked or disliked. For example, politicians know that we have fears about privacy and identity theft in cyberspace, so they tie these fears to their own causes by stating that, if elected, they intend to enact strict controls over the use of cyber-information. Advertisers associate a certain kind of athletic shoe with a well-known professional, with everyday people who exercise, or as Nike did, with a person in a wheelchair. These associations intensify the good aspects of the shoe and show that one needn't be an athlete to benefit from its features.

Composition. The third and final tactic of intensification uses physical composition of the message to emphasize one's own good points or the other guy's bad points. This usually involves the use of nonverbal or visual means and takes several forms. Altering the makeup of the printed word (as in changing "U.S.A." to "U.$.A.") sends the message that the nation is only interested in money. Altering the composition of a candidate's publicity photo often manipulates meaning. A low camera angle makes the candidate look larger than life and tells us to look up to him or her. Altering the layout of an advertisement intensifies persuasive outcomes. For example, the upper-right and lower-left corners of a magazine page or a poster are considered *fallow*, or less likely to get full reader attention. The eye only glances at them momentarily, so guess where the cigarette manufacturers usually put the health warning? These cases also exemplify the use of the peripheral route of the ELM in persuasive appeals, and we don't put much time, effort, or research into processing them.

B O X 1.3   Cultural Diversity and Persuasion

 To become familiar with the many issues that are intertwined with our increasing diversity as a country, go to www.newsreel.org/nav/ topics and explore the content and authors of various diversity-related documentary videos. Visit the video by Jean Kilbourne entitled "Killing us Softly," which addresses the many ways in which advertising forces women to value attractiveness, sexuality, and gender stereotypes, thus making women and children vulnerable to violent abuse. Kilbourne claims that

advertisers are the real pornographers of our times. Other interesting options include: "The Politics of Love in Black and White" which explores the problems of interracial couples; "Colorism" which investigates the caste system that operates in Black communities based on features, hair, and skin shade. Take a look at "Tough Guise," which focuses on the relationship between gender and violence. Other titles will interest and sensitize you to persuasion and diversity.

Persuaders also use composition to compare and contrast. For example, a candidate for political office is pictured against some dramatic setting such as the Statue of Liberty. To intensify an incumbent politician's bad points, an ad superimposes his or her image on a picture of a polluted river or harbor in the home district. To emphasize the negative identification and to encourage further emotional interaction with the spot, a muted version of "America the Beautiful" might accompany a voice-over talking about the incumbent's lack of social responsibility. The polluted river or harbor, the background, the music, and the voice-over combine to "compose" the ad's meaning. Use Rank's intensification as a starting place in becoming a critical receiver.

Downplaying

Sometimes persuaders want to avoid intensifying or calling attention to something because it undermines their persuasive goal. They avoid advertising the strong points of the competition. Politicians don't tell us what a good job their opponent did recently. This strategy also can downplay the persuader's bad points while downplaying a competitor's good points. Let's now look at the tactics used in the strategy of downplaying: omission, diversion, and confusion.

Omission.   Sometimes persuaders simply leave out critical information to avoid highlighting their own shortcomings. For example, politicians leave

out the fact that the statistics supporting their position are not official. Most advertisements for foods are staged in some way. Live photographs of food are frequently unappetizing—lettuce wilts, red meat color fades, and so on. As a result, there is an occupation known as "food cosmetics" in which the expert uses a variety of techniques to make the food look better. Salads look crisper if coated with hair spray just before photographing. Photographs of floor tile adhesive look more appetizing than actual chocolate pudding. A soup manufacturer makes its chunky version look chunky by filling the bottom of the bowl with marbles so that the chunks float higher. The officials of a charitable organization omit telling the administrative costs for dispersing the charitable donations.

The Claussen pickle company intensified its own good points by advertising that its pickles are refrigerated rather than cooked. As a result, they are much crisper than competitor Vlasic pickles. They used a TV ad showing the two pickles being bent in half. The "snap!" of the Claussen pickle and the burst of juice from it really intensified Claussen's good points and demonstrated Vlasic's soggy bad point, but Claussen omitted telling consumers that the brand contains far more sodium than Vlasic pickles (their own bad point) and that refrigeration isn't necessary for Vlasic pickles (the other's good point).

It is clear that Claussen intentionally chose to omit mentioning the sodium content of its product because people need to reduce their intake of sodium for health reasons like avoiding strokes or heart attacks, so the omission has ethical implications. What would you say? What about the recent claim that Cheerios are now high in fiber? Although the claim is true, the fact that they always were high in fiber is omitted. Here the omission doesn't endanger one's health, but it is misleading and part of a marketing strategy.

Diversion. Diversion consists of shifting attention away from another's good points or one's own bad points by using substitute issues. Persuaders frequently use humor to divert attention. For instance, the Energizer "Bunny" ads use humor, and this diverts attention from the fact that all alkaline batteries have about the same life. Ford used emotional appeals to divert attention away from the poor design of its Explorer, which had a tendency to roll over, resulting in a number of deaths and injuries. Ford redirected blame to the factory-installed Firestone tires. Splitting hairs diverts attention from the major issues of the debate and siphons valuable time away from discussion and interaction between the persuader and persuadee.

Confusion. Another downplaying tactic creates confusion in the audience's mind. Using technical jargon that the receiver doesn't understand creates confusion. Weaving an intricate and rambling argument that evades the real issues results in audience confusion, as does the use of faulty logic. Consider the claim that "She's Beautiful! She's Engaged! She Uses Earth Balsam Hand Creme!" It implies a "logical progression" that, because she used the hand cream, she became beautiful, and because of that, she met and won the man of her dreams.

Intensify own good	Intensify others' bad
1.	1.
2.	2.
Downplay own bad	**Downplay others' good**
1.	1.
2.	2.
3.	3.

FIGURE 1.6 Intensify/downplay scorecard.

SOURCE: By permission of Hugh Rank.

A METHOD OF SELF-PROTECTION

In his discussion of doublespeak, Rank (1976) offered some advice about how to detect the flaws of persuaders who use various tactics to intensify or downplay: "When they intensify, you downplay. When they downplay, you intensify."

Beginning in 2004, politicians exploited audience fears about retirement benefits by claiming that the Social Security System faced a crisis in funding. Supposedly, this justified setting up private investment accounts using some of the Social Security dollars regularly paid by employees and employers. The "crisis" claim was an exaggeration that backfired when opponents demonstrated that there were several alternatives to meet the shortfall, all of which involved less drastic changes. The word "crisis" caused an initial emotional reaction and thus encouraged audience interaction. However, receivers looked deeper into the issue using the central information processing route of the ELM, and the "crisis" dissipated.

A way to follow Rank's advice systematically is to divide a sheet of paper into quarters, as shown in Figure 1.6, and then enter the kinds of downplaying and intensifying going on in the message(s). Simply seeing these items makes you more alert to the kind of manipulation going on. Try using the self-protection method on an advertisement or a political speech. When the ad or speech downplays something, you intensify its shortcomings. And when it intensifies something, you downplay the intensification. We will discuss a number of other tools of analysis as we proceed, but Rank's intensify/downplay tool seems a useful general tool of analysis to employ when first faced with a persuasive blitz.

REVIEW AND CONCLUSION

If you now feel more alert to the possible ways persuaders manipulate you, congratulations! You're already on your way to becoming a more critical receiver. You now need to arm yourself with some tools of analysis that make for wise consumers. There is a bonus for learning them. Seeing what works—in what circumstances, with what kinds of people—helps you prepare to persuade others. Skillful consumers of messages learn to be more effective producers of messages. As we move ahead, apply the tools of persuasive analysis

on your own and in the study questions at the end of each chapter. Use the diversity and interactive media boxes as well as the learning goals, key terms, and applications of ethics. Also, explore the InfoTrac College Edition sites sprinkled throughout the text. Examine the ways in which persuasion operates on the interpersonal level. Every day you make decisions in nonpublic settings. Your parents may try to persuade you to avoid certain occupational fields, to seek a summer job, or to put off a purchase. You decide to heed or reject your parents' advice on the basis of your interpersonal communication with them. Rank's model helps here too. Identify what your parents intensify and downplay. Do the same thing with other interpersonal relationships— roommates, friends, colleagues, or your boss. Then try to spot the kinds of symbols that lead to or discourage identification. Critical analysis of interpersonal persuasion helps you to make informed decisions. People are persuaded daily in the public arena through advertisements, speeches, radio and TV programs, newspaper and magazine articles, and the Internet. But we need to remember that persuasion also takes place in our personal lives.

KEY TERMS

When you are finished with this chapter, you should be able to identify, explain, and give examples of the following terms or concepts.

persuasion	ethos	elaboration likelihood model	hidden agenda
interactive media	pathos		SMCR model
cultural diversity	logos	central information processing route	tactics
response-ability	common ground	peripheral information processing route	strategies
doublespeak	enthymemes		goals
rhetoric	identification	influence	intensify
artistic proof	co-creation	coercion	
inartistic proof	self-persuasion		

APPLICATION OF ETHICS

The Ethics of Omission. A homeowner needs to sell his home but is hesitant to inform realtors or prospective buyers that there is mold in the basement that could be toxic. The homeowner has been able to get rid of the mold from time to time by spraying the basement with household bleach. What should the homeowner do? (1) Spray the basement and list the house for sale and not mention the mold problem. (2) Spray the basement and mention the problem and a solution to both buyers and realtors. (3) Hire a toxic mold expert to find out if the mold really is toxic and discover what can be done about it if is indeed toxic. (4) Don't spray the basement and simply list the house as "For Sale by Owner."

QUESTIONS FOR FURTHER THOUGHT

1. If you or someone you know recently made a major purchase (for example, an automobile, an MP3 player, or a digital camera), identify the context in which persuasion occurred. Where did the persuasion take place? In the showroom? Through a television ad? Interpersonally, such as in discussing the purchase with a friend? What kinds of appeals were made? What characteristics were intensified? Downplayed? Was the persuasion emotional or logical, or both? What did you learn from the careful examination?

2. Much persuasion occurs in interpersonal contexts. Examine one of your interpersonal relationships, such as that between you and your parents, your roommate, a teammate, or a fellow member of an organization or church. Describe how, when, and where persuasion operated in the relationship. What characteristics about yourself have you intensified? Downplayed? What about the other person's intensification? Downplaying? Which tactics worked best? Repetition? Association? Omission?

3. Beginning with the definition of persuasion offered in this chapter, create your own model of persuasion that reflects all the important elements of the definition given here.

4. Identify three types of persuasion you recently processed, and analyze each according to the definition offered in this chapter and the ELM. What verbal and/or visual symbols were used? Did you interact with the message? What did the persuader intend? Which information-processing route (peripheral or the central) operated for you? What created identification? What was intensified? Downplayed? Using which tactics? Repetition? Association? Composition? Omission? Confusion? Diversion?

5. Describe the tactics of intensification, and explain how they work. Give examples of their use on television, in print, on radio, by politicians, and by advertisers.

6. Describe the tactics of downplaying and explain how they work. Give examples of their use on television, in print, on radio, by politicians, and by advertisers.

7. Identify a current "propaganda blitz" going on in the media coverage of an event or issue. Which route in the ELM was employed? Describe current examples of the strategies of intensification and downplaying that seem central in the "war on terrorism." What tactics of intensification or downplaying are used regarding environmental issues? Are they ethical or unethical?

8. List some of the interactive media you use. How many of them came about in recent times—say since 2000? How many of them preceded the Internet?

9. Have you noticed the ways in which we are becoming a more diverse culture? How do they affect the persuasive process?

 For online activities, go to the *Persuasion* book companion website at http://communication.wadsworth.com/larson11.

5

The Making, Use, and Misuse of Symbols

LEARNING GOALS

After reading this chapter, you should be able to:

1. Identify significant human developments that were made possible via language.
2. Identify several unique facts about the English language.
3. Explain and give examples of eloquence.
4. Explain why language is symbolic action.
5. Give examples of the use and misuse of linguistic symbols.
6. Discuss Langer's theory about language use.
7. Discuss the general semanticists and their theories and goals.
8. Demonstrate how an emotion laden sentence can be defused using the extentional devices suggested by the semanticists.
9. Discuss Burke's notions of identification, substances, and the role of language as a cause of guilt.
10. Explain semiotics and its use of terms such as *text, code, signifiers,* and *signifieds.*

Author, language columnist, and critic Richard Lederer (1991) observes:

> The boundary between human and animal—between the most primitive savage and the highest ape—is the language line. The birth of language is the dawn of humanity; in our beginning was the word. We have always been endowed with language because before we had words, we were not human beings. [Words] tell us that we must never take for granted the miracle of language (p. 3).

Throughout history, the uniquely human ability to create **symbols** made possible all our major cultural advances. Symbols can be many things, such as words, pictures, art works, music, and others. The dictionary definition reads "Something that represents something else by association, resemblance or convention." (*American Heritage Dictionary*, 1985). Thus our national flag represents or stands for the 13 colonies that became the original United States and also for the present 50 United States. The most widely used type of symbol is probably language. The words stand for or represent things, ideas, feelings, and so on. Before the development of the spoken word, humans resembled the beasts. But the ability to use symbols for communication enabled us to live very differently. Tribes formed using the communicative power of symbols—especially linguistic symbols. Communication facilitated the specialization of labor, the recording of history, and allowed humans to create culture. But, like the opening of Pandora's box, the use of visual and verbal symbols to communicate also allowed humans to engage in less-constructive behaviors such as lying, teasing, breaking promises, scolding, demeaning, and propagandizing. And with the development of writing and print, people found that promises, treaties, and legal contracts could be both made and broken, and laws could be used for evil as well as good. The title of the book *Deeds Done in Words* (Campbell & Jamieson, 1990) indicates that language serves as a frequent surrogate for action. Researcher and professor Neil Postman (1992) maintains that language is an "invisible technology" or a kind of machine that can "give direction to our thoughts, generate new ideas, venerate old ones, expose facts or hide them" (p. 127). Language theorist Kenneth Burke (1966) said it best when he noted that humans are "symbol making, symbol using, and symbol misusing" creatures.

This ability to use symbols—whether words, pictures, or art—lies at the heart of persuasion and so deserves our attention. We've seen that receivers must get to the bottom of persuasive meanings by carefully analyzing the verbal and nonverbal symbols being used or misused by persuaders. We need to ask whether the symbols prompt logical or emotional meanings and if they are centrally or peripherally processed in the Elaboration Likelihood Model (ELM). For instance, imagine a TV advertisement for a brand of beer. It probably uses verbal, visual, and musical or lyrical symbols. Together, they show that people who drink the brand enjoy a certain lifestyle and are happy-go-lucky.

Persuaders frequently use metaphors (which are a kind of symbol, such as "Marlboro Man") to emphasize their points. Two recent books on the right to privacy issues use metaphors in their titles: *No Place to Hide* by Robert O'Harrow (2005) and Daniel Solove's *The Digital Person* (2005). Both titles imply that we face two dangers—a loss of privacy and becoming mere ciphers or digits. Recent research on metaphors shows that their use increases persuader credibility, and they operate best when their theme is reiterated throughout the persuasive message and especially if used initially and in the conclusion (Sopory & Dillard, 2002).

By examining various metaphors and other symbols used in persuasion, we accomplish several things:

1. We discover the persuader's use or misuse of symbols.

2. We discover the persuader's stylistic preferences and what they reveal about his or her motives.

3. We can anticipate the kinds of messages likely to come from this source in the future.

One reason we can infer so much is that the making of symbols is a highly ego-involving and creative act. When we make a symbol, we own it—it belongs to us, and it reveals a good deal about us and our motives. The same thing occurs when others try to persuade us. They make symbols (usually language) and as a result they "own" their creations, and ownership can be revealing. Critical receivers need to know something about language and how to read it for clues regarding the persuader's motives. Let's look a little deeper into our own language.

THE POWER OF THE ENGLISH LANGUAGE

Lederer (1991) also offers many examples to help us avoid taking the English language (the common denominator for most persuasion we process) for granted. Consider just a few of them:

1. Of almost 3000 languages in existence today, only 10 are the native language of more than 100 million people, and English ranks second in the list only behind Chinese (pp. 19–20).

2. Users of English as a second language outnumber native users (p. 20).

3. English is the first language of 45 countries (p. 20).

4. Most of the world's books, newspapers, and magazines are written in English, and two thirds of all scientific publications and 80 percent of all stored computer texts are in English (p. 20).

5. English has one of the richest vocabularies—615,000 words in the *Oxford English Dictionary*—not including slang, many technical and scientific terms, newly invented words like iPod, BlackBerry, rurban, and blog). Compare that with French, which has about 100,000 words; Russian, which has about 130,000; or German, which has about 185,000 (p. 24). At the same time that it is so rich in vocabulary, English is remarkably economical. It requires far fewer syllables to translate Mark's gospel into English than into any Romance, Germanic, or

Slavic language (p. 29). The King James version of the Bible uses only about 8000 words, the entire works of Homer contain about 9000, and all of Milton has only about 10,000.

6. English is now the international language of science, business, politics, diplomacy, literature, tourism, pop culture, and air travel. Japanese pilots flying Japanese airliners over Japanese air space must communicate with Japanese flight controllers using English, and the same is true of the airspace over every other country in the world (p. 30).

7. English is a hospitable language—more than 70 percent of our words come from other anguages (for example, boss, kindergarten, polka, sauna, canoe, zebra, alcohol, jukebox, camel, tycoon, tundra, ketchup, pal, vodka, sugar, tattoo, and flannel, to name a few) (pp. 24).

8. Nonnative speakers report that English is the easiest second language to learn (p. 28). Lederer also demonstrates the power of a permanent aspect of the English language—its syntax. He asks students to arrange five words—"Lithuanian," "five," "scholars," "Shakespearean," and "old"—so that they make syntactical sense. Inevitably, they all come up with the same syntax or word order. Try this exercise, and discover that you and most, if not all, of your classmates come up with "five old Lithuanian Shakespearean scholars." The order of adjective strings begins with the most specific and continues to the least. There are Shakespearean scholars in countries other than Lithuania just as there other kinds of scholars. Our language use is also very sophisticated and differs in its spoken and written forms. For instance, consider the following

> InwritingandreadingtheEnglishlanguage, weneedvisualcuestodeciphermessages.

There are two visual cues in that first string of words—the comma and the capital E—and both of them shout out, "Here is a word break!" We get no such help in the second string. In written

---

BOX 5.1   **Interactive English**

 Go to www.englishforum.com/00/interactive/ (or www.englishforum.com 00 interactive) and explore the many interesting and fun ways interactive media can help you improve your use of the English language. One of the many activities at the site is the daily display of a new idiom. If you don't know what an idiom is, consider this one: "As different as chalk from cheese." What do you suppose it means? At the site there is a daily famous quote and a chat group where you can leave or receive a message about the use of English. You can trade English language lessons with students from other countries. For example, Oman will trade lessons in Arabic with you. You can leave your term papers or other texts there for free critiques. Try to solve the word puzzles and learn new slang words. The site also lists good English schools in eight countries and offers students budget travel hints. And there is even an online wizard who can read your mind. You will learn much about the English language there, and you may want to invent your own words as Shakespeare did (see Figure 5.1).

English, those cues really help, but in spoken English, we lack visual cues and consequently become baffled sometimes when trying to interpret words. In spoken English, try to determine the difference between "no notion" and "known ocean," or between "buys ink" and "buys zinc," between "meteorologist" and "meaty urologist," and between "cat's skills," "cats' kills," and "Catskills," or between "tax" and "tacks." This last example resulted in a humorous student blooper. The student wrote, "The American Revolution came about because the British put tacks in their tea." So, as persuadees, we must consider whether the persuasion is coming to us in written or spoken language or via visual symbols—the channel plays an important part in our development of meaning and deciding how to react to it.

LANGUAGE, ELOQUENCE, AND SYMBOLIC ACTION

Eloquent persuasion always seems unique and fresh. It strikes us as capturing the moment, and it may even prophesy the future. The speech made by Martin Luther King, Jr., on the night before he was assassinated had elements of prophecy. King said that God had allowed him "to go up to the mountain top," that he had "seen the Promised Land," and that he doubted that he would get there with his followers. He concluded, "But, I am happy tonight! I'm not fearing any man! Mine eyes have seen the glory of the coming of the Lord!" Although the words were not wholly original (they were drawn from the Old Testament and Julia Ward Howe's "Battle Hymn of the Republic"), his use of them was prophetic in the context of the movement he was leading. They certainly were emotional and probably were processed in the peripheral channel of the ELM.

Today we find many groups using and misusing linguistic symbols in dramatic ways on buttons, badges, or bumper stickers. Consider a few: "Think Globally; Act Locally," "Guns Don't Kill; People Do," or "Da Bulls." Others use license plates as a medium to make symbolic declarations about themselves and their philosophies: "IM N RN," "REV BOB," "COACH," "I M SX C," "MR X TC," "XME OME," or "TACKY." Each of these messages symbolically makes a revealing statement about its user. Researchers know that persons displaying bumper stickers or wearing T-shirts with product or candidate labels imprinted on them will buy the products or vote for the candidate they are promoting far more often than those who don't display the labels. Making the symbolic statement means they already took action in their minds, and

EXPERTS STATE THAT SHAKESPEARE USED A VOCABULARY OF 17,677 WORDS IN HIS WRITINGS!

10% OF THESE WORDS WERE HIS OWN INVENTIONS!

SOME OF THE WORDS WE OWE TO SHAKESPEARE ARE...

BAREFACED LEAPFROG SNOW-WHITE LONELY HURRY BRITTLE HINT

©ATCHISON 6-29

FIGURE 5.1   Other words coined by Shakespeare include "amazement," "bump," "clangor," "dwindle," "fitful," "majestic," "obscene," "pious," "road," "flibbertygibbet," "slugabeat," and "useless." Can you invent some words of your own?

SOURCE: Used by permission of Wide World Photos.

their words become deeds or substitutes for action. As Burke (1966) observed, "Language is symbolic action," and we often act out what we speak.

Language can also be misused. The deaths of Afghani and Iraqi civilians became "collateral damage," in operations Rolling Thunder and Enduring Freedom (both names are also double-speak), while "surgical air strikes" made the enormous damage sound neat and clean. Market researchers decided to use the words "recipe for success," for example, to assure working women who use Crisco that they are indeed "cooks" and not merely "microwavers" who thaw and reheat meals. A great pair of words—"Budget Gourmet"—describes an inexpensive, okay, prepackaged meal, but not one of gourmet quality.

Another reason language requires careful analysis is that it tells us a lot about the persuader's motives and reveals much by its particular verbal and visual symbols. Consider the demeaning and dehumanizing language used by anti-Semitic persuaders in the past (and perhaps in the present) in referring to Jews and other minorities as "vermin," "sludge," "garbage," "lice," "sewage," "insects," and "bloodsuckers." The recent influx of immigrants from the Middle East spawned similar linguistic venom: "camel jockey," "dot head," "pak head" or "Q-tip," all of which demeaned and dehumanized others. We need to remember that "ethnic cleansing" still occurs in many places in the world, and language serves as the major weapon for instigating dehumanization and worse. In less-dramatic settings, words create emotional responses and devalue people. What do the words "lady doctor" imply? That the doctor is not as good as a male physician? That the doctor is in the business only for the fun or sport of it? Why does "lady" convey so much meaning and evoke emotional responses? Communication scholar Dan Hahn (1998) points out how language depicts males as sexual aggressors and females as stalked prey or passive entities. Consider a few examples in which the language of seduction becomes the language of stalking: the male is described as "a real animal" or unable to "keep his paws off her," while the female is "a real dish" or "a real piece of meat" to be "turned on" or "cranked." Recently we have become sensitized to the use (and misuse) of Native American references in athletics—the Braves, the Redskins, the Chiefs, the Fighting Illini, and the Seminoles.

For an interesting peek into how emotionally involved people can get over language issues, access InfoTrac College Edition, and enter the words "language style" in the search engine. Read a few of the items dealing with language and religion, language and feminism, and language and marketing and salesmanship. Report your findings back to the class.

FIGURE 5.2 As this cartoon demonstrates, language used in its spoken form can be quite different from its use in its written form.

SOURCE: Reprinted by permission of Aaron Johnson.

The world of marketing provides many examples of the persuasive power in language choice. Brand names often reveal manufacturers' attitudes toward customers. For instance, Oster Corporation markets a "food crafter" instead of a "food chopper," which tells us that Oster takes a gourmet approach. (Chopping sounds like work. Crafting? Now, that's art.) Smoking certain brands of cigarettes can make a gender statement—Eves and Virginia Slims are for her not him. At one time, the brand names of American-made automobiles suggested status, luxury, power, and speed—Roadmaster, Continental, Coupe de Ville, and Imperial. Later, new brands coming on the market suggested technology, speed, and economy—Rabbit, Colt, Fox, Jetta, and Laser. When the baby boomers started hitting midlife, auto brand names suggested wealth, quality, durability, and long lives—Sterling, Infiniti, Sable, Probe, and Escalade.

LANGER'S APPROACH TO LANGUAGE USE

We need to identify the uses and misuses of symbols, especially in the language used by politicians, advertisers, employers, and other persuaders. A useful approach to the study of language is based on the work of philosopher and language pioneer Suzanne K. Langer (1951). She recognized the power of language symbols, and like Lederer and others, she believed that the ability to create symbols distinguishes humans from nonhumans. Language

lets us talk and think about feelings, events, and objects even when the actual feelings, events, or objects are not physically present. Langer associates two concepts with this capacity—signs and symbols. Signs indicate the presence of an event, feeling, or object. For instance, thunder signals lightning and usually rain. My dog goes into a panic at the sound of thunder—lightning struck close to her as a pup, so she tries to hide from it. If she could process symbols, I might talk to her about thunder and explain the futility of trying to hide from it. Only the comforting tone of my voice (another sign) seems to calm her down. We know that the red traffic light at an intersection signals potentially dangerous cross traffic. Guide dogs recognize the red light by its location on the top of the traffic signal and even learn to stop the person they are leading, but you cannot teach them to recognize the symbolic link between the red light and the words "cross traffic"—a much more complex connection. As Langer (1951) put it, "Symbols are not proxy of their objects, but are vehicles for the conception of objects" (p. 60). Because of our ability to use symbols, you and I understand the presence of danger by such things as the color red, the word "danger," or the skull and crossbones on a bottle. Using symbols seems to be a basic human need. Even persons unable to write, hear, or speak make symbols using visual signs, hand motions, and other symbolic means. Some symbols have a common meaning upon which most people agree. Langer called such symbols **concepts**, in contrast to **conceptions**, which she used to refer to any particular individual's meanings for the concept.

B O X 5.2   Brand Names: Discursive or Presentational?

Developing brand names entails more effort than you would think. It is no accident that Snuggle—a fabric softener—has a teddy bear as its logo. When you see Snuggle on the shelf, you probably do not think of actually "snuggling" up with a good book and a cup of coffee, but you might put a package of it in your shopping cart and feel good about having done so. There is no string of words to be followed when you look at the brand, its logo, or its packaging. The brand's name is a presentational symbol.

Observe the brand on your next shopping trip. Now consider another brand name—TheraFlu, a cold medicine meant to be taken as a hot drink before going to bed. There is no evidence that the brand works any better than any other nighttime cold medicine having similar ingredients. However, the brand is threatening sales of NyQuil, the first over-the-counter nighttime cold medicine on the market. Why? Perhaps there is a presentational explanation (Feig, 1997).

All human communication and hence persuasion relies on concepts and conceptions. So, naturally, the possibility of misunderstanding always presents itself.

Langer introduced three terms to be used when discussing meaning: "signification," "denotation," and "connotation." **Signification** means a sign that accompanies the thing being considered. So a skull and crossbones on a bottle signifies "Danger—Poison!" **Denotation** refers to the common and shared meaning we all have for any concept. **Connotation** refers to my or your private and emotional meaning for any concept such as "danger." The denotation of the word would be the dictionary definition of the word danger as "Exposure or vulnerability to harm or loss." (*American Heritage Dictionary*, 1985). The connotation of the word is my or your personal and individual conception of danger. Because of my Minnesota background, I find blizzards to be dangerous. Someone from Florida might not, and the obverse would be true for my connotation for the word "hurricane." And of course, we are increasingly facing culturally diverse connotations for words and concepts. For example, China thinks of itself as extraordinarily egalitarian. However, professor and marketing consultant Barry Feig (1997) reports that a flourishing trade exists there for counterfeit labels for high-priced and high-status brands of bicycles. Few persons in China own autos, but most have bicycles, and most of them are quite ordinary—

almost generic. The fake labels are symbols that communicate status in a society where status differences supposedly don't exist,

Langer also maintained that meaning is either "discursive" or "presentational." **Discursive symbols** are usually made up of sequential, smaller bits of meaning. Musically, this would be equivalent to movements in a symphony. In a drama it would be the unfolding of a plot. For our purposes, discursive symbols usually occur in the form of language. **Presentational meaning**, on the other hand, occurs all at once and the message must be experienced in its entirety, such as when one looks at a painting, architecture, or a statue, or experiences a ritual. Thus, some of the "meaning" in any advertisement is discursive (the slogans, jingles, and ad copy), and some is presentational (the graphic layout, fonts, and pictures). Similarly, some of the meaning in a political campaign occurs discursively (the speeches, press releases, and interviews), and some is presentational (the way the candidate looks, his or her "image," and the pictorial and music in spot ads).

GENERAL SEMANTICS AND LANGUAGE USE

Beginning with the landmark work *Science and Sanity* by Count Alfred Korzybski (1947), scholars known as general semanticists began a careful and systematic study of the use of language and meaning. They intended to devise tools for improving the understanding of human communication and to encourage careful and precise uses of language. Most of them were from academic departments of English or psychology, though Korzybski was originally a military intelligence officer who debriefed spies and double agents. His theory grew out of the difficulty in determining what these persons *really* meant when they communicated something. The semanticists wanted to train people to be very specific in sending and receiving words, to avoid the communication pitfalls such as stereotyping that had led to the rise of demagogues in many countries prior to WW II. For instance, the general semanticists believed people needed to learn to be aware that the appeals made by most persuaders were **maps** or inner perceptions and not **territories** or realities. A map is what exists in my or your head, but a territory is what exists in the real world. For example, you might have an image of a certain place, experience, or event. That image is only a map. That place, experience, or event may not resemble your map of it at all. With the advent of such interactive media as virtual reality, Internet gaming and dating, the home shopping network, and telemarketing, receivers face an increased blurring of map and territory. As a result, we need to heed the advice of the **semanticists** more than ever because much of the interactive world is virtual. In other words, interactive messages are maps, not territories.

Take the case of stereotyping. Stereotypes are supposedly unreliable. No member of a class or group is exactly like any other member. To counter the miscommunication that can result from stereotyping, receivers need to heed Korzybski's reminder that "the map is not the territory." In other words, our internal conceptions of other persons, ethnic groups, and ideas will differ widely from the actual persons, groups, things, and ideas. Korzybski and his colleagues recognized the difference between an event, object, or experience and any individual's conception of it. In their scheme, the word "map" equates to Langer's "conception," and the word "territory" equates to "objective reality" or close to Langer's "concept."

Our faulty maps get expressed through the language we create to convey them, and they usually miscommunicate in some way. For the general semanticists, the real problems occur when people act as if their maps accurately describe the territory, thus turning the map into the territory. Korzybski believed that we all carry thousands of maps around in our heads that represent nonexistent, incorrect, or false territories. To demonstrate this concept for yourself, write down the name of a food you have never eaten, a place you have never been, and an experience you have never had. These words serve as maps for unknown territories. You probably think that fried brains would feel slimy and gooshy in your mouth. In reality, they have the texture of well-scrambled eggs. What about your map for skydiving or for being a rock star? What about your maps for various ethnic groups? What about your map for places that you have only visited via the Internet?

Access InfoTrac College Edition, and enter the word "psycholinguistics" in the search engine. Psycholinguists are persons who try to get at what is in our heads, using our language use as their raw material. Go to the subdivisions options and select the analysis option. Examine the items referring to "Fatal Words" (which concerns the crash of ValuJet flight 592), "Words, Words, Words," "Linguistic Virtual Reality," and the language used by schizophrenics. How do the items heighten your awareness of the power of word choice?

In most cases, your maps will be very different from the territories as they really exist. Our mental, visual, and word maps present a real problem in communication, and especially in persuasion. Just as persuaders must discover the common ground of ideas so they can persuade us, they also must identify the maps we carry around in our heads. Then they must either play on those maps (using our misperceptions to their advantage) or try to get us to correct our faulty maps. Only then can they persuade us to buy, vote, join, or change our behavior. Our faulty maps are frequently expressed through language.

WAY UP NORTH, WHERE THE HUSKIES GO BY AL O

HEY EVANS, DID YOU EVER GET A RESPONSE FROM THE NORTHERN STAR ABOUT THE ARTICLE YOU SUBMITTED?

YEA, GRANT, I JUST GOT AN EMAIL FROM ONE OF THE EDITORS, "DEAR BOB"...

MY NAME AIN'T BOB..

HA HA HA! WHAT AN IDIOT, LOOK, HE SPELLED "BOB" WITH TWO "O"s

FIGURE 5.3 It is clear that Bob doesn't understand the map/territory distinction.
SOURCE: Used with permission of Al Ochsner.

We create and use words to communicate and to build our maps. We react to these words as if they are true representations of the territories we imagine. To the semanticists, this **signal response** is equivalent to my dog trying to hide from lightning whenever she experiences the sign or signal of thunder. Signal responses are emotionally triggered reactions to symbolic acts (including language use), and these responses play out as if the act were actually being committed. In a recent example of the signal response, an official in the Washington, D.C., city council and aide to the African American mayor was removed from the council because he used the word "niggardly." Now, the dictionary definition of the word is "unwilling to give, spend, or share . . . stingy, scanty, or meager" (*American Heritage Dictionary*, 1985). But because the word sounds similar to a racial epithet—the "N" word—it prompted a signal response among members of the council, even after a definition of the word was given. The semanticists were accurate about the power of the signal response (National Public Radio, 1999).

The semanticists wanted to train senders and receivers to be continually alert to the difference between signals and symbols. Semanticists also try to isolate meaning in concrete terms. Let's examine a fairly inflammatory sentence and then try to defuse it using the techniques of the semanticists. Suppose I tell you, "Your generation of college students is conservative, selfish, and lazy." Your response will probably be negative because of the connotations of some of the words used—"selfish" and "lazy" for sure, and maybe "conservative" as well. Semanticists would advise us to use what they call **extensional devices**, or techniques for neutralizing or defusing the emotional connotations that often accompany words by adding information that makes my meaning clear to you and others. One extensional device in my language use would be to identify the specific college students I have in mind. Semanticists call this **indexing**. In this case, my statement would change to something like, "Your generation of college students, who have everything paid for by their parents, is conservative, selfish, and lazy." That would calm some of you because you probably know fellow students who have everything paid for, including lots of extras that you don't get.

But I still would not be as clear as I could be, according to the semanticists. They would further urge me to use an extensional device called **dating**, or letting you know the time frame of my judgment about college students. Using dating, I might say something like, "Generation X college students who have everything paid for by their parents are conservative, selfish, and lazy." That might cool you down a little more. Here is where the extensional device semanticists call **etc.** comes into play. This device is meant to indicate that we can never tell the whole story about any person, event, place,

---

BOX 5.3   Language and Cultural Diversity

 Did you know that only four countries in all of Latin America have populations greater than the Latino population of the United States, which is now about 22.5 million? Or did you know that there are more Asians in the United States than there are in Cambodia, Laos, Hong Kong, or Singapore? Or did you know that at some point in this century, Latinos will outnumber non-Latinos? These are just a few of the many facts mentioned by Nido R. Qubein. He is an internationally known consultant, award-winning speaker, president of High Point University, and he sits on the boards of several Fortune 500 companies and is chairman of a national public relations firm, Business Life Inc., and CEO of the Great Harvest Bread Company. He came to the United States as a teenager, with no contacts, no English language skills, and less than $50 to his name. He travels the globe and urges his audiences to remember that "people from different backgrounds send and receive messages through cultural filters" and that the same words, facial expressions, and gestures have different meanings depending on one's cultural heritage. You may want to access his home page at www.nidoqubein.com/index. There you can listen to him speak, get samples of his video and audio tapes, and get free articles written by him.

---

or thing. Using this device, I might say, "Generation X college students who have everything paid for by their parents are conservative, selfish, and lazy, among other things." Now conservatism, selfishness, and laziness aren't their only attributes. For example, they also might be "societally concerned about environmental issues," "worried about honesty," or any of a number of other positive attributes.

Finally, the semanticists would advise using an extensional device called **quotation marks**, which is a way to indicate that I am using those flag words in a particular way—my way, which isn't necessarily your way. For example, my use of the word "selfish" might relate to the students' unwillingness to help other students succeed in class. Or it could relate to their unwillingness to volunteer in the community or to do any of a number of other things that wouldn't necessarily match your meaning for the word "selfish." My sentence might now read, "Generation X college students who have everything paid for by their parents are 'conservative,' 'selfish,' and 'lazy,' among other things." Now you would probably probe for my meanings for the emotional words, or you might even agree with the sentence.

Using extensional devices in decoding persuasion helps us make sure the maps in our heads more closely resemble the territory to which we refer. Persuaders need to design specific, concrete extensional messages, especially when using emotionally charged words or abstract words for which there can be many meanings. More important, persuadees need to consider whether they are being appealed to via the map or the territory. Abstract words such as "power," "democracy," "freedom," "morals," and "truth" are particularly vulnerable to misunderstanding. Unethical persuaders often intentionally use abstract or emotionally charged language to achieve their purposes. It is our task to remember the map/territory distinction and to use extensional devices as we attend to symbols. We must remember that receivers also have "response-ability."

To learn more about the power of words, access InfoTrac College Edition, enter the word "newspeak" in the key word option, and explore the item titled "Pomobabble" by Dennis Arrow, referring to postmodernism. Make a list of your top ten examples, make copies for your classmates, and pass them out.

BURKE'S APPROACH TO LANGUAGE USE

Perhaps no language theorist or critic wrote as many treatises in as wide a variety of fields or with as broad a knowledge of human symbolic behavior as Kenneth

Burke did. Burke focused on language as it is used to persuade people to action. Burke (1950) defined persuasion as "the use of language as a symbolic means of inducing cooperation in beings that by nature respond to symbols" (p. 43). This active cooperation is induced by what he termed **identification**, a concept similar to Aristotle's "common ground" and our use of "co-creation," as noted in Chapter 1.

According to Burke, the development of identification occurs through the linguistic sharing of what he called **sub-stances**. He divided the word into its prefix *sub*, meaning "beneath," and *stances*, which refers to "grounding" or "places." In other words, identification rests on the beliefs, values, experiences, and views of the self that we share with others. Burke noted that these sub-stances or "places" emerge in the words we use to define things, persons, and issues. Critical receivers of persuasion need to pay particular attention to the words, images, and metaphors that persuaders use to create (or undermine) identification. Our self-concepts are made up of various kinds of symbolic and real possessions, including physical things (clothing, cars, books), experiential things (work, activities, recreations), and philosophical possessions (beliefs, attitudes, values). Identification with others develops to the degree that we symbolically share these possessions. In other words, we identify with persons who articulate a similar view of life, who enjoy the same kinds of activities, have similar physical possessions, lifestyles, beliefs, attitudes, and so on. If we identify with persuaders, we naturally tend to believe what they say and probably follow their advice. Thus, the job of persuaders is to call attention to those sub-stances that they share with receivers. The receivers' job, in turn, is to critically examine these sub-stances to see whether they truly are shared values and beliefs or whether the persuader merely makes them appear to be shared. In other words, persuadees need to decode persuaders' messages for their authenticity, and determine whether the messages reflect persuaders' real beliefs and values or are merely convenient concoctions.

The dictionary defines substance as "the essential part of a thing—its essence." The definition is especially meaningful with regard to identification. We identify with others because we share their essential beliefs, values, experiences, and so on. I am like you and you are like me to some degree; hence, I will believe you when you try to persuade me. For example, consider the Academy Award–winning film *Million Dollar Baby*. The manager character played by Clint Eastwood shares certain experiences and values with the coach character played by Morgan Freeman. Freeman relies on these shared substances to help convince Eastwood to coach and manage the aspiring young boxer played by Hillery Swank.

To Burke, most persuasion attempts to describe our "essential parts," and this description is always revealing. All words have emotional shadings and reveal the feelings, attitudes, values, and judgments of the user. Examining persuasive language can tell us about ourselves and *about* the persuaders who solicit our interest, support, and commitment. Burke also suggested that symbolic activities like the use of language inevitably cause people to have feelings of guilt. From the beginning, language automatically led to rule making and moralizing. Because we all break the rules or don't measure up to moral standards at some time, we experience some degree of guilt. Burke argued that all human cultures exhibit patterns that help explain guilt, and the development of language in each of us is foremost. For example, the word "puppy" is clearly not an actual puppy, so language that names what something is inherently leads to the idea of what something is not—**the negative**. The negative then leads to sets of "thou shalt nots," whether supernatural, parental, spousal, or societal. Inevitably, we fail to obey some of these negatives and again experience shame and guilt. "No" is one of the first things we learn as children, and we realize that it means we just displeased someone. We hear "No, no, no," over and over, and then we begin to use it ourselves. It gives us power, and we go about testing the extent of that power during the "terrible twos" and, in fact, throughout life.

The second behavioral pattern that contributes to guilt relies on the principle of hierarchy, or "pecking order." It happens in all societies and groups, and it leads to either jealousy of others or to competition. We rarely (perhaps never) reach the top of the pecking order, and we feel guilty about that as well. A third source of guilt is our innate need to achieve perfection. Unfortunately, we all fall short of our goals and so feel inadequate and ashamed for not doing our best. This shame makes us feel guilty about not living up to our own or others' expectations. How do we rid ourselves of guilt? In most religions, guilt is purged symbolically—we offer up a sacrifice or engage in self-inflicted suffering, penance, and so on. And these cures are used in our self-persuasion as well: "I'll be good, God, if only I get out of this dilemma." But the handiest and most flexible, creative, artistic, and universal means to whip guilt is through language. We usually try to get rid of guilt by talking about it—in prayer, to ourselves, to a counselor or authority figure, or to someone with whom we identify. Consider how frequently persuaders offer us symbolic ways to alleviate our guilt. The parents who feel guilty take their family on a vacation to Disney World. The imperfect child tries to do better at school by using the Internet and spending more time studying and doing extra credit assignments.

In summary, persuasion via identification works because we all share sub-stances and because we all experience guilt. In processing persuasion, try to recognize that persuaders create identification by referring to shared sub-stances—preferred beliefs, lifestyles, and values. They motivate us by appealing to our internal and inevitable feelings of inadequacy or guilt. Examine the language and images in advertisements, sermons, political appeals, and other messages, reminding yourself of the strategies being used to create identification, and also feelings of imperfection, shame, and guilt.

To see how critics have used Kenneth Burke's theories, go to InfoTrac College Edition, and select the Powertrac option. Enter the words "Kenneth Burke" in the search engine. Read the "Kenneth Burke—R.I.P." item to get a feel for the importance of his work. Access any of the items listed to learn how others have applied Burke's theories in language analysis. Report your findings to the class.

THE SEMIOTIC APPROACH TO LANGUAGE USE

Semiotics is also concerned with the generation and conveyance of meaning. A number of scholars are associated with this "science" of meaning, including Umberto Eco. Semiologists apply the tools of linguistics to a wide variety of texts. Almost anything can be a text that has one or more meanings—semioticians talk about the "meaning" of a doctor's office, a meal, a TV program, a circus, or any other verbal or nonverbal symbolic event. According to semiotic theory, all texts convey meaning through **signs** or **signifiers**. A signifier in a restaurant could be the presence or absence of a hostess. It signifies that we are to wait to be shown to our seat or that we can select our own in the case of the absent hostess. **Signifieds** are the things (events, rules, etc.) to which the signifiers refer. These signifiers interact with one another in meaningful and sophisticated, but not obvious, relationships, or sign systems, which make up the "language," or "code," of the text.

These codes can be inferred from a text. For example, consider your classroom as a text having its own signifiers and signifieds—some linguistic and some visual, some logical and some emotional. The room usually has an institutional "meaning" signified by the type of walls, lighting, boards, and so on. Blackboards and plaster walls usually signify that the building is an old one. Green or white boards and cinder block walls signify a newer building. The kinds of student desks (with or without arms), the arrangement of the room (for example, desks in rows versus groups), and the physical objects (an overhead versus a video projector) are all signifiers that tell us about what to expect when entering this "text." There may be a clock on the wall, signifying that time is important here, and it may be in view of the students or only to someone facing the back of the room (usually the teacher).

Consider several of the codes embedded in various texts. For example, a simple code is the use of black and white hats in old cowboy movies to indicate the good guy and the bad guy. Pages

FIGURE 5.4 Bob doesn't get the meaning of the word "euphemize."
SOURCE: Used with permission of Al Ochsner.

being blown off a calendar in a movie signify the passage of time. What meanings are conveyed by drinking out of mugs as opposed to Styrofoam cups or fine china? Each type of cup is a signifier, and each coffee drinker, consciously or unconsciously, is communicating a different message, yet words aren't necessarily involved.

In a semiotic approach to the study of meaning, we try to read each message from several perspectives: (1) the words that are or are not spoken, (2) the context in or from which they are spoken, and (3) the other signifiers in the message—visuals, colors, tone of voice, furnishings, and so on. Indeed, semioticians approach any communication event as if it were a text to be read by the receiver or analyst. More and more marketing and advertising research is being conducted from a semiological approach, according to Curt Suplee (1987) of the *Washington Post*. He quotes advertising and design celebrity George Lois as saying, "When advertising is great advertising, it fastens on the myths, signs, and symbols of our common experience and becomes, quite literally, a benefit of the product.... As a result of great advertising, food tastes better, clothes feel snugger, cars ride smoother. The stuff of semiotics becomes the magic of advertising" (p. 3).

For an excellent discussion of how semiotics can be applied and for insight into how the worlds of advertising and marketing use semiotics,

access InfoTrac College Edition, and enter the word "semiotics" in the search engine. Select the analysis option, go to the item drawn from the *Journal of Advertising Research*, and learn how agencies like Saatchi and Saatchi use the tool to market entertainment products. Now go to the research option, and select the article from *The International Journal of Market Research* to learn how Guinness beer uses semiotics in designing its advertising.

Semiotics also can help us understand where a persuader is coming from and what his or her agenda might be. What is the semiotic meaning of the following letter sent to the chair of my department?

Dear Professor Jones,

I am interested in directives as to how one may proficiency out of the speech requirement. Having been advised to seek counsel from you "specifically"—I sincerely hope you will not be displeased with my enthusiasm by asking this indulgence. There is a basis for my pursuing this inquisition as I am an adept speaker with substantiating merits. I will be overburdened with more difficult courses this fall—at least they will be concomitant with my educational objectives in the fields of Fine Arts and Languages. It would be a ludicrous exercise in futility to be

FIGURE 5.5 As this cartoon illustrates, language is fun to experiment with as well as being important in persuasion.

SOURCE: *Frank and Ernest.* ©United Feature Syndicate Inc. Used with permission.

mired in an unfecund speech course when I have already distinguished myself in that arena. I maintained an "A" average in an *elite* "advanced" speech course in High School. I am quite noted for my bursts of oratory and my verbal dexterity in the public "reality"—quite a different platform than the pseudo realism of the college environs. There is a small matter of age—I shall be twenty-two this fall. I am four years older than the average college freshman. I am afraid that I would dissipate with boredom, if confined with a bunch of *teenagers*. Surely you can advise something that would be a more palatable alternative?

Yours sincerely,

P.S. Please do not misconstrue this "inquiry" as the enterprise of an arrogant student, but one who will be so immersed in *serious* intellectual pursuits that the "speech" requirement will be too nonsensical and burdensome.

If ever a student needed to learn about communication, it was this individual. But what does the language usage here tell you about the writer of the letter? She uses sixty-four-dollar words—perhaps a code for insecurity—but she seems unsure about her choice of words, as shown by her putting words into quotation marks, which indicates that she has her own special meaning for them. She also uses italics to signify that this word has special meaning and importance. She also misuses some words. For example, she says that she is pursuing an "inquisition" when she means an "inquiry." An inquisition is a tribunal for suppressing religious heresy. She says she has "substantiating merits" when she probably means that she has "substantial reasons" for being excused from the course. These and other signifiers add up to the semiotic meaning of the letter, which is that the author is insecure and hopes to impress the recipient of the letter. As Figure 5.5 demonstrates, semiotic meanings can be toyed with for fun.

To explore the fascinating work of Berger on the semiotics of cartoons (he is a cartoonist himself), go to InfoTrac College Edition, and select the Powertrac option. Enter the words "Arthur Asa Berger" in the search engine. Then access the item titled "Scratches from a Secret Agent," and enjoy.

REVIEW AND CONCLUSION

By now, you probably have deeper appreciation for human symbol making, use, and misuse, and for the power of language as a tool of persuasion—especially the English language. You might realize how much meaning you can uncover when you critically analyze the symbols used in persuasion. It takes time and effort to decode discursive and presentational persuasion, to locate the meanings being used to create a state of identification, to determine the difference between the map and the territory, and to learn the many codes operating in various kinds of texts. To become a responsible persuadee, you need tools to assist you in analyzing the many persuasive messages targeted at you. Chapter 6 focuses on some tools for doing this.

KEY TERMS

When you have read this chapter you should be able to identify, explain, and give an example of the following words or concepts.

symbols	discursive symbols	extensional devices	sub-stances
concepts	presentational meaning	indexing	the negative
conceptions	maps	dating	semiotics
signification	territories	etc.	signs
denotation	semanticists	quotation marks	signifiers
connotation	signal response	identification	signifieds

APPLICATION OF ETHICS

Here is the situation: An interpreter arrives a few minutes before a court of law is called to order. He wants to speak to the defendant, who is a non-English speaker, to determine if using Spanish instead of English will be acceptable. The defendant lets the interpreter know that Spanish is a second language for him (his first language is an indigenous dialect), but that he understands the interpreter and proceeding in Spanish is acceptable. The interpreter has three options: (1) Tell the judge of the situation and that Spanish interpretation is acceptable to the defendant. (2) Say nothing and proceed with the interpretation in Spanish since the defendant has said it is OK with him. (3) Inform the defendant's attorney and let him decide how to proceed. Which option seems most ethical to you? Does the interpreter have any ethical obligation to inform the Judge? Is he ethically obliged to say anything?

QUESTIONS FOR FURTHER THOUGHT

1. Why is symbol making such a powerful human activity? Give several examples of how symbols create high involvement in people. Are symbols logical or emotional? Are they processed centrally or peripherally?

2. What is meant by Burke's phrase "symbol misusing"? Give some examples of the misuse of symbols.

3. Why is the English language so powerful?

4. Why is a red stoplight a sign to a leader dog, and how is that "meaning" different from the words "red stoplight" or "dangerous cross traffic"?

5. What did Suzanne Langer mean when she said that symbols are the "vehicles for the conception of objects"?

6. What is the difference between signification, denotation, and connotation?

7. What is the difference between a presentational and a discursive symbol?

8. What is the difference between a map and a territory, according to the general semanticists? Give an example of one of your food maps.

One of your geographic maps? One of your experience maps?

9. Was Bill Clinton's meaning for "sexual relations" (with Monica Lewinsky) an ethical use of language? Why or why not?

10. What is a signal response? Give several examples.

11. What are the extensional devices recommended by general semanticists? What purpose do these devices serve? Give examples.

12. What did Kenneth Burke mean by "identification"? By "sub-stance"? By the "need for hierarchy"? By "guilt"? How do these concepts explain why language is so important in persuasion and in living life?

13. What is the difference between a signifier and a signified? What is a code? Give examples of simple codes from the worlds of sports, politics, and/or advertising.

14. Is it ethical for advertisers to use guilt to get us to buy? Why or why not? Give some examples.

 For online activities, go to the *Persuasion* book companion website at http://communication.wadsworth.com/larson11.

6

Tools for Analyzing Language and Other Persuasive Symbols

LEARNING GOALS

After reading this chapter, you should be able to:

1. Identify the three dimensions of language focused on in this chapter and give examples of each that you have found or invented.

2. Discuss the powers of symbolic expression in persuasion.

3. Give examples of tools of analysis for each of the dimensions of language.

4. Explain the pentad and give examples of each term in contemporary persuasion.

5. Explain and give examples of god, devil, and charismatic terms in contemporary persuasion.

6. Explain and give examples of archetypal metaphors being used in contemporary persuasion.

7. Explain the difference between the pragmatic and unifying styles and give examples of each from contemporary persuasion.

8. Explain semiotics and discuss how texts and codes work.

Now that you have some perspective on the making, use, and misuse of symbols and an appreciation for the power of language (and the English language in particular), let's consider several ways to analyze both verbal and nonverbal persuasive symbols. Such analysis helps us to reject misguided, fallacious, and deceptive messages. We mentioned several recent examples such as the divided "official" stances on Social Security, the non-existent "W.M.D.s" in Iraq, and the lies of CEOs of corporations who bankrupted their companies while getting rich in the process. All of these used persuasive language, and we'll face many more examples in the future, so receivers need to learn about language use and how to uncover deceptive persuasion.

The cube in Figure 6.1 represents three of the many dimensions of language. They are (1) the **semantic dimension** (the meanings for a word), (2) the **functional dimension** (the jobs that words can do, such as naming), and (3) the **thematic dimension** (the feel and texture of words like "swoosh"). Following our consideration of these dimensions, you will find a discussion of several tools useful in analyzing each dimension and several example analyses. Notice that the cube consists of many smaller cubes, each representing a word or set of words having its own unique semantic, functional, and thematic dimensions. Now consider this line of ad copy: "Sudden Tan from Coppertone Tans on Touch for a Tan That Lasts for Days." On the functional dimension, the words "Sudden Tan" name a product. Semantically, much more is suggested. The word "sudden" describes an almost instantaneous tan, and, indeed, the product dyes skin "tan" on contact. The ad's headline—"Got a Minute? Get a Tan"—is superimposed over before-and-after photos of an attractive blonde who has presumably been dyed tan. On a thematic level, the words do even more. The word "sudden" sounds and feels like the word "sun," so the brand name sounds like the word "suntan."

Consider these examples of thematic language use.

- The "Kero-Sun" heater burns kerosene and warms your house like the sun.
- Have a "Soup-erb Supper" with a package of Hamburger Helper's beef-vegetable soup.

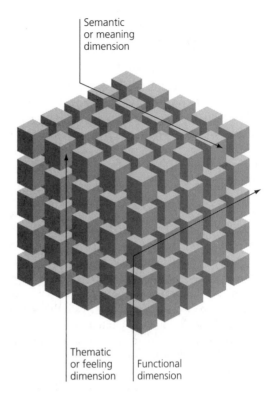

FIGURE 6.1 This figure shows three of the many dimensions of language that are at work when persuadees decode persuasive messages.

- Try My Mom's Meatloaf mix—Meat Loaf that Tastes Like Home.
- Presto named its popcorn popper "The Big Poppa," which sounds like popcorn being popped.

THE FUNCTIONAL DIMENSION: WHAT DO THE WORDS DO?

Words can do many things. They can motivate action, identify causes and effects, and lay blame. During a trial in which an abortionist and the woman who had the abortion faced charges of manslaughter, language functioned in several ways.

The defense referred to attempts to abort the fetus earlier in the pregnancy, saying, "After two unsuccessful attempts. . . ." The prosecutor used active verbs and pronouns, saying, "They tried twice, . . . they were unsuccessful," to lay blame on the woman and the doctor. In one case, the function of the words blunted the accusation—in the other, it focused blame. The functional dimension has powerful potential to simply shift our focus (Andrews, 1984). Take, for example, the function of defining, which can "frame" or set the perspective for the persuasive appeal. As communication scholar Dan Hahn (1998) observes, "Definitions are like blinders on a horse: They focus attention on some aspects while blinding us to others" (p. 53). For example, consider the quarantining of trade to a country to stop shipping into and out of its ports. You could call such an action a "blockade," which is considered an act of war. Now, call the actions "sanctions" That's what the United States did when it outlawed trade by American companies with Iran, Iraq, and North Korea, portraying these nations as part of an "axis of evil" that had sinister worldwide motives. This word choice served at least three functions. First, it signaled the three nations that the United States wasn't necessarily interested in all-out war with them (though we ultimately invaded Iraq). Second, it gave a justification for the resulting hardships being endured by their populace. Finally, it vilified the nations as "outlaws" in the world community. In another example, Hahn points out the meanings associated with the label "middle class." For some, the term means those earning between $17,000 and $64,000 per year (pp. 61–62). To others it means a lifestyle that includes a house, two late model cars, and membership in the local YMCA. So an important dimension of persuasive language is the functions, tasks, or jobs that the words perform.

Communication researcher Robert Cialdini (2001) observes that some language functions to compensate for our personal feelings of insecurity or low self-worth. He notes that "the persistent name dropper" is a classic example (p. 173); name droppers bolster their own self-esteem by knowing important personalities. Sometimes, words create

fear. Consider the underlined words in this sales pitch that functioned to instill fear in the small business owner:

> We've been talking with businesses in the area, and they tell us that they're afraid of three things. The area is growing so fast that they fear that they'll miss out on the new movers coming into the area. Research shows that twenty percent of the country is on the move at any one time, and they worry about the competition getting to these folks first. Then they tear their hair out when they hear that people who have lived in the same area for years don't even know where their business is located. And finally they're terrified that their brand loyal customers will go to the competition because of price or some other reason.

The underlined words functioned to induce fear about what might happen to the business owner's existing and potential customer base. The words interact with preexisting ideas and fears in the prospect's mind. Then he or she co-creates the possibility of loss. In another successful example, a "Got Milk?" ad claimed, "One in five osteoporosis victims is male. Luckily, fat free milk has the calcium bones need to beat it." The words create fear in the male reader who uses this new knowledge to change his behavior. So naming potential problems interacts with the reader and prompts fear and a motivation to take action—drink more milk.

Cialdini (2001) identifies several functions that language can perform other than building fear. These include the function of creating deference or blind obedience to authority (p. 182). Cialdini says that the use of titles can also function to convey authority (p. 188). Today, we hire an "administrative assistant" not a "secretary," and the new name functions to build the employee's self-worth. Another function Cialdini identifies is the power of language to create "the scarcity effect" (p. 205). Consider the words "Price Good Only While Supplies Last!" or "Act Now! Only a Few Left at this Price!" These phrases function to convince the persuadee that the product is in short supply. This creates "a sense of urgency" and prompts the prospect to take action.

THE SEMANTIC DIMENSION: WHAT DO THE WORDS MEAN?

The semantic dimension explains the various shades of meaning given to language. For example, in the abortion case discussed earlier, the defense won a ruling censoring the use of the terms "baby boy" and "human being" and allowing only the word "fetus" to be used by the prosecution. We react very differently to the word "fetus" than we do to "baby boy." Clearly, choosing words with the proper semantic meanings can be critical to the interactive co-creation of persuasive meaning.

Word choice also provides clues about the source's underlying intentions. It is not surprising that words like "questionable business practices" and "insider trading" convey different meanings than the words used by critics, which include terms like "looting" the company's pension fund, "destroying employee security," "auditing flimflams," and "corporate sharks drawn by blood." The impeachment trial of Bill Clinton produced many examples of carefully chosen language characterizing Clinton with terms such as "perjurious," "willfully corrupted," and "betrayed." They encourage certain kinds of co-created persuasive meanings. For example, receivers could infer from these words that Clinton was a habitual liar who didn't even respect the office he held or the oath of office to which he swore (Democracy Project, 1999).

Let us now turn to the thematic dimension of language to discover how words can convey feelings, sometimes even via one of the five senses.

THE THEMATIC DIMENSION: HOW DO THE WORDS FEEL?

In addition to having functional and semantic meanings, some words also have a feeling, a texture, or a theme to them. You almost physically sense them. Onomatopoeic words sound like their meaning. For example, listen to the feel of "shush," "whir," "rustle," "buzz," "hum," "ding," or "boom." Some-what less obvious thematic examples rely on **assonance**, or the repetition of vowels or vowel sounds—for example, "the low moans of our own soldiers rolled across the battlefield like the groans of the doomed." **Alliteration** is similar except that it relies on the repetition of consonants, as in "Smoke Satin Cigarettes—Sense Their Silky Smoothness." Both alliteration and assonance are favorite tools of the advertising copywriter. They're fun to hear and repeat. Sometimes, figures of speech produce a texture or theme. For example, the use of powerful metaphors creates thematic meaning or texture. According to communication researcher Michael Osborn (1967), wartime British prime minister Winston Churchill, repeatedly used what Osborn termed archetypal (universal) metaphors of "light" to characterize the British military and citizenry and "dark" ones for the enemy. In a speech during WWII, he said,

> If we stand up to him (Hitler), all Europe may be free and the life of the world may move forward into broad, sunlit uplands. But if we fail, then the whole world, including the United States, including all that we have known and cared for, will sink into the abyss of a new Dark Age made more sinister, and perhaps protracted, by the lights of perverted science.... Good night then: sleep to gather strength for the morning. For the morning will come. Brightly will it shine on the brave and the true, kindly upon all who suffer for the cause, glorious upon the tombs of heroes. Thus will shine the dawn (pp. 115–126).

Archetypal metaphors usually refer to common substances or events like light and dark, birth and rite of passage, and frequently are associated with the sacred or profane. Some familiar ones include references to fire, water, and blood. President George W. Bush repeatedly used the fire metaphor to characterize the rise of democracy in the Middle East and elsewhere in the world where freedom's "flames need to be fanned." Opponents of the invasion into Iraq declared that it would take a long time to "wash the blood" from America's hands. So metaphoric language can carry a lot of persuasive cargo.

By carefully considering the functional, semantic, and thematic dimensions of any persuasive message, we exercise our response-ability as receivers. Even if our interpretation of a message doesn't match the persuader's, the analytic process we apply to persuasive messages helps ensure the responsible reception of persuasion.

THE POWER OF SYMBOLIC EXPRESSION

Symbolic expression affects emotions and/or the intellect, but it sometimes has actual physical effects. For example, the kinds of symbols people use and respond to can affect their health. People who use expressions such as "I can't stomach it," "I'm fed up," or "It's been eating away at me now for a year" are more likely to have more stomach ulcers than do others (*Chicago Daily News,* 1972). Symbolic days like birthdays have dramatic effects. In nursing homes, more persons die during the two months after birthdays than during the two months before (Lewis & Lewis, 1972). Thomas Jefferson and John Adams both died on the Fourth of July, a date of tremendous significance for both of them (Koenig, 1972). Some people die soon after the death of a loved one—and sometimes from the same disease. Symbolic sympathy pains can become real (Koenig, 1972). According to Seigel, the words we say to ourselves can also cure disease and even stop hemorrhaging (1989).

Burke (1960) makes an argument that language is symbolic action, and that may be an explanation of why words have almost magical possibilities. We know that words are central to most religious beliefs (e.g., see John 1:1, and in Genesis God speaks with each act of creation) and are usually spoken at sacramental enactments (i.e., marriage or the burial of the dead) in most if not all religions. Words are also important in law (e.g., the defendant must plead "guilty" or "not guilty" unless handicapped, and the verdict and sentence must also be spoken).

Not only do symbols deeply affect individuals, but they also serve as a kind of psychological cement for holding a society or culture together. Traditionally, a sacred hoop representing the four seasons of the earth and the four directions from which weather might come served as the central life metaphor for the Lakota Indians. The hoop's crossed thongs symbolized the sacred tree of life and the crossroads of life. A Lakota holy man named Black Elk (1971) explained the symbolic power of the circle for his people:

> You have noticed that everything an Indian does is in a circle, and that is because the Power of the World always works in circles, and everything tries to be round. In the old days when we were a strong and happy people, all our power came to us from the sacred hoop of the nation and so long as the hoop was unbroken the people flourished.... Everything the Power of the World does is done in a circle.... Even the seasons form a great circle in their changing and always come back again to where they were. The life of a man is a circle from childhood to childhood and so it is in everything where power moves. Our tipis were round like the nests of birds and these were always set in a circle, the nation's hoop, a nest of many nests where the Great Spirit meant for us to hatch our children (p. 134).

Black Elk believed that his tribe had lost all its power or "medicine" when forced out of traditional round tepees and into square reservation houses.

What symbols serve as the cultural cement for our way of life: the flag, the Constitution, the home, competition, and sports? What are the symbols that unite our diverse cultural segments? What might someone of Chinese heritage use for cultural cement? References to wisdom and age occur frequently in Chinese literature from the past to the present. What about someone of Indian extraction? East European? A good place to find the central symbols of our culture is in the language used in advertisements. Most ads promise a benefit to the consumer, elaborate on it, provide proof, and give a call to action. Benefits must reflect our wants and needs. Elaboration and proof probably reflect our need for knowledge. And we are an action-based society, as we shall see when we discuss cultural premises.

IN LOW TRACTION CONDITIONS, QUADRA-DRIVE™ FINDS AN ELIGIBLE RECEIVER AND SENDS ALL THE POWER* TO IT.

(AND YOU THOUGHT QUARTERBACKS HAD TO THINK FAST.)

Now there's a revolutionary new four-wheel drive system that does the thinking, and the work, for you. Introducing Quadra-Drive, our most advanced four-wheel drive system ever. If only one wheel has traction, Quadra-Drive seeks that wheel out, then transfers all the power* to it. And, unlike some other systems, it works both front-to-rear and side-to-side. In fact, Quadra-Drive is the only system in the world that delivers maximum power all the time. So Jeep, Grand Cherokee can pull you out of situations other 4x4s just couldn't handle.

For further information about our newest, most capable sport utility ever,** please visit us online at www.jeep.com or call 1-800-925-JEEP.

Jeep.
THERE'S ONLY ONE

THE ALL-NEW JEEP. GRAND CHEROKEE
THE MOST CAPABLE SPORT UTILITY EVER"

*Sends 100% of the developed engine torque. **Based on AMCI overall on- and off-road performance tests using Grand Cherokee with available Quadra-Drive™ and V8 engine. †Optional. Jeep is a registered trademark of DaimlerChrysler.

FIGURE 6.2 Consider the cultural values underlying this ad for Jeep. Notice the "chalk talk" imagery and the references to football.

SOURCE: The marks JEEP® and QUADRA DRIVE™ are trademarks of DaimlerChrysler and are used with permission from DaimlerChrysler Corporation.

To be short and concise, the ads and slogans "distill" or simplify complex ideas. This boiling down of meaning is called **synecdoche**, and politicians frequently use it. They know that concise words and phrases often become part of the evening news, thus acting as unpaid advertisements. The words also suggest a common denominator between persuader and persuadee. In an ad in *Newsweek,* the AARP used the slogan "Let's Not Stick Our Kids with the Bill!" referring to its opposition to proposed changes to the Social Security system. The phrase unified members and nonmembers of the organization to object to the proposed changes. Consider the verbal and nonverbal symbols in Figure 6.2, such as the words "Quadra-Drive™," the football "chalk talk" image, and the picture of the Jeep taking a corner. Do these words and symbols reflect any of the central values of our culture? What about AARP's use of the word "stick" in its slogan?

Political rhetoric also reflects our cultural values. Two important words used by politicians are "freedom" and "equality." As columnist David

---

B O X 6.1   Meet Mediamatic.Net

 Go to www.mediamatic.net and find numerous examples of how our new digital world is changing not only the persuasive symbols in language but in other forms of symbol making such as interactive film, virtual reality, diagramming a speech in space, mob-tagging discourse, architecture as a criminal act, video letters, and many other fascinating items on language and other symbols. Be sure to visit the Mediamatic Supermarket while you're there and learn how to get a Mediamatic t-shirt.

Broder (1984) noted, "Words are important symbols, and . . . 'freedom' and 'equality' have defined the twin guideposts of American Democracy" (p. 41). The words have the thematic qualities to stir patriotic emotions. However, they are not rated the same by all persons. As Broder notes, "Socialists rank both words high, while persons with fascist tendencies rank both low; communists rank 'equality' high but 'freedom' low, and conservatives rate 'freedom' high but 'equality' low" (p. 41).

Considerable power in linguistic symbols resides in their functional, semantic, and thematic dimensions. Not only do words reveal motives, but they also affect our self-image and express cultural ideals. Let's examine tools for analyzing these dimensions of language in persuasion.

TOOLS FOR ANALYZING PERSUASIVE SYMBOLS

Becoming aware of the three dimensions of language and nonverbal symbols helps us to become responsible receivers of persuasion. We can use various tools for the analysis of persuasion to focus our critical eyes and ears on more specific aspects of language symbols.

Tools for the Functional Dimension

Two tools for analyzing the functional dimension of language symbols in persuasion are language critic Richard Weaver's grammatical categories (especially regarding sentence and word types) and the effects of word order or syntax in sentences.

Weaver's Grammatical Categories. Language theorist and pioneer Richard Weaver (1953) suggested that the type of sentence preferred by an individual offers clues as to that person's worldview (the way the person uses information and comes to conclusions). Weaver discussed some persuaders' preference for simple sentences, compound sentences, or complex sentences.

Simple sentences express a single complete thought or point and must contain one subject or noun and one action word or verb and an object ("He hit the ball"). Persuaders who prefer simple sentences don't see the world as a very complex place. Such a person "sees the world as a conglomerate of things . . . [and] seeks to present certain things as eminent against a background of matter uniform or flat" (p. 120). The simple sentence sets the subject off from the verb and object. There is a clear foreground and background in simple sentences, and they highlight cause and effect.

Compound sentences consist of two or more simple sentences joined by a conjunction such as "and" or "but." Weaver observed that the compound sentence sets things either in balance ("He ran, and he ran fast") or in opposition ("He ran, but she walked"). The compound sentence expresses either resolved or unresolved tension. According to Weaver, it "conveys that completeness and symmetry which the world ought to have" (p. 127). Persuaders using compound sentences see the world in terms of opposites or similarities. When you encounter compound sentences, try to identify the tension and the symmetry (or lack of it) in them.

Complex sentences also contain two or more distinct components, but not all the components stand alone as complete simple or compound sentences. Some of the elements in the sentences rely on another element in the sentence to be fully understood. Once, in speaking about word choice, Mark Twain used a complex sentence: "Whenever we come upon one of these intensely right words in a book or a newspaper, the resulting effect is physical as well as spiritual and electrically prompt" (Lederer, 1991, p. 128). The first portion of Twain's sentence ("Whenever . . . newspaper") could not stand alone; it is dependent on the last half of the sentence ("the resulting . . . prompt"), which could stand alone. The complex sentence features an intricate world with multiple causes and effects at the same time—dependency and independency or completeness and incompleteness. Weaver (1953) said it "is the utterance of a reflective mind" that tries "to express some sort of hierarchy" (p. 121). Persuaders who use complex sentences often express basic principles and relationships, with the independent clauses more important than dependent ones, as in this description by an ex-Olympic athlete:

> But after having represented the United States in five Olympic track and field teams from 1980 to 1991, I certainly have a feel for what the next class of Olympians is doing now. . . . if you are lucky enough to make it, there is the singular drama of Olympic competition (Lewis, 1999, p. 56).

Weaver (1953) also had some observations about types of words. For example, people react to **nouns** (which are defined as the name of a person, place, or thing) as if they were the things they name. Nouns "express things whose being is completed, not . . . in process, or whose being depends upon some other being" (p. 128). A persuader's noun use can reveal clues to his or her perceptions of things. When persuaders reduce persons to the level of things or objects by name calling, they do so for a reason—to deal with the people as objects, not as subjects or human beings.

According to Weaver, **adjectives** function to add to the noun, to make it special. The dictionary defines adjectives as "words that modify nouns . . . by limiting, qualifying or specifying" (*American Heritage Dictionary,* 1985). For example, "the little

blue Ford hybrid with the Alabama plates" limits, qualifies, and specifies which vehicle we mean. For Weaver, adjectives were "question begging," and showed uncertainty. If you must modify a noun, you're uncertain about it in the first place. To Weaver the only certain adjectives are dialectical (good and bad, hot and cold, light and dark). Examining a persuader's adjective use can reveal his or her uncertainty and what they see in opposition to what.

Adverbs, to Weaver, are words of judgment. The dictionary defines adverbs as "words that modify verbs, adjectives, or other adverbs" (*American Heritage Dictionary,* 1985). Adverbs represent a community judgment that helps us to agree with what the persuader thinks we believe. For example, adverbs such as "surely," "certainly," and "probably" suggest agreement. When persuaders say, "Surely we all know that thus-and-such is so," they imply that the audience agrees with them. Such adverbs encourage interactive co-creation.

Syntax. In addition to using word or sentence types to analyze persuaders' messages, we can look at the syntax used. **Syntax** is defined as "the pattern or structure of the word order in sentences or phrases." How can that have a persuasive effect? Word order can either alert or divert the reader/listener. Consider the difference between these two sentences:

- Before bombing the terrorist headquarters, we made sure the target was the right one.
- We were sure the target was the right one before bombing the terrorist headquarters.

In the first sentence, the dependent element occurs at the beginning of the sentence ("Before . . .") and alerts the reader/listener to the conditions needed before taking action. The independent element expresses the main point of the sentence. In the second sentence, the action comes first, and the dependent element focuses the attention of the listener/reader on the justification for the action.

Some persuaders place emotional or surprising words at the beginning of a sentence to reduce the impact of what follows. The audience focuses on the evidence because of the emotionality of the claim. For example, the speaker might say, "There is no greater hypocrite than the animal rights advocate who opposes the use of animals in research labs during the day and then goes home and has beef, pork, or chicken for dinner!" The reader/listener knows beforehand that the claim is about hypocrisy, and they focus on the reasons for the claim. The sentence is dramatic and creates a puzzle—"There is no greater hypocrite than whom?" we ask ourselves.

The other side of the coin is the speaker who diverts attention from the evidence by hiding the claim at the end of the sentence. This makes the audience wonder where all this evidence is leading. The speaker says, "The animal rights advocate who opposes the use of rats in the research lab and then goes home to eat beef, pork, or chicken is the kind of hypocrite we don't need in this country!" The drama of the sentence is reduced, and the power of the evidence diminished because the audience wonders about the speaker's destination.

Communication scholar L. H. Hosman (2002) notes that language variations affect one of three elements of the persuasion process: "judgment of speaker, message comprehension and recall, or attitude toward the message" (p. 372), and that these effects are crucial in information processing. This, of course, brings us back to the Elaboration Likelihood Model (ELM), and the old debate over the comparative effectiveness of emotional appeals (peripheral processing) and logical ones (central processing). Hosman also reports that active sentence structure influences perceived believability, clarity, appeal, and attractiveness in print advertisements in different ways than does passive sentence structure. "The nature of a sentence's grammatical construction or of a narrative's construction has important persuasive consequences" (p. 374). Sentence structure and word choice can reveal the persuader's motives and act as indicators of information-processing channels being used in the ELM.

To learn more about how sentence structure is used in evaluating such potentially important messages as hate letters, access InfoTrac College Edition, and enter the words "sentence structure" in the search engine. Read the article titled "More Than a Figure of Speech" by Jerrold Post. Report to the class what you discover about using sentence structure to evaluate threats. Also enter the words "hate mail" in the search engine, and examine a few of the articles listed there. What do you think about the use of language in hate mail?

Tools for the Semantic Dimension

While the functional dimension carries important verbal and nonverbal meanings, the semantic dimension of co-created interactive meaning carries the bulk of persuasion in most messages.

Strategic Uses of Ambiguity.   Some think it unethical for persuaders to communicate in intentionally ambiguous ways, but they quite often do just that. They try to be unclear, vague, and general to allow for the broadest possible degree of common ground, identification, and co-creation of meaning. They want each receiver to fill in his or her own private meanings or connotations for the particular words or symbols. This strategy results in the largest number of interpretations and thus creates the largest potential audience for the persuader's brands, candidates, or causes. It also pleases as many and offends as few persons as possible. Receivers need to identify intentional ambiguity and analyze the reason(s) for the lack of clarity.

Persuaders use several methods to create strategic ambiguity. One is to choose words that can be interpreted in many (often contradictory) ways. A politician may support "responsibility in taxation and the cost of educating our youngsters." Those who think teachers are underpaid might hear this as a call for increasing funding for education. Those who hold the opposite view could as easily interpret the statement as meaning that education spending needs to be cut. The key word that increases ambiguity is "responsibility." The speaker or writer does not say what cause he or she favors. Another ambiguous word is "astronomical," as in "The budgetary implications of the war in Iraq are astronomical." Does this mean millions or billions or hundreds of billions of dollars? Depending on one's position, several meanings might result. Another way to create strategic ambiguity is to use phrases like "noted authorities on the subject seem to concur that, . . . ," which appear to lend support and credibility to the persuader's point. Communication scholar E. M. Eisenberg (1984) held that strategic uses of ambiguity can help get agreement on things like mission statements and at the same time allow individuals to interpret the statements as the persuader hopes.

In some cultures ambiguity is considered offensive. Listeners want to "cut to the chase" and stop wasting time. Persuadees in other cultures (such as Japan) value talking around the point and establishing a relationship before talking business. Still others want to mull things over and look at the issue from several perspectives.

Persuaders also create ambiguity when they juxtapose or combine words or phrases in startling ways that present issues in a new light. For example, the term "born again" is persuasive to many people. It suggests that the person's earlier religious beliefs were weak, and that their conversion caused the person to be spiritually re-created. Some born-again lobbyists labeled themselves the "Moral Majority," creating persuasive intentional ambiguity. The term was ambiguous because the group wasn't a majority but a minority, yet it had great persuasive appeal as media preachers created what political researchers Dan Nimmo and James Combs (1984) called "the Electronic Church." Another highly ambiguous term is "Moral Decay." It reminds us of "tooth decay," which nobody likes.

How can we defend ourselves against ambiguous language? The semanticists advise using increasing specificity about and concrete elaborations on any ambiguous term by using extentional devices to clarify meaning. Semioticians advise us to seek meanings in persuasive "texts" by digging into various verbal and nonverbal codes and signifiers in the text. Doing this helps determine the real thing being "signified." Advertisers use semiotics to devise global marketing and advertising strategies (Domzal & Kernan, 1993). Examining the denotations and connotations of persuasive symbols also helps us study the semantic dimension of language. Other tools address the semantic dimension of language. Among the more useful tools addressing the semantic dimension of language is the dramatistic approach suggested by Kenneth Burke.

To learn more about the uses of strategic ambiguity, access InfoTrac College Edition, and type the words "strategic ambiguity" in the search engine. Select one of the periodical references by Jim Paul, and learn how business uses strategic ambiguity.

Burke's Dramatism. In addition to his ideas on language discussed in Chapters 1 and 5, Burke offered students of persuasion a theory and a tool for analyzing the semantic dimension of language. He called his theory **dramatism**, and his tool of analysis the **pentad**.

Dramatism maintains that the basic model used by humans to explain various situations is the narrative story or drama. Burke (1960) thought of the drama as "a philosophy of language" capable of describing and analyzing a wide variety of human symbolic acts such as language use. He focused on the differences between action (which is motivated) and motion (which is not motivated). Basic bodily functions, such as sweating or digestion, are unmotivated nonsymbolic acts. Action requires motivation and the ability to use language symbolically. We bring the action into being, and language use is thus a kind of symbolic action—it is motivated. Burke believed that we choose words because of their dramatic potential and that different individuals find certain elements in the drama more potent than others.

Burke's model, the dramatistic pentad, as its name implies, has five central elements: scene, act, agent, agency, and purpose (see Figure 6.3). **Scene** includes physical location, the situation, time, social place, occasion, and other elements. The scene could be something like "Campaign 2008," "the Oval Office," a website, or *The Oprah Winfrey Show*." Scenically oriented persons feel the scene should be a "fit container" for the action, and believe that changes in the scene will cause other changes—drilling for oil in the Arctic National

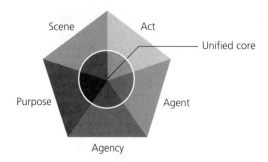

FIGURE 6.3 The five elements of dramatism ultimately affect one another, and each emerges from a common unified core—the drama itself.

FIGURE 6.4 In Burke's terms, the agent is the focus of this ad, as you can see by the two fishermen, but other elements of the pentad are apparent also.

SOURCE: Reprinted by permission of Southern Comfort Company.

Wildlife Reserve can result in a change in the ecology, perhaps a catastrophic change. They also believe that if gays are permitted to join the armed forces there will be less discrimination. The Clinton–Lewinsky scandal was distasteful because the Oval Office was the container for the act—not a fitting scene for sexual dalliance. The Lincoln Memorial was a "fit" scene for Martin Luther King, Jr.'s, "I Have a Dream" speech. The setting helped make the speech memorable.

Act refers to any motivated or purposeful action. In persuasive messages, the verb is the best indicator of the act. After all, verbs are defined as words that describe acts or actions, so looking at the verb is the best place to start applying the term *act* to your analysis. The words and actions taken by a person, and their appropriateness for the scene, ultimately affect outcomes.

Access InfoTrac College Edition, and enter the words "word choice" in the search engine. Examine the items regarding word choice in advertising from InfoTrac; the item from *ETC,* the journal of general semantics; and the item in the *Journal of Direct Marketing* entitled "The Future of 'force communication'" are especially insightful.

Agent is Burke's term for the person or group of persons who take action in the scene. They are the actors or characters who make things happen (the police officer, the corrupt politician, the terrorist, Howard Stern, and so on). Figure 6.4 has an agent focus, as can be seen from the two youthful fishermen who are the central agents in the ad. Factors such as hatred, instinct, greed, or jealousy sometimes motivate agents. Countries and organizations (e.g., UN peacekeeping forces, the N.R.A., or pro-choice groups) also act as agents. Agent-oriented persuaders believe that strong, honest, and well-intended individuals determine the outcome of important events and even of history. And, on the other hand, they also believe that unthinking, deceitful, or dishonest agents cause bad outcomes.

Agency is the tool, method, or means used by persuaders to accomplish their ends. Some auto companies now focus on development of the fuel cell and hydrogen energy as the agencies to solve our dependence on fossil fuels. Shakespeare's

Hamlet used the play within a play as the agency to establish his uncle's guilt. Calvin Klein used nudity and prepubescent females as agencies to draw attention to Obsession Night for Men. Wheaties uses pictures of famous athletes on its packages to promote the brand as "the Breakfast of Champions." Communication strategies also act as agencies (such as intensifying one's own good points or others' bad ones).

Purpose is the reason an agent acts in a given scene using a particular agency. The persuader's true purpose can be more, or less, apparent. The U.S. Army's old recruiting slogan, "Be All That You Can Be," suggested that the purpose for enlisting was improving your skills to maximize your potential. Its new slogan, "Join the Army of One," suggests a different purpose for enlisting: you can make an individual difference and develop your skills. When the amount of aid sent by the United States to victims of a disastrous Indonesian tsunami was low compared to that sent by much smaller countries, critics in this country and abroad interpreted the action as meaning that the administration was less interested in helping others than in saving money.

These five elements can help develop a persuasive strategy in interpersonal relationships. For example, if you were trying to get a date for a rock concert, you might emphasize the scene, describing the auditorium, crowd, sounds, costumes, lighting, colors, and so on. An alternative strategy would be to focus on the act, describing the kinds of music and the interactions between performers and audience. You might also choose to focus on the agent, describing the musicians, their reputations, and their appearance. If you chose to feature agency, you might mention the new digital sound system, the unique instruments used, and special effects. Finally, you could feature purpose by telling your prospective date, "to be really 'cool,' you shouldn't miss attending the concert, and you might meet other interesting people, too."

In any given situation, all these elements of the pentad operate simultaneously to a greater or lesser degree (see Figure 6.5). Burke compared them in pairs, or "ratios," to identify a persuader's "key" term. For example, the scene can be compared

with each of the other terms one at a time and we can determine which term seems most important by a process of elimination. For instance, if scene supercedes act, agent, and agency but not purpose, we can then infer that purpose is a good candidate for the persuader's key term. But purpose must be compared to act, agent, and agency to see if it supercedes those terms of the pentad.

There are ten possible ratios or pairs of terms. In *Hamlet,* for example, the dramatic tension created in the scene–act ratio comes from the fact that Hamlet's mother has married his uncle (the act) during the period of mourning (part of the scene) for Hamlet's father, the king, who has died mysteriously. His uncle inherits the throne and marries Hamlet's mother less than one month after the funeral (also part of the scene). Clearly the scene was tainted by the act. Disturbed by this imbalance, Hamlet curses his mother, saying, "She married. O, most wicked speed, to post with such dexterity to incestuous sheets!" Later, Hamlet asks Horatio whether he came to court for the funeral or the wedding, and expresses his anger in these bitter words: "Thrift, thrift, Horatio! The funeral baked meats did coldly furnish the marriage tables."

We also frequently see the persuasive power of the scene–act ratio in advertisements. For example, in Figure 6.6, the scene—the state of Alaska—offers tourists great fishing with the words "If you like your fish wild" and "twelve native species, all of them pugnacious." It notes that Alaska has "two oceans, two seas, and hundreds of bays," thereby improving the scene–act balance. After all, where but in the biggest state would you expect the biggest fight with the biggest fish?

Scene can also interact with the other elements of the pentad. In the scene–agent ratio, balance or imbalance again can indicate potent persuasion or high drama—comedy, tragedy, or melodrama. In Hitchcock's classic film *Psycho,* viewers see a scene–agent imbalance when Anthony Perkins tells Janet Leigh that he has "stuffed" all the animal specimens in the motel office. Then we see him spy on her through a secret peephole in the eye of one of the specimens. This is not the behavior of a normal motel owner. It makes the audience uneasy. This uneasiness

F I G U R E 6.5 This ad demonstrates the use of all the elements of Burke's pentad. The scene is a family home. The agents are father and daughter. The act is nurturing, and the purpose is planning for the future. As is often the case, the product being advertised is the agency. This ad was designed in response to another ad Kemper ran in which a father is planning for his son to go to college in response to criticisms that the company was sexist in suggesting that only males were destined for college. Knowing this, what are the purpose and agency in the current ad?

SOURCE: Used by permission of Kemper Financial Services.

Your tomorrows depend on the consistent performance of your long-term investments. And that's why investors have made Kemper one of America's largest asset managers. For over forty years, the Kemper Family of Mutual Funds has been dedicated to the kind of steady, long-term performance that builds tomorrows today. To learn more, talk to your financial representative at this location.

We're Building Tomorrows Today™

Fund performance cannot be guaranteed and will fluctuate. Before you invest in a fund, carefully read the brochure and prospectus for more complete information, including management fees and expenses. © 1994 Kemper Financial Services, Inc.   219631

NAT-72B 1/94

implies the strong possibility of danger. The tension caused by the scene–agent imbalance is increased when we hear Perkins and his "mother" (whom he also "stuffed") arguing at the Victorian house near the motel (see Figure 6.7). We want to warn Leigh to go to another motel or at least to "lock the bathroom door." Hitchcock uses scene–agent tension throughout the rest of the film and keeps the audience on the edge of their seats.

Any of the other ten possible pairs of elements of the pentad (act–purpose, act–agency, scene–purpose, scene–agency, and so forth) might be examined to discover a persuader's key term or element. Burke believed that a persuader's key term infuses every aspect of life—home, family, job, political choices, and philosophy of life. Identifying a persuader's key terms or elements alerts us to the motives of and reasons for the persuasion and helps us predict

FIGURE 6.6 How are the scene and the act balanced in this ad?
SOURCE: Used by permission of the Alaska Division of Tourism.

future persuasive appeals. As you encounter persuasion, try to listen for the key term being used.

Tools for the Thematic Dimension

We've seen that the thematic dimension of language is that quality in certain words or sets of words that gives them a texture or "feel." While the words do have a variety of semantic meanings and syntactical functions, their most important persuasive aspect is their ability to set a mood, a feeling, or a tone or theme for the persuasion. For example, Abraham Lincoln set the theme for his famous Gettysburg Address with these words: "Fourscore and seven years ago our forefathers brought forth on this continent a new nation, conceived in liberty and dedicated to the proposition that all men are created equal." How far less stirring the speech would have been if he had said,

FIGURE 6.7 The imbalance in the scene/act ratio in Hitchcock's film classic *Psycho* heightens dramatic tension.
SOURCE: Used with permission of Doug Walker.

"Eighty-seven years ago the signers of the Declaration of Independence started a new country designed to assure us of freedom and equality." The two sentences have equivalent semantic and functional meanings, but the obvious difference between them lies in their texture.

We also noted how the repetition of consonants (alliteration) or vowels (assonance) carries thematic meaning. The advertisements for Satin cigarettes, for example, used alliteration to create a thematic meaning for the brand—"Smooth. Silky. Satin. Cigarettes." Or consider the slogan for Lexus: "The Relentless Pursuit of Perfection." It sounds unstoppable.

Sometimes parallel sentence structure communicates a thematic meaning. For example, consider the no-nonsense theme in the parallel sentences in an ad promoting MTV to advertisers. The copy accompanies a picture of a male in his twenties in an easy chair holding a TV remote, and reads,

> If this guy doesn't know about you, you're toast. He's an opinion leader. He watches MTV. Which means he knows a lot more than just what CDs to buy and what movies to see. He knows what clothes to wear, and what credit card to buy them with. And he's no loner. He heads up a pack. What he eats, his friends eat. What he wears, they wear. What he likes, they like. And what's he never heard of . . . well . . . you get the idea. MTV. A darn good way to influence the MTV Generation (*Advertising Age*, 1993, p. S-3).

Thematic meaning also can come from the use of metaphors or onomatopoeia. Let's turn now to several other tools for discovering the thematic meaning in persuasive messages. These include finding metaphorical themes; noting the use of sensory language; looking for god, devil, and charismatic terms; identifying the pragmatic and unifying styles; and use of semiotics to determine the thematic meanings of nonverbal symbols or "signifiers."

Metaphorical Style.   Persuaders set the mood for persuadees by repeatedly using certain sounds, figures of speech, and images. Recent research on the effects of metaphors shows that using them increases the credibility of the persuader because they make the persuader seem more dynamic and interesting. This is especially so when the source uses only a single metaphor instead of multiple ones (Sopory & Dillard, 2002). Dan Hahn (1998) applies another archetypal metaphor—that of water as a dangerous image. Notice the positivism and the negativity of the underlined water images:

> Due to foggy thinking, the tide has been running against freedom and we are sinking in a swampland of collectivism. Therefore, despite the detractors who say don't rock the boat, the campaign we launch here will set the tide running again in the cause of freedom. The past will be submerged, and we will travel democracy's ocean highway where freedom will accompany the rising tide of prosperity (p. 115).

Hahn reminds us of other associations we have with the water metaphor. It is life giving and is also the basic element from which life emerged (p. 115). Other archetypal metaphors include references to wind and windstorms, blood and blood bonds, the locomotive as representative of the economy, and the boxing ring or the horse race as stand-ins for any of life's contests and struggles. Roads and maps also serve as metaphors for planning (e.g., "the roadmap to peace" in the Middle East).

Metaphors also help in **framing** the issue or topic to give the audience a way of seeing things. For example, imagine a persuader trying to inform the audience about the AIDS crisis in Africa, where grandparents are now raising most children due to the premature deaths of the parents. A good metaphor might be warfare, with the persuader saying, "We're in the early stages of the battle here with the veterans of past battles having to fight to the bitter end. It's not going to end with a single decisive weapon." The audience sees the fight against the disease is likely to be a long one with no real miracle cures.

To learn more about the power of metaphor, access InfoTrac College Edition, and type the word "metaphor" in the search engine. Peruse the more than fifty periodical titles, and choose some articles to read. Report your findings to your class.

Sensory Language.   Courtroom communication expert Stephanie L. Swanson (1981) maintained that most effective lawyers rely on words relating to one or more of the five senses: sight, sound, touch, smell, and taste. She speculated that jurors respond to the particular sensory information channel they prefer. How could a persuader use these preferences? Suppose an attorney asks three witnesses to describe an automobile accident. The witness preferring the auditory channel might say something like, "I was walking down Oak Street, when I heard the screech of brakes, and then a sickening sound of crashing glass and metal, and someone screamed." The witness who prefers the visual channel might say, "I saw this blue Beamer coming around the corner practically on two wheels. Then he hit the brakes, and it looked like the car slid sideways toward me. Then I saw his front end make a mess of the little Geo." The witness who prefers the kinesthetic channel might say, "I had this feeling that something was about to happen, and when it did I felt frightened and helpless, and I cringed as the cars crumpled up like scrap paper." Swanson advised attorneys to "listen closely to the sensory language used by your clients...try to respond in kind—matching the sensory language of the other person" (p. 211). She suggested attending to the kinds of words used by individuals during the juror selection process—then "tailor your language to your listeners' primary sensory channel. You can 'paint a picture' for a visual person, 'orchestrate the testimony' for an auditory person, and 'touch the heart' of the

FIGURE 6.8 It is clear that giving tickets is a god term for the evil queen, but getting a parking ticket from any of her helper dwarfs is a devil term for her.

SOURCE: Used with permission of Al Ochsner.

kinesthetic individual. Using sensory language lets the jurors feel that your discourse is directed toward them individually" (p. 211). The use of sensory language acts like an interactive medium, and it increases the likelihood for the co-creation of meaning.

Thus, in trying to identify a persuader's use of the thematic dimension of language, explore the sensory language used in the persuasion.

God, Devil, and Charismatic Terms. Another thematic or textural element of style in persuasion is the development of families of terms. Persuaders like to divide the world into tidy categories that prompt co-created meanings. Richard Weaver (1953) held that one of these category sets is made up of **god terms** and **devil terms**. Although terms or labels make up only parts of propositions, they often link with other terms or labels to shape a message or a persuasive argument. Weaver defined a god term as an expression "about which all other expressions are ranked as subordinate and serving dominations and powers ... its force imparts to the others their lesser degree of force" (p. 211). Weaver saw a god term as an unchallenged word (or phrase) demanding sacrifice or obedience. He used three terms as examples of god terms: "progress," "fact," and "science." *Progress* still persuades, but is hampered by negative associations—pollution, for example. *Science* lost some of its credibility in recent

times also, due to negative associations such as nuclear power or genetic engineering.

Devil terms are just the opposite. They are "terms of repulsion" and express negative values. As Weaver put it, "They generate a peculiar force of repudiation" (pp. 210–215). Today's god and devil terms include "the environment," "green," "the family," "security," "terrorism," "deficit spending," "politically correct," "technology," "dittoheads," "surfing the Web," and "budget surplus." God and devil terms can vary in a diverse culture. For example, Western culture places considerable value on the term "forgiveness," considering it the correct response when one is wronged. Other cultures believe "forgiveness" is a devil term—the sissies' way out For them the god term when wronged is "revenge." Such god and devil terms alert you to potential persuasive appeals aimed at you or that you might choose to use in your own persuasion.

As we move further into the new millennium, other god and devil terms are emerging. Some of the more recent god terms include "family/family values," "low fat," "rule of law," "green vehicles," "air security," "financial security," "education," "phased retirement," "weight loss," "nutrition," "fuel cell," and "hybrid car." Try to discover others as you search for the thematic dimensions of words or terms used in advertising or political and ideological statements.

Weaver said that the connotations of certain negative terms can sometimes be reversed, making the terms neutral or even positive. Take, for example, the expression "wasted" or "getting wasted." Its use during the 1970s referred to killing Viet Cong or others perceived to be the enemy. Later, it referred to getting drunk or "stoned." Today, "wasted" has recovered its original meaning of "squandered" and refers to such topics as corporate trust, energy, and credibility.

Weaver described **charismatic terms** as "terms of considerable potency whose referents it is virtually impossible to discover. Their meaning seems inexplicable unless we accept the hypothesis that their content proceeds out of a popular will that they shall mean something" (p. 48). His examples are the words "freedom" and "democracy," which have no apparent concrete referent but still seem to have great potency and serve as god terms for U.S. foreign policy.

The terms "budget surplus" and "fanning the flames of freedom" became charismatic recently, and most agreed that a "budget surplus" was great after decades of "budget deficits" (a devil term). Nearly everyone agreed on the wisdom of "saving Social Security." Another candidate for a charismatic term is "recycling." With the growing awareness of declining natural resources, the concept of recycling applied to a host of things, such as paper, plastic, aluminum, glass. "Patriot" and "patriotic" recently became charismatic terms, but they were devil terms during the Vietnam era.

Pragmatic and Unifying Styles.   Persuaders tend to rely on one of two persuasive styles—pragmatic or unifying. **Pragmatic** persuaders want to convince neutral or opposition listeners. They want to change minds instead of reinforcing existing beliefs. Politicians speaking at a news conference rather than at a rally of their supporters tend to favor the pragmatic style. **Unifying** persuaders use a different style because they want to motivate people who already believe what they're going to say; they just reinforce beliefs to whip up enthusiasm, dedication, or encouragement. Thus, when Rush Limbaugh, Howard Stern, Bill O'Reilly, and others speak to their respective television and radio audiences, they use the tactics of the unifying speaker—their audiences already believe them. The problems for pragmatic persuaders are clear—they must change opinion before they can expect action. Unifying persuaders can be much more idealistic, and use more emotional, less objective claims and evidence than the pragmatic persuader.

What stylistic devices typify these extremes? The unifying persuader focuses on the "then-and-there"—on the past or future—when things were ideal or when they might become ideal. Because the audience fills in the blanks, abstract language choice works well for unifying persuaders; their language frequently is poetic, emotional, and filled with imagery that excites the audience's imagination. Although there is little intellectually stimulating or requiring logical examination, lots of emotional and stirring things emerge. The unifying persuader is a sounding board for the audience and provides them with the gist of the message but not the details. The audience participates with unifying persuaders in the co-creation of the message. In fact, audiences sometimes participate actively by yelling encouragement to unifying persuaders or by repeating phrases to underscore their words—"Right on" or "Amen, brother" or "Tell it like it is."

Pragmatic persuaders, because they need to win the audience, avoid appealing to abstract ideals. They use concrete words, focusing on facts instead of images and undisputed things. They avoid depicting an ideal situation in "then-and-there" terms. Rather, they focus on real aspects of immediate problems of the "here-and-now"— things that seem realistic, not idealistic. Pragmatic persuaders orient their message to the present instead of the future, and tend to focus on facts and statistics instead of imagery. Their messages pass through the central information-processing route of the ELM instead of the peripheral route, as is probably the case for unifying persuasion. Consider these words of a pragmatic persuader describing skydiving:

> When I stand in the door of an airplane in
> flight, I alone am responsible for the decision
> to jump. If the winds, clouds or any other

conditions are unfavorable, I have the option of riding down in the plane—something I have done on several occasions. Neither the pilot nor the drop zone operator forces me to jump if I choose not to. Once a skydiver exits the plane there's no going back. One person and one person only has the responsibility of deploying the parachute . . . and executing a safe landing. . . . Skydiving is not a preprogrammed carnival thrill ride with simulated risk. . . . While the trend in American society is to find someone else to blame for your own mistakes; that is not the way it is in skydiving. To suggest otherwise indicates total misunderstanding of the sport on the part of your reporters (Kallend, 2002, p. 8).

The language is concrete and prosaic, the references are here and now, and the persuader is trying to change the audiences' mind instead of uniting them. The pragmatic and unifying styles depend on the needs of the audience and the demands of the occasion, not on the needs of the speaker.

Semiotics and Signifiers.   We referred to the field of semiotics earlier as a way to study meaning. Its most important contemporary theorist is Umberto Eco. He proposed that the process of "signification" (or the giving of meaning to a "sign") has four elements: (1) the objects or conditions that exist in the world, (2) the signs available to represent these objects or conditions, (3) the set of choices among signs, or the repertoire of responses available for use, and (4) the set of rules of correspondence that we use to encode and decode the signs we make and interpret when we communicate.

This final characteristic most directly relates to the goal of this course—the discovery of the various **codes** or sets of rules used by persuaders and understood by persuadees in the process of co-creation. We know that when a stage manager lowers the lights and asks us to turn off our cell phones and pagers, the event is about to begin; this is an example of a code. We participate in our own persuasion by "agreeing with" the code(s) the persuaders use. We become critical consumers of persuasion by continually striving to uncover and reveal these codes (Eco, 1979).

We find more subtle examples of codes in some advertisements. For example, consider the ad for Bostonian shoes in Figure 6.9. What codes operate in this ad? Some seem obvious, but others are more subtle. In fact, some codes found in the ad embed themselves within other codes. The most obvious code is that the ad tries to sell the product, although the kind of product is not so clear. But we soon discover that the product is men's shoes. Another less obvious code is that the product is an upscale one, as indicated by the composition and copy of the ad and the price of the shoes—$105. The ad is understated, with little actual ad copy. Finally, the illustration is distinctively "fine art" in its composition. Within these codes, we find a more subtle code that is only implied and never directly stated. This code signifies the lifestyle that goes with the product. The shoes merely serve as an emblem of that lifestyle. What do we see in this photograph? Clearly, it is the "morning after" a satisfying night of lovemaking (notice the coffee cups and pastries on the bed, the negligee on the well-rumpled bedding, the indentations on both pillows). The lifestyle includes a fine home (notice the expensive furniture and the framed photographs on the nightstand in the upper left corner). This lifestyle includes expensive accessories such as the Rolex watch and the Mont Blanc pen on the dresser. The stylish suspenders, the theater ticket stubs slipped into the frame of the mirror, and the picture of a beautiful wife under the tickets signify a lifestyle that values the arts, stylishness, beauty, and physical attractiveness (note the snapshot of the man, bare-chested and muscular). Clearly, this ad carries a lot of meanings, "signified" by the verbal and nonverbal symbols being used (or perhaps misused). Its persuasive message must be co-created based on agreed upon and shared semiotic codes. The signifiers, or collection of objects in the room, probably trigger emotional values that the audience holds dear.

Although analyses like this intrigue us, they are difficult to carry out without some kind of systematic methodology. The fields of theoretic semiotics and applied semiotics (for example, advertising and image/political consulting) expanded rapidly in

---

B O X 6.2   Semiotics and the Culture of Circuses

Semiotician Paul Buissac (1976) offered some fascinating examples of codes in his semiotic analysis of circus acts, illustrating this idea of an easily discernible code understood by "children of all ages" around the world:

> Wild animal, tightrope, and trapeze acts never occur back to back in the circus...they are always interspersed with clown acts, small animal acts, magic acts, or the like. If a daring act is canceled, the entire order of acts needs to be altered because of audience expectations, tension reduction, and the need to communicate that the world is alternately serious and comedic.... Death-defying acts also have a code— usually a five-step sequence. First, there is the introduction of the act by the ringmaster (a godlike figure able to control not only the dangers but the chaos of the circus). This introduction, with its music, lights, and revelation of dazzling and daring costumes, is followed by the "warm-up," in which minor qualifying tests occur: The animal trainer, dressed as a big-game hunter, gets all the animals to their proper positions; the trapeze artist, with his beautiful assistants, can easily swing out and switch trapeze bars in mid-air; the tightrope walker dances across the rope with ease. Then come the major tests or tricks: getting the tiger to dance with the lion, double trapeze switches, and walking the wire blindfolded. Having passed these tests, the circus performer then attempts the 'glorifying,' or 'death-defying,' test. It is always accompanied by the ringmaster's request for absolute silence and, ironically, by the band breaking the critical silence with a nerve-tingling drum roll. Then comes the feat itself: The animal tamer puts his head into the lion's mouth; the trapeze artist holds up a pair of beautiful assistants with his teeth, demonstrating his amazing strength; and the blindfolded tightrope walker puts a passenger on his shoulders and rides a bicycle backward across the high wire. Frequently, there is a close call: An unruly tiger tries to interfere with the "head-in-the-mouth" trick, there is a near miss on the trapeze or a stumble on the high wire, and so on. Once the glorifying test is passed, the ringmaster calls for applause as the act exits and then returns for a curtain call. This sequence is a 'code' we all understand. (n. p.)

Suppose the circus tent caught fire. What would be the appropriate code for the ringmaster to use in order to reduce panic?

---

recent times, and as receivers we need a simplified way to pin down their uses (or misuses) of symbols.

This brief discussion of the semiotic approach to language and meaning gives us another tool for discovering the important first premises emerging from language preferences and the images molded from them.

To learn how semiotics is used in advertising and marketing, access InfoTrac College Edition, and enter the word "semiotics" in the search engine. Look at the article by Frank and Stark in the *Journal of Advertising Research*. Read the abstract, and then read the article and reference its footnotes through the InfoTrac College Edition system. You might also look under the related–subjects category and go to the discourse analysis option. Some fascinating titles can be found in the signs and symbols option as well.

TUNING YOUR EARS
FOR LANGUAGE CUES

Consumers of persuasion need to become vigilant when processing and responding to persuasive messages. In the course of this vigilance, one of the most important things persuaders can do is tune their ears to language for various clues to style and motives. Using some of the tools described in this chapter helps. Applying the study questions at the end of this and other chapters also helps. There are at least three specific strategies you might use to make yourself more critical of style and to "decode" persuaders:

1. *Role-play the persuader.* Assume that you are the persuader. Now, shape the persuasion you wish to present. For example, if you favor high

Perfectly fitting and proper. This day. Every day.

Every decision should be as clear-cut as your choice of Bostonian. These wingtips are trimmer, more richly detailed. And more comfortable. With cushioned innersoles and glove-soft leather linings. About $105. For nearby stores, call 1-800-444-2624.

perfectly fitting and proper

BOSTONIAN
since 1899.

FIGURE 6.9 What messages are implied by the "code" of physical objects in this ad (theater tickets, rumpled bedclothes, articles of clothing that seem to have been hurriedly discarded, an empty cocktail glass, and so on)?

SOURCE: Reprinted by permission of the Bostonian Shoe Company.

salaries for baseball players, frame a pragmatic message for half-hearted believers, those who are neutral, or others who are only moderately opposed. Would you mention the shortness of most players' careers? After all, they receive a relatively low overall salary across a lifetime. You might compare ballplayers to entertainers, who also make several million dollars per year for relatively little actual work time. If your audience were the players' union, you might bypass the numbers and use highly emotional and abstract language to motivate them—create images of club owners as rich bloodsuckers who use up the best years of an athlete's life, use then-and-there language, and refer to new goals of the group or to past abuses by the owners.

2. *Restate a persuasive message in various ways.* Ask yourself, "What other ways could I say this?" Try to determine how these alternatives change the intent and effects of the message.

B O X 6.3 Diversity and Semiotics

 Semiotics and cultural diversity are a particularly hot topic just now, and many websites will pop up when you enter the words into any search engine. If you want to try a favorite of mine go to www.aptalaska.net/~ron/FOOD%2005/glob/irrealis.htm, which is the website for Globalization Theory. Sample the links found there (e.g., modality irrealis depicts a variety of global images and contradictions such as the superimposition of Chairman Mao's face on the U.S. Capital building) and discover how many things apply to semiotics. You might also enter the words "semiotics" and "cultural studies" in any search engine and discover more.

Communication scholar Arthur Asa Berger (2005) offers a methodology for doing semiotic analysis, and he provides a fairly simple checklist. First, he advises us to consider the persuasion aimed at us as "texts" to be read, and then to start looking for clues. He has a checklist of questions to ask when trying to read persuasive texts:

1. Isolate and analyze the important signs in the text.
   a. What are the important signifiers?
   b. What do they signify?
   c. Is there a system that unifies them?
   d. What codes can be found (for example, symbols of status, colors, or music)?
   e. Are ideological or sociological issues being addressed?
   f. How are they conveyed or hinted at?

2. Identify the central structure, theme, or model of the text.
   a. What forces are in opposition?
   b. What forces are teamed with each other?
   c. Do the oppositions or teams have psychological or sociological meanings? What are they?

3. Identify the narrative structure of the text. (That is, if a "story" is being told, what are its elements?)
   a. How does the sequential arrangement of events affect the meaning? What changes in meaning would result if they were altered?
   b. Are there any "formulaic" aspects to the text (for example, hard work leads to success, justice prevails, or honesty gets its reward)?

4. Determine whether the medium being used affects the text, and how.
   a. How are shots, camera angles, editing, dissolves, and so on used?
   b. How are lighting, color, music, sound, special effects, and so on used?
   c. How do paper quality, typefaces, graphics, colors, and so on contribute?
   d. How do the speaker's words, gestures, and facial expressions affect meaning?

5. Specify how the application of semiotic theory alters the original meaning ascribed to the text.

Try using the parts of Burke's pentad. For example, take the following slogan for Grand Marnier Liqueur—"There Are Still Places on Earth Where Grand Marnier Isn't Offered After Dinner." The words appear on a photo of a deserted island. The appeal is scenic. An agent-oriented version of this slogan claims that, "People of Taste Offer Grand Marnier." A purpose-oriented version might read, "Want to Finish the Conference? Offer Grand Marnier." An agency-oriented version might say, "Grand Marnier—From a Triple-Sec-Ret Recipe." The act-oriented message emphasizes action by saying, "Make a Move—Offer Grand Marnier."

3. *Attend to language features in discourse.* Don't allow yourself to passively buy into any persuasive advice. Instead, get into the habit of looking at each message's style. Analyze messages on billboards, in TV commercials, the language used by your parents when they try to persuade you, the wording on product packages, or in the phrases used in discussions between you and friends, enemies, or salespersons. Start listening not only to ideas but to word strategies—the packaging of those ideas. Focusing on these features gives you an intriguing pastime, and helps develop an ear for stylistic tip-offs.

WHAT DO YOU CALL A WOMAN WHO'S MADE IT TO THE TOP?

FIGURE 6.10 Using the semiotic approach in Berger's checklist, uncover the meaning of this ad. Note that the woman has "lost" items from her pockets—a passport, the keys to an Audi, credit cards, a picture of herself drawn by her child, jewelry, aspirin, a champagne cork, a $100 bill, and other signs. What do they signify? How old is this woman? Is she sentimental? Busy?

SOURCE: Reprinted by permission of Ms. Magazine, ©1992.

Ms.

She's a better prospect than ever. Because we've turned the old *Ms.* upside down to reflect how women are living today. And you're going to love the results.

The new *Ms.* is witty and bold, with a large-size format that's full of surprises. Whether it's money, politics, business, technology, clothing trends, humor, or late-breaking news … if it's up-to-the minute, it's part of the new *Ms.*

So if you want to reach the top women consumers in America, reach for the phone. And call Linda Lucht, Advertising Director, *Ms. Magazine*, One Times Square, New York, N.Y. 10036. Tel: (212) 704-8581.

The new Ms. As impressive as the woman who reads it.

REVIEW AND CONCLUSION

Responsible receivers of persuasion relate to the language persuaders choose. They gain insight by looking at the semantic connotations of the words being used. They look at word order, or syntax, and at the frequency of various parts of speech. The degree of ambiguity used by the persuader is often revealing, as in the dramatistic analysis suggested by Burke. The motifs and metaphors chosen by persuaders often reveal motives. Persuadees also need to look at the god, devil, and charismatic terms used, as well as the choice of pragmatic versus unifying styles. Finally, try to apply the semiotic approach to the interpretation of persuasive messages. All these critical devices improve with role-playing, restating, and developing awareness of the words, styles, and ideas used in co-created speech, TV ads, films, political slogans, social movements, or package designs.

KEY TERMS

When you have completed this chapter, you should be able to identify, explain, and give an example of the following words or concepts.

semantic dimension	complex sentences	act	devil terms
functional dimension	nouns	agent	charismatic terms
thematic dimension	adjectives	agency	pragmatic style
assonance	adverbs	purpose	unifying style
alliteration	syntax	metaphorical style	semiotics
synecdoche	dramatism	framing	codes
simple sentences	pentad	sensory language	
compound sentences	scene	god terms	

APPLICATION OF ETHICS

Considering Richard L. Johannesen's description of ethical standards in Chapter 2, do you consider the strategic use of ambiguity ethical, unethical, or dependent on the persuader's goal and the ultimate outcome? What if ambiguity convinces you to make an unwise purchase decision? What if government reports are ambiguous about sources of intelligence to protect their sources or to protect national security? What if optimistic but incomplete research about possible cures for a disease gives the individual sufferer a reason to hope?

What might be some ethical standards for the strategic uses of ambiguity? Support your proposed standards and apply them to sample cases like those in the preceding paragraph to demonstrate how well they might work. What shortcomings, if any, did you discover in your proposal?

QUESTIONS FOR FURTHER THOUGHT

1. Transcribe the lyrics of a popular song. Now analyze them according to the functional tools presented in this chapter. Is there a preference for a certain word type? A certain sentence structure? Is the message ambiguous or concrete? Explain.

2. Describe several semantic tools. What do you think is the pentadic perspective of the president of the United States? Of your instructor?

3. Describe the tools for a thematic or textural analysis of language, and use them to analyze the persuasion occurring in a recent political campaign. What do these analyses tell you about the candidate? Try the same thing with a recent advertising campaign.

4. What god terms work for your parents? What about their devil terms? Shape a request for something from your parents expressed in their god terms. What god terms motivate the user of the interactive medium being sold on www.livehunt.com?

5. How do unifying persuaders differ from pragmatic ones? Find examples of each type of persuader in your class, in persuasive attempts

of the past, or in defenders and opponents of some issue in your community. What differences exist between these two types? Which style seems more or less likely to carry unethical persuasive appeals? Describe the differences between semantics and semiotics. Which seems more objective? When might it be appropriate to use each approach? Do you use semantics and semiotics to both analyze and create persuasive messages and, if so, how?

6. What is the difference between a text and a symbol? What is the difference between a signifier and the signified?

7. If language use serves as a medium of communication, describe its interactivity. How is it used when delivered via interactive media? Describe some cultural differences in symbolic language use within subcultures.

 For online activities, go to the *Persuasion* book companion website at http://communication.wadsworth.com/larson11.

Identifying Persuasive First Premises

U nderlying all means of analytically processing the symbols of persuasion is the ancient Aristotelian concept of the enthymeme and his triad of ethos, pathos, and logos. The enthymeme serves as the analytical metaphor or organizational device for Part II. Part II is a search for the types of major premises that work in enthymemes. We identify those major premises that most audiences believe and those that audiences can be convinced of to prompt action or change.

The first category of major premise is studied in Chapter 7. It is called the process (or psychological and emotional) premise. Process premises rely on psychological factors that operate in nearly all persuadees. Persuaders tie their product, candidate, or idea to these process premises, which are then used as the major premises in enthymematic arguments that have wide appeal. In terms of the Elaboration Likelihood Model (ELM), most process or emotional premises are dealt with in the peripheral information-processing path.

Chapter 8 covers a second category of major premises called logical or content premises. Their persuasiveness lies in the audience's belief in the truth or validity of the argument, and they get processed in the central channel of the ELM. You have probably noticed that there is considerable similarity between process premises and content premises. Process premises rely on psychological or emotional needs, whereas content premises rely on logical or rational patterns. We learn these patterns of inference beginning in early childhood, and they are reinforced throughout our lives. For instance, suppose we tell two-year-old children that if they continue to cry they will have to take a "time-out" or go without television or a particular toy. What we really are using is "if...then" reasoning, or the rational pattern that actions have consequences.

Chapter 9 examines cultural premises that rely on patterns of behavior or beliefs taught to us by our society. They resemble articles of faith for audiences. For example, Americans learn that when faced with a problem they must seek a solution to it, perhaps by establishing a task force or swallowing a pill. This seems so obvious that we are dumbstruck to discover that people from some other cultures prefer simply to accept the inevitable when faced with a problem. Problem solving is a culturally transmitted pattern for us. Knowing that, persuaders motivate us to take actions by portraying the actions as solutions. Clever persuaders can create problems and then sell us a cure. Cultural premises consist of the myths and values our society holds dear. Cultural premises are probably processed in the peripheral information-processing route of the ELM.

Chapter 10 explores nonverbal premises, which are sometimes more potent than sophisticated verbal premises. Often, nonverbal premises contribute to the ultimate success or failure of persuasion. These premises are usually processed almost unconsciously following the peripheral path of the elaboration likelihood model, and they can vary widely depending on one's culture or subculture.

As you read Part II, think of yourself as searching for major premises that you and an audience hold in common. Identifying these major premise types helps you to become a more skillful persuader, but also—and more important—a better and more critical consumer of persuasion.

7

Psychological or Process Premises: The Tools of Motivation and Emotion

Needs: The First Process Premise

Packard's "Compelling Needs"
Maslow's Hierarchy of Needs
Uses of the Needs Process Premise

Emotions: The Second Process Premise

Fear
Guilt
Anger
Pride
Happiness and Joy

Attitudes: The Third Process Premise

Attitudes, Beliefs, and Opinions
The Functions of Attitudes

Attitudes and Intention
Attitudes and Interpersonal Communication/Persuasion
Attitudes and Information Processing

Consistency: The Fourth Process Premise

Cognitive Dissonance Theory
Sources of Dissonance
Sources of Consonance

Review and Conclusion

Key Terms

Application of Ethics

Questions for Further Thought

LEARNING GOALS

After reading this chapter, you should be able to:

1. Identify, explain, and give examples of Packard's hidden needs. Give current examples.

2. Identify, explain, and give examples of Feig's hot buttons. How do they operate in your life?

3. Identify, explain, and give examples of several positive and several negative emotions. Which are most powerful for you?

4. Explain the difference between attitudes, opinions, behavioral intentions, and behavior.

5. Explain and give examples of each of the levels in Maslow's pyramid of needs. Who do you know who seems to be self-actualizing?

6. Explain and give examples of cognitive dissonance. Where is it operating in your life?

7. Explain and give examples of consonance. Where is it operating in your life?

8. Discuss the ethics of appealing to the emotions, needs, and attitudes held by persuadees.

This chapter examines what are commonly called appeals to the emotions or the will. We will look at four kinds of emotional appeals:

1. Appeals to deeply held needs, physical or psychological

2. Appeals to positive and negative emotions

3. Appeals to attitudes and opinions

4. Appeals to psychological states of balance or consonance and imbalance or dissonance.

Some persuasion theorists distinguish between logical and emotional appeals, arguing that they represent opposite ends of a continuum and that the "better" appeals are the logical ones. This explanation assumes that persuasive appeals are either one thing or another and that the two types of appeals operate separately and independently. It is easy for us to think that both "rational" and "emotional" persuasion occur all at once as a result of some key phrases, statistics, qualities of the persuader, or other factors. While some persuasion does occur this way, far more often it occurs over time.

We've seen that most persuasion depends in part on self-persuasion, usually occurs incrementally or bit-by-bit, and often includes many kinds of communication. One "emotional" appeal might serve to capture receivers' attention. A series of "logical" arguments might reinforce the first appeal and lead to the final decision or behavior. For example, an organization called Volunteers in America asks you to donate your car to them because the money earned from selling the car helps place neglected and abused children in safe and nurturing homes. Is the appeal emotional or logical? Well, it has elements of both. The emotional appeal is about helping kids get better treatment in a good environment. Helping others makes most of us feel good about ourselves. But there are some logical reasons for donating your car. For instance, you can get a tax deduction for the donation (something you need), and you don't even have to bring the car to them or get the car in running order—the organization has free pick-up within 48 hours and they repair it before sale. The real question is not whether this is a logical or emotional appeal, but whether you process the message centrally or peripherally. In this case, the peripheral route processes—the "feeling good" part—and the central route processes—the tax break, the 48 hour pick-up, and repair—are the emotional and logical parts of the persuasion respectively.

In this chapter, we examine several emotional appeals or premises that tap into the psychological or emotional processes operating in the peripheral route of the ELM. These appeals rely on human needs, emotions, attitudes, and the psychic comfort we feel over decisions we make. We call these appeals **process or emotional premises** or appeals because they target psychological and emotional processes that operate in most people. When we call them premises, we are referring to their uses in enthymemes. When we refer to them as appeals, we are talking about how they operate in the worlds of politics or advertising. It is probably okay to think of the words *premises* and *appeals* as nearly synonymous. Both are subtypes of persuasion that gets at our psychological processes rather than our logical or reasoning processes. For example, most of us have fear-based emotions that cause psychological tension, and we eagerly take action to relieve this tension. So, persuaders work to generate fears about our grooming and then offer us products that relieve those fears and tensions. Consider the mouthwash Listerine. Initially it was used as a powerful surgical antiseptic, a floor cleaner, and a cure for gonorrhea. It wasn't until the 1920s that it was marketed as a cure for halitosis— an obscure word for bad breath (Leavitt & Dubner, 2005). A headline in one of its early ads read, "Got halitosis? Listerine mouthwash makes your breath kissing sweet." Psychological appeals or process premises operate in business, marketing, advertising, sales promotions, politics, interpersonal communication, and ideological persuasion. Process or emotional premises operate when we buy a product because of brand loyalty, brand name, a memorable slogan, a catchy jingle, or even packaging. Recall the Snuggle fabric softener example from Chapter 5? The brand name was cuddly, as was its logo of a stuffed teddy bear. Process premises also operate in more serious situations such as enactment of homeland security laws and appeals from prison reform candidates and from advertisers trying to convince you to make major purchase decisions for a new car or home. Emotional premises appear in everyday interpersonal persuasion between neighbors, spouses, parents and children, siblings, lovers, bosses, and employees.

NEEDS: THE FIRST PROCESS PREMISE

Each of us has our own set of individual needs. Some of them are critical—we can't live without things like food, water, clothing, and shelter. Others are not critical—we can get along without

approval from others. And not everyone's needs have the same priority. Diverse cultural roots can influence the priority of our needs, but most needs resemble those of lots of other people, so various theories of motivation apply to the general population. Many appeals focus on needs, which when satisfied lead to our overall sense of well-being (for example, success on the job, being liked, or having religious faith). Without the satisfaction of these needs or some substitute, we feel frustrated, anxious, afraid, even angry, and tension results. We infer these needs from patterns of behavior that presumably satisfied and happy people exhibit. Because people seem concerned about being successful, we quickly infer a need for physical symbols of success like a Jaguar, a summer place, or a large home.

Persuasion in today's changing world usually focuses on promoting or selling symbolic ways to meet people's physiological and emotional needs. Some products, such as self-improvement courses, really can help individuals make a better impression on the boss, but what people buy, vote for, or support doesn't usually have such direct effects. They drive a BMW and enjoy what they believe to be the admiring looks they get from other drivers. Our support for a candidate may relate to a need for approval from others or a need for self-esteem—the candidate's supporters are our friends or neighbors, and they appreciate our support. And we feel good about ourselves because our support for the good candidate just might "make a difference."

If the persuader relying on the needs process premise analyzes audience needs or emotions incorrectly, persuasion sometimes boomerangs. For example, an advertiser, assuming that travelers needed tough luggage, produced an expensive TV spot in which the luggage was handled roughly while being loaded onto an airplane and then falling out of the plane in flight, plummeting down 30,000 feet, landing on some rocks, and bouncing into the air. When the luggage was opened the camera showed the undamaged contents. The ad seemed persuasive. However, sales dropped following its airing. Why? Focus group interviews revealed that most people have fears that their flight might crash, and they resented the idea that their luggage would survive when they wouldn't. The emotions of fear and resentment served as powerful motivators, as do emotions like anger, jealousy, hatred, joy, or love.

To discover why consumers respond as they do, **motivation research**—based on the social sciences and the study of marketing rather than on our traditional political, ideological, or rhetorical traditions—grew rapidly after World War II. In his best-selling book *The Hidden Persuaders* (1964), Vance Packard, author and advertising theorist, reported that a majority of the hundred largest ad firms in the country used psychoanalytic motivation research to discover deep-seated psychological needs and responses. Other persuaders such as public relations executives and fund-raisers also turned to psychological theories to discover receivers' motives, emotions, or needs, and then they tied products, candidates, and causes to those motives and needs. Packard held that much motivation research

> seeks to learn what motivations or **hidden needs** influence people in making choices. It employs techniques designed to reach the subconscious mind because preferences generally are determined by factors of which the individual is not usually aware. In most buying situations the consumer acts emotionally and compulsively, unconsciously reacting to images which they subconsciously associate with the product (p. 5).

One expert said, "The cosmetic manufacturers are not selling lanolin; they are selling hope.... We no longer buy oranges, we buy vitality. We do not buy just an auto; we buy prestige" (p. 5). Packard says that motivation researchers assume three things about people: (1) they don't always know what they want when making a purchase; (2) you can't rely on what they say they like or dislike; and (3) they don't usually act logically when they buy, vote, or join.

Motivation research reflects the symbolist tradition in psychology rather than the experimental tradition. Advertising and marketing researchers use focus group interviews to get consumers to describe the fears, pleasures, or fantasies they associate with brands and ads. Other researchers ask people to complete sentences or do word associations about the brand. This trend continues, and recent research about consumer behavior confirms many of the claims made by Packard. This kind of motivational research is still with us but now uses more sophisticated techniques that take cultural diversity into account and use interactive media to involve the receiver. N.Y.U. professor Neil Postman (Freedman, 1988) long ago observed that "Advertisers,... desperate to keep you tuned to their pitches, (are) trying some new tricks. Many of these commercials have more impact on the subconscious level" (p. 5).

Ad agencies often enlist psychologists and neurophysiologists to produce the desired effects (Freedman, 1988). For example, Amherst Incorporated, developed a research instrument called the Motivation and Attitude Profile (MAP) and used it to market goods, services, and politicians. Amherst's creative director describes the idea behind MAP this way: "People are driven by their emotions—it's not about fact or logic. Increasingly, the only button you press is an emotional one. You find out what their needs are and you discover how to reflect those needs" (Booth, 1999, p. 32). Products as varied as Haagen-Daz ice cream, Volkswagen, and life insurance rely on psychographics, which is a research technique that identifies the psychological reasons for purchase behavior. Whether we call it motivational research, lifestyle research, hidden persuaders, or psychographics, using the process amounts to the same basic idea—finding hidden or obvious needs and developing the products and ads to fulfill those needs.

To learn more about the fascinating field of motivation research, access InfoTrac College Edition, and enter the words "motivation research" in the search engine. Read several of the articles listed there. The two articles by Jerry Thomas provide a thorough description of some research techniques used. Enjoy the article "21 Meaningful Motivational Messages."

B O X 7.1   Consumer Insight—Getting Into Your Head

A Chicago-based nationwide marketing company, Claritas, used psychographics and lifestyle data to develop its PRIZM system. PRIZM is a marketing tool that identifies more than 60 market segments across the United States with names that reflect the inner psychological needs of the consumers in each. Take, for example, the segment called "Pickups and Gun Racks." Persons in "Pickups and Gun Racks" tend to live in manufactured housing or mobile homes and are heavy users of generic or house brands of sweetened soda pop. If they purchase lingerie, it tends to be from Frederick's of Hollywood. Their most recent financial transaction is the purchase of a lottery ticket. They obviously have different needs from those of the people in the segment "Town and Gowns" (you may be living there right now), and these needs, in turn,

differ from those of the people in the segment "Red, White, and Blue Collar." For persons in "Town and Gown," the most frequent financial transaction is the use of an ATM. If they purchase lingerie, it is frequently at a department store or Victoria's Secret, and most of them live in houses, apartments, dorms, or fraternity and sorority houses. PRIZM is a popular tool among many consumer marketing firms.

 Do you think marketers know too much about us? How much of this information came from government data? How much have we ourselves given away? If you want to learn more, go to www.claritas.com and view the video presentation explaining the segmentation system and other options on the company homepage.

Packard's "Compelling Needs"

One approach to the needs premise was Packard's **"compelling needs,"** which were based on his observations on the rapidly evolving advertising industry of the motivation research era. He claimed that these needs were so powerful that they *compelled* people to buy, and he identified eight such compelling needs that advertisers used to sell products. We still see them in use today, although with far more sophistication than Packard described. Marketers design ads promising that the product or service will provide real or symbolic fulfillment of these compelling needs.

Marketing consultant Barry Feig (1997) says advertisers are looking for the **hot buttons** that will motivate people and prompt purchase behavior. Feig defined hot buttons as appeals that cause receivers to become emotionally involved with a product rather than responding rationally to product reality. For example, he claims that new car purchases frequently result from the test drive and the new car smell. The purchaser becomes emotionally involved with the feel and smell of a new car and puts aside other factors like performance. Some clever persuader found a way to package that

smell in an aerosol spray can so that it can be used to sell used cars more effectively. Feig's own work in the 1990s verified Packard's hidden needs, and he found other needs not noted by Packard.

The Need for Emotional Security. Packard's first compelling need was for **emotional security**, which is defined as feelings of anxiety about the future and feelings of insecurity about our personal welfare and and safety, as seen in Figure 7.1. These feelings emerge whenever our world becomes unpredictable, and we then try to dispel them in symbolic ways. Packard attributed this need for emotional security to the Great Depression. Following W.W.II., people desperately wanted to avoid the insecurity of unemployment, the inability to make ends meet, and so on, so when they had employment, they saved regularly and bought home freezers to preserve food for the possibly uncertain future. The need still operates, but for different reasons. Terrorism seems unstoppable and is certainly unpredictable. Identity theft is mushrooming, making everyone feel insecure. AIDS threatens the economic future of the continent of Africa and elsewhere, and dangerous pollution fouls our environment hourly. The world economy

FIGURE 7.1 This ad plays on our inherent feelings of insecurity, especially in an age of identity theft and other means used to defraud people.

SOURCE: Used by permission of Sanford Corp.

seems precariously balanced. If oil prices continue to escalate, the stock market might crash, resulting in another Great Depression. With mergers, downsizing, and outsourcing, job security now concerns many people, and literacy rates have dropped to less than 70 percent from earlier highs over 90 percent, making it hard for many people to get any job other than flipping burgers.

No wonder we search for substitute symbols of security. Deodorants promise us secure social relationships. Self-improvement courses promise better job security. Retirement planning programs offer financial security. These products and services act as minor premises in enthymemes mentioned in previous chapters that have as a major first premise the belief that "security is good." Even in interpersonal relationships, the need for security causes people to search for commitment. At first, "living together" seemed to be a liberating lifestyle, but this is now questioned by some because there is no security without commitment. Author Stephanie Staal (2001) points out that the divorce rate of those who live together before marriage is 50 percent higher than the rate for those who did not. We all face unpredictable change, and that makes us vulnerable to persuasion that promises some symbol of security—a good investment program, membership in respected social groups, safety derived from security systems, owning a weapon, or interpersonal confidence stemming from trusting and reliable relationships. Feig (1997) equates this need for security with a universal hot button he calls the "desire for control." This need for security or control varies within our culture. For example, in some subcultures, security is put off until tomorrow in favor of gratification today.

The Need for Reassurance of Worth. We live in a highly competitive and impersonal world in which we often feel like mere cogs. Packard noted that people need to feel valued for what they do whether it is at a factory, a desk, a classroom, or a day-care center. Homemakers, blue-collar workers, managers, and others need to feel that they are accomplishing something of value and are appreciated by others. Packard called this the need for **reassurance of worth**, which is defined as a feeling that we are valued by others. This need forms the basis of many persuasive appeals, from ads promising to make us better parents, spouses, or friends to appeals for volunteers in good causes. A study asked managers and workers to rate ten factors in job satisfaction. Managers rated wages, fringe benefits, and working conditions at the top, but workers placed them at the bottom. They rated "appreciation for work done" at the top, followed by "my boss listens to me," and "fellow workers." Feig (1997) verified the existence of the reassurance of worth need, saying "Consumers need to feel good about themselves and fulfill their self-images—it's a basic human need" (p. 14).

Based on hundreds of interviews, sociologist Robert Bellah and colleagues (1985) concluded that most contemporary Americans see themselves in a race for material goods, prestige, power, and influence. They separate themselves from others and find self-worth in material things. Ethics author Kathleen Sibley (1997) noted the feelings of distrust felt by many employees when they learned of a company policy of monitoring employee email.

To learn more about how this perception can affect brands and businesses, access Info-Trac College Edition, enter the words "corporate ethics," and examine some of the articles there.

When we feel less and less important as individuals, we become vulnerable targets for persuasion that promises reassurance of worth. Reassurance of worth has its cultural implications also. Schiffman and Kanuk (1997) observed that Asian Americans are very brand loyal, but especially so when the brand lets it be known that they are welcome and that their patronage is appreciated by offering preferred customer cards, premiums, and so on. Other ethnic subcultures value bargaining, and still others value quality over price.

The Need for Ego Gratification. Packard found that many consumers not only needed to be reassured of their basic worth, but they also needed **ego gratification**, which he defined as feelings of self-importance and having one's ego stroked. As you can see in Figure 7.2, the traveling business woman gets special treatment from Courtyard by Marriott, including Internet access, fine furnishings, and even a cup of coffee served in a china cup instead of a plastic one. Also notice that Marriott emphasizes they cater to female business travelers and those from different ethnic groups, thus reinforcing the growing importance of females and ethnicities in the workplace. Earlier ads usually showed white male executives as customers.

Satisfaction of the need for ego gratification comes from a variety of sources—friends, co-workers, neighbors, parents, groups, institutions, and ourselves. Feig (1997) called this need the "I'm better than you" hot button, and emphasized that consumers display possessions that build their egos and meet this need. Persuaders often target groups whose members feel that they have been put down for some time, such as teachers, police officers, firefighters, and postal or social workers. After 9/11, the media brought many of these groups into a well-deserved public spotlight. They got ego gratification from being featured on TV, in newspapers and on the covers of news weeklies. Such groups can also

LOG ON AND ON.
FREE HIGH-SPEED
INTERNET ACCESS
IN EVERY ROOM.
Surf, search, chat, upload, download, e-mail, e-conference, live stream, podcast, webhost, webdesign, webzine, blog .... The free high-speed Internet access in our rooms is designed to make our guests as comfortable as possible online. Everything else in it is designed to make them as comfortable as possible off. Courtyard.® Our rooms were made for you.℠

IT'S THE MARRIOTT WAY.℠

To reserve a room
with Free High-Speed
Internet Access,
call 1-800-MARRIOTT
or visit Marriott.com.

Marriott
REWARDS.

© 2005 Marriott International, Inc.

FIGURE 7.2 Marriott promises to fulfill the need for ego gratification by giving special attention to its business executive customer base, and thus caters to gender and ethnic diversity.

SOURCE: Used by permission of Marriott International, Inc.

now get special rates on their mortgages, grants in aid to help them buy homes, and other benefits showing national appreciation for public service. Persuaders frequently sell products, ideas, and candidates by targeting an out-group's ego needs in personal ways that appeal to self-perception.

Take family values, for example. From the late 1960s until the late 1980s the traditional family was out of style. Communal living was popular, as was living together. Those who remained committed to the ideal of the traditional family felt like outcasts. From the 1990s to the present, persuasive "pro-family" appeals succeeded in presidential campaigns, religious appeals, public relations, and the marketing of products promising a restoration of family values. Feig (1997) called this need the "family values" hot button, and noted that marketers sell a vision of the family as we all wish it would be.

If this issue interests you, go to InfoTrac College Edition, enter the words "living together" or "family values" in the search engine, and peruse some of the related articles.

Note that the ad copy in Figure 7.2 stresses the importance Marriott places on the individual—in this case, the female executive, whose needs traditionally have been largely overlooked by the hotel/motel industry. Similarly, politicians know how to stroke the egos of appropriate groups of potential voters. One Republican female candidate for governor used ego gratification with two widely differing audiences. For a GOP women's luncheon she arrived by limousine, wearing a conservative dress and scarf, and ate chicken salad for lunch. Afterwards, she changed her clothes to a black leather jacket, boots, gloves, and pants, and then drove a Harley to the Young Republicans club at a nearby college. She got rave reviews at both events (National Public Radio, 2002).

The Need for Creative Outlets. In our modern technocracy, few products can be identified with a single artisan. This was not always the case. For example, until the Industrial Revolution craftsmen such as cabinetmakers created a piece of furniture from beginning to end—it was their unique product. The same applied to blacksmiths, craftsmen, silversmiths and others. They all could point with pride to their product. That is not often the case today, which is why we feel a need for **creative outlets**. Packard saw this need being met by offering substitute creative activities that would replace the creations previously produced by individuals. They felt less and less creative in many ways, and they needed to find ways to express their own unique creativity. Packard said persuaders targeted this need for creative outlets by promoting products and brands related to hobbies, crafts, and social activities.

FIGURE 7.3 The Fluid Milk Promotion Board strokes the ego of average citizens by making them feel special, hinting that they are sophisticated, and suggesting that they can avoid health problems by drinking three glasses of milk a day.
SOURCE: Reprinted by permission.

Today more than half the population works in the service and information industries, where most important products are intangible and not really very creative. There is no actual creation of anything, and more work is now being accomplished through technologies such as robots. People still need to demonstrate their own creativity—a need that Feig (1997) identified as the "excitement of discovery" hot button—so they engage in gardening, gourmet cooking, home decorating, collecting and restoring antiques, art, or music.

To see how the need for creativity operates today, access InfoTrac College Edition, and enter the words "need for creativity" in the search engine. Browse some of the items listed there.

FIGURE 7.4   This cartoon is based on a true incident. A wounded goose was taken in and nursed to health by an assistant to NIU's president, who was single and nearing retirement.

SOURCE: Used by permission of Al Ochsner.

The Need for Love Objects.   Packard noted that people whose children have grown up often feel a need for **love objects**. These "empty-nesters" feel lonely and unneeded when the last kid goes off to college, gets a job, or gets married. Empty-nesters fill their love needs in various ways such as doing volunteer work, devoting more time to their jobs or hobbies, or becoming a big brother or sister or a foster grandparent. Persuaders target these empty nesters in a variety of ways. For instance, many older persons get pets to serve as substitute love objects. They coddle them, spoil them, and even dress them up. The pet food industry targets "gourmet" lines to such persons who bring home Premium Cuts, Tender Vittles, Beef 'n Gravy, Tuna Surprise, or Chicken Spectacular. The food sounds and even looks like something a human might consume. Feig (1997) calls this the "revaluing" hot button, and he predicts a major increase in products that attempt to fill this need as the baby boomers approach retirement and an empty nest (see Figure 7.4).

The Need for a Sense of Power or Strength.   More than members of other cultures, most U.S. citizens seek emblems of potency or a **sense of power or strength** in symbolic ways. Packard defined this as the need for a personal extension of one's *perceived* power or strength rather than true power or strength. The bigger the car or outboard motor, the better.

Snowmobiles, ATVs, jet skis, and Harleys sell because they give the user this sense of power. Whether the brand is a double-triggered chain saw or a Hummer, an increased perception of power is the central issue. Stanley Tools sells "heavy duty" tools, not wimpy, "light duty" hammers and wrenches. Similarly, Americans seem to elect politicians who do macho things. In fact, any major candidate for the presidency must demonstrate physical strength in some way. And as males approach midlife, they often engage in macho activities like bungee jumping or bodybuilding.

The Need for Roots.   One of the predominant features of modern society is mobility. Individuals employed by any large firm will probably have to move several times during their careers, and most persons have three or more careers during their lifetime. In the decade following graduation from college, the average graduate moves a dozen times, usually crossing state lines at least once. As a result, most persons feel a **need for roots**, symbolic or real. The need for roots is defined as feelings of homesickness and a yearning for family-centered activities. When individuals move away from home, especially if it is some distance, there are some pieces of home that they can bring along with them. One is brand loyalty, which develops most strongly between the ages of 18 and 24. Recent college graduates have one of the highest levels of brand loyalty, which is why my university inked an agreement to give Pepsi exclusive "pouring rights" on campus. Only Pepsi products such as Mountain Dew, Lipton Iced Tea, or Fruitopia can be sold or served on campus. All materials used to serve the brands (cups, straws, napkins, and so on) must have the Pepsi logo imprinted on them. Pepsi gave over $8 million to the school's scholarship fund for this right, knowing that brand loyalty would develop.

The need for roots and the sense of brand loyalty also helps explain *line extensions* or the development of new products based on old and familiar brands. We feel more at home buying the new Quaker Oats Squares than another brand because of the familiar, friendly, and old-fashioned face of the Quaker Man promising "An honest taste from an honest face." He serves as an emblem of our tradition, our need for an "old-fashioned" hearty breakfast, and our need for a sense of roots. The nice thing about brand names is that they are portable—we can take them to a new home anywhere. The Lane Furniture Company appealed to the need for roots and emotional ties to home by offering newlyweds a Lane cedar chest to "take part of home" with them when they marry. We've already noted the appeal politicians make to family values. The trend toward increasingly mobile and fragmented lives is likely to continue. As a result, the need for roots remains an important motivator, and advertisers, politicians, and ideologues continue to use it in their persuasive appeals to us. Feig (1997) equates this need with his "family values" hot button and notes, "Quality time with families is still of utmost importance to Americans." Schiffman and Kanuk observe that in some subcultures (such as Asian American and Latino) family and roots stretch across several generations. In this regard, The *New York Times* noted the trend of bringing generations of family on road trips (Feig, 1997).

Brand loyalty can be further investigated in InfoTrac College Edition by typing the words "brand loyalty" in the search engine. Examine a sample of the articles listed.

The Need for Immortality. None of us wants to believe in our own mortality. The fear of growing old and dying clearly drives the healthy-living industry, which promotes such things as good nutrition, stress reduction, exercise, and a healthy lifestyle. Packard suggested that a need for immortality grew out of the need to maintain influence over the lives of family members. The breadwinner is made to feel that by purchasing life insurance he or she obtains life after death in the form of continuing financial security that will help the kids go to college even if he or she isn't there.

Other products make similar appeals to the fear of death. For instance, Promise margarine will keep you healthy longer because "Promise is at the heart of eating right." And Nivea's Visage face cream will make your skin "firmer, healthier, and younger" for only pennies a day. As the ad executive noted in an earlier quote, we aren't buying lanolin, we are buying hope—hope for a little more immortality. This need for immortality seems particularly relevant in our modern technocracy. The much-talked-about midlife crisis is an example. This occurs when people realize that "time marches on" and that they have probably passed the halfway point in their lives or when they confront some other major life event such as the death of a parent. So they get divorced, quit or lose their job, buy a sports car, run off with someone half their age, and speed away in the sports car, as if to underscore their indestructible youth. They want to be young again, or at least to enjoy some of the experiences they missed along the way. Frequently, they engage in dangerous activities such as skydiving.

There are many other persuasive appeals that succeed because they are somehow tied to the desire for immortality (Lafavore, 1995). Feig (1997) calls this the "self-nurturance and the ability to stay ageless and immortal" hot button, and noted that older persons are more willing to spend money on things that make them feel better about themselves.

If you are interested in needs and how motivational research can identify them, go to InfoTrac College Edition, and enter the words

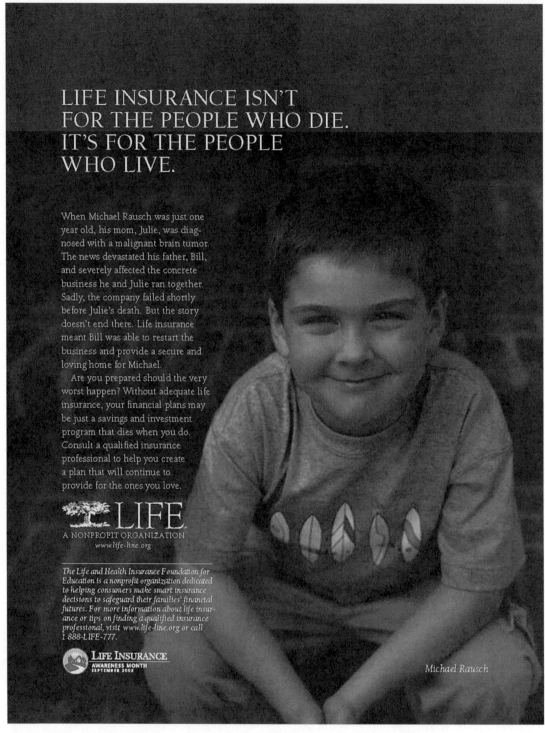

FIGURE 7.5 This ad appeals to the need for immortality by assuring readers that even if they are no longer there, they will still be able to influence the lives of their survivors.

SOURCE: Reprinted with permission of the LIFE Foundation.

"needs" and "motivation research," and explore the options there.

We now turn to perhaps one of the most well-known models of human needs. It was first described more than 50 years ago, and it is still going strong.

Maslow's Hierarchy of Needs

Abraham Maslow (1954), a well-known psychologist and pioneer in the discipline, long ago offered a simple starting point for examining people's needs. His theories about the power of human needs are judged by many to be as relevant for persuasion today as they were when he first described them. Nancy Austin (2002), a California management consultant, maintains that, though the theory may be over a half-century old, "for modern managers looking to pump up performance, it still has zing." Robert Zemke (1998), the senior editor of the journal *Training*, notes, "It's ironic that this '50s psychologist with no head for business played such a central role in the development of the psychology of management and the thoughts of modern managers." In 1998, Maslow's daughter published a revision of his work, entitled *Maslow on Management*, which was greeted with rave reviews (Rowan, 1998). And Schiffman and Kanuk (1997) say that in spite of its age, "Maslow's hierarchy is a useful tool in understanding consumer motivations and is readily adaptable to marketing strategy," (p. 100). Some of Feig's (1997) hot buttons equate to Maslow's need levels. Despite its vintage, Maslow's hierarchy still has much to teach us.

Maslow theorized that people have various kinds of needs that emerge, subside, and then reemerge. In his hierarchy of needs the lower levels of the hierarchy represent the strongest needs and the higher levels the weaker ones (see Figure 7.6). Maslow did not believe that higher needs are superior to lower needs—rather, they are less likely to emerge until the stronger lower needs have been met. The base of the pyramid represents universal needs or beliefs about which there is unanimous agreement. As we move up the pyramid, we find

FIGURE 7.6 **Maslow's hierarchy of needs.**

needs or beliefs on which there may not be unanimous agreement and on which individuals place varying degrees of value. As a result, there is an upward dynamic in Maslow's hierarchy, which means that as powerful needs are met, less potent ones emerge. Maslow called this upward dynamic **prepotency**. In other words, weaker needs (such as the need for self-respect) emerge only after stronger needs (like food or shelter) have been filled. Don't try to persuade a dehydrated person to dress up before having a drink of water. The need to slake our thirst is prepotent; and until it is fulfilled, we ignore other needs. As time passes, the earlier needs also reemerge again. For example, the needs for food or water emerge and then recede as we eat or drink, but they reemerge at a later time.

Basic Needs.   The bottom level of Maslow's pyramid contains the strongest needs we have—our **basic needs**, which he defined as the physiological things required to sustain life—regular access to air, food, water, shelter, sleep, and so on. Until these needs have been met, we don't usually concern ourselves with higher needs. However, basic needs can motivate behavior. For example, the person who is starving can be motivated to do all sorts of

BREAST CANCER BEGINS EVEN SMALLER THAN THIS. THAT'S WHY YOU NEED A YEARLY MAMMOGRAM, ESPECIALLY AS YOU GET OLDER. MAMMOGRAMS CAN DETECT LUMPS TOO SMALL FOR YOU TO FEEL AND EARLY DETECTION MAY SAVE YOUR LIFE, SO CALL 1-800-ACS 2345.

GET A MAMMOGRAM.
EARLY DETECTION IS THE BEST PROTECTION.

 A Public Service of
This Publication   AMERICAN CANCER SOCIETY®

FIGURE 7.7 The need for security is the appeal used in this ad from the American Cancer Society.

SOURCE: Reprinted by permission of the American Cancer Society.

unusual things to secure food, ranging from stealing it to eating insects. And we know that the need for air can cause drowning victims to panic and drown not only themselves but also their would-be rescuers.

Security Needs. The second level of Maslow's pyramid is the **need for security**, which he defined as the ability to continue to fill the basic needs of life. We can look at these needs in several ways. If we fear losing our jobs, we have a strong need to obtain income security, and we try to find a more secure job, or we save money for hard times. Even if we have job security, we still might feel insecure about maintaining our personal safety because of the rising crime rates in our neighborhood. We might take drastic action to ward off criminals by keeping a gun on the nightstand or perhaps by moving to a gated community. Even when we feel secure in our community, we still might feel insecure because of world politics. We fear that our country is vulnerable to terrorists, who may manage to soon acquire nuclear and biological or chemical weapons. Or we fear that our leaders are considering unwise military actions against some country. Those not technically trained for the computer age have a realistic fear of being out-of-date and soon out of a job. Political analysts explained several recent election results as related to fears of economic displacement. In the interpersonal realm, we have a need for "social security," or the continuing acceptance by others. In other words, the need for security emerges and reemerges as various threats to our security become evident (see Figure 7.7).

Today, insecurity, like change, is one of the few predictable things in life. Eight of every ten jobs being filled by tomorrow's college grads don't even exist today. It's almost impossible for you to prepare for the future because the rate and pace of change is accelerating so quickly. Computer technology now becomes obsolete in less than a year. No one can keep up with all the new (and frequently essential) information about jobs, health, communities, and a host of other personal and social issues. This need is similar to Feig's (1997) "desire to control" hot button. Feig says this need explains home-based businesses because you can become own boss and avoid layoffs.

Belongingness and Affiliation Needs. Once our security needs have been met, we become aware of needs on the third level of the pyramid—**belongingness or affiliation needs**, which are defined as the need to interact with others and to identify with some group. A number of options are open to us to meet our need for association. Usually, individuals go beyond the family and workplace and become members of groups with which they want to affiliate, such as service groups, places of worship, the PTA, bowling leagues, or golf and health clubs. Generally, we limit the number of groups we join, and we are active members in only a few. Feig (1997) identified the "need for belonging" as another of his hot buttons and noted that "Americans are the 'joiningest' people in the world." He advises doubters to examine the number of membership cards in their wallets if they don't think this is so (p. 29).

The flip side of belonging and affiliation needs is the trend toward isolation. A number of people and organizations are concerned about the tendency of people to cocoon or isolate themselves. In his article "Bowling Alone" (1995) and his follow-up book, *Bowling Alone: The Collapse and Revival of American Community* (2000), Robert Putnam observed that more and more persons join what he calls checkbook groups such as the Citizen's Utility Board, The Sierra Club, or the American Association of Retired Persons. Belonging only requires that you write a check, because the groups rarely if ever meet. Membership is down in civic and fraternal groups like the Lions, Elks, and Moose Clubs, and fewer people bowl in leagues, preferring to "bowl alone."

Like physiological and security needs, the need to belong often interacts with other needs and continues to reemerge throughout our lives. Also, what fulfills our belonging needs differs at various points in our lives and will probably change across time. It may be important to belong to a fraternity or sorority when we are in college, but after graduation, these affiliations fade and are replaced

by job-related associations or other social activities. Later, when we have families, other affiliations tend to be more important to us, and we join community groups and a church or other religious organization. In this context, a recent trend is the emergence of "mega-churches" like the Mariners Church of Newport Beach, California. This church offers programming for various market segments— grief therapy, Gen X activities, and seminars on a variety of topics like twelve-step recovery, divorce dynamics, and the parenting of adolescents—all served up with cappuccino and snacks. The need to belong will always be with us because humans by nature are social beings.

Love and Esteem Needs. Once we satisfy our affiliation or belonging needs, we feel the emergence of needs in the fourth level of Maslow's model, which he called **love and esteem needs**, defined as the need to be valued by the members of the groups with which we affiliate—our families, fellow workers, friends, church congregation, and neighbors. Once we are part of a group, we want to feel that the group values us as a member and as an individual. We are happy when our families understand and admire the things we do. In her recent book *My Life So Far*, Jane Fonda quotes Oprah Winfrey as naming this need the "Please Disease" (2005) and describes it as a lifelong and unending desire to do things that will please our parent(s) and bring us love or esteem. The esteem need is also a reemerging one. That is, when we find that we are needed, loved, and esteemed by our family, our need for esteem does not fade away— instead, its focus shifts, and we now want to feel needed by our co-workers, our boss, and our friends.

Many product appeals offer a kind of symbolic substitute for esteem. For example, as Figure 7.8 shows, the kids will hold Mom in high esteem if she uses a certain brand of gas grill.

At various times, esteem seems rooted in conspicuous consumption for purposes of display. At other times (such as wartime), conspicuous consumption borders on being unpatriotic. However, important events and life experiences can change the way people satisfy esteem needs. For instance,

THE GRILLER: MARATHON MOM

No time to waste, right? So a gas grill has to perform quickly, easily. Enter MasterFlame². It's built with your schedule in mind: easy push button ignition, sturdy shelves for extra work space, a cooking system that virtually eliminates uneven heat, and multi-level cooking to prepare the main course and side dishes at one time. Give it a try... you'll find you've made a delicious dinner for your family and it wasn't a chore at all. In fact, it's our guess you'll find you even had fun.

To locate Char-Broil MasterFlame² gas grills, and find out about a free gift with purchase, just call

1-800-477-0118

THE GRILL: MASTERFLAME²™ FROM
Char-Broil

FIGURE 7.8 Esteem needs are the key appeal in this ad claiming a Char-Broil gas grill allows the mother to whip up a great meal for her kids, and she feels good about that.

SOURCE: Reprinted by permission of Char-Broil.

recent political, financial, and religious scandals have shaken people's faith in traditional institutions and their leadership's ability to show esteem. What kind of esteem for employees and stockholders does the crooked CEO have? Schiffman and Kanuk (1997) note that the Asian American subculture is highly motivated by esteem needs and therefore they are strivers, particularly in terms of education. People realize that working in community can help them meet their esteem needs. In fact, "community" has become a kind of God term.

Self-Actualization Needs. Maslow put **self-actualization needs** at the top of his pyramid (thereby implying that they rarely emerge). He defined self-actualization as the achievement of one's full potential or capability. At first, Maslow believed that individuals could live up to their potential only when all four of the lower needs had been met. It is hard for young people on the way up to think about self-actualization, just as it is difficult to meet love or esteem needs if individuals don't belong to some group that can offer love or esteem. But in reality, self-actualization is an integral part of everyone's life. Feig (1997) labeled this need "the desire to be the best you can be" hot button, and he identifies several examples, including the pride we all had as children when we brought home our gold-starred papers from school—they were proof of self-actualization.

FIGURE 7.9 The humor here is based on Cardinal Sicola's inability to self-actualize.

SOURCE: Used with permission of Al Ochsner.

Maslow later came to see self-actualization as occurring through what he called "peak experiences" in life. These events allowed individuals to enjoy and learn about themselves, or experience something they had only dreamed of previously. Thus, the person who ventures into the wilderness and learns to be self-reliant and not to fear isolation enjoys a peak, or self-actualizing, experience. When people take their first job after high school or college and discover that they have abilities that are of value, they probably experience a degree of self actualization. Cultural trends also affect the ways in which we seek to satisfy our self-actualization needs. Social critic T. J. Jackson Lears (1983) noted that the search for ways of identifying ourselves and our potential came about when the United States shifted from being a culture of production to a culture of consumption; that is, in moving from a secure farm existence to an unsettling urban isolation, we experienced a loss of traditional values and chaotic changes in our lifestyles. The result, Lears claimed, was the search for a "therapeutic ethos" or an identity that would let us be at ease with ourselves—that would permit us to self-actualize. To a large extent, this therapeutic ethos offers inner harmony, reduced feelings of emptiness, and hope for self-realization through patterns of consumption.

To examine the culture of consumption in which we live, access InfoTrac College Edition, and enter the words "consumption culture" in the search engine. Be sure to read the reviews of *Consuming Desires: Consumption, Culture and Happiness*, a book of essays on consumption edited by Ed Rosenblatt. They may make you want to read the entire book.

As you are exposed to various persuasive events, whether public or interpersonal, try applying Maslow's model to them. See whether it sheds light on the needs that people feel and that may motivate their actions. You may want to experiment with persuading another person using several levels of Maslow's model. If the person doesn't seem motivated by appeals to security, try appealing to basic or belongingness needs.

Uses of the Needs Process Premise

In our search for the first premises that serve as springboards for persuasion in enthymemes, human needs demonstrate one area of our vulnerability to persuasion. Whether we identify them using Packard's compelling needs, Maslow's hierarchy, Feig's hot buttons, or some other model, we all experience strongly felt needs that require some sort of satisfaction. Persuaders frequently tie minor premises to these powerful needs and allow audiences to complete the enthymematic argument by drawing the conclusion. As persuadees, we must consider the persuasive requests made of us from the perspective of our own needs. And as persuaders,

---

BOX 7.2   Interactive Marketing and Human Needs

Go to www.everybodysinteractive.com and discover how marketing experts are delving into human needs using interactive media. The home page you will discover there will show you how marketers use interactive media to appeal to human needs and emotions. Explore the various options, including how The Watson Communication Group plans and executes advertising strategies for various clients such as Levi Straus, Microsoft, cosmetic dentists, skin care specialists, and others. You will see how human needs and emotions are being tapped by persuaders of all sorts.

---

we should examine the current needs of those we wish to influence. If we do that, we are more likely to succeed and to do our audience a service by giving them a way to satisfy their needs.

It is important, however, to be ethical in appealing to audience needs. As persuadees we need to ask, "Is this appeal to my needs ethical or not?" thus practicing our response-ability, and we need to ask the same questions when we take on the role of persuader. A good way to train yourself to evaluate appeals from this critical perspective—as persuadee or persuader—is to restate persuasive messages, such as TV commercials or political appeals, from the perspective of the Packard, Maslow, Feig, or other need models. As first premises on which persuasion can be built, psychological and physiological needs are powerful motivators.

EMOTIONS: THE SECOND PROCESS PREMISE

Another kind of psychological or process premise relates to our emotions. Appeals to our emotions are the second of four such process premises including needs.

What does it mean when, in the midst of a discussion, someone says, "You're just being too emotional about this"? It may mean they have noticed a physical change in your behavior. Perhaps your voice changes in timbre or volume, your face gets red, you begin to show a nervous tic, or your eyes reveal anger. Or they might be responding to the fact that you have started rattling off statistics, sounding like a courtroom attorney. Borchers (2005) refers to these two interpretations of being emotional as demonstrating the physiological and the cognitive dimensions of emotion. In the physiological dimension you feel a change in the way your body is responding to the situation. You feel your voice's change in timbre, your face flushing, and your change in facial expression. With the cognitive dimension of emotions, the changes in you are not physical responses—they are perceptual changes in the way you think about a person, an issue, or a situation. These cognitive changes are usually expressed verbally. We are probably born with the physiological dimension of emotions hardwired into our brains. However, we must *learn* the cognitive dimension and how to express what emotions we are feeling. We learn these things from experiences, parents, authority figures, friends, or role models whom we observe in films, on television, or elsewhere. In both the physiological and the cognitive dimension, there are cultural variations (Porter & Samovar, 1998), particularly when our emotions are publicly displayed. We can see this in ethnic stereotypes of the emotional, gesticulating Italian or the authority-driven German. You learn that British are very polite even when expressing anger whereas other ethnicities might be outright rude.

In both the physiological and the cognitive dimension, we are dealing with models for understanding and reacting to our feelings and beliefs. Nabi (2002) maintains that emotions have five basic components: (1) cognitive evaluation of a situation, meaning that we are aware and have thought over the situation; (2) physiological arousal, or a change in bodily functions, such as an adrenalin rush; (3) motor expression, or what we physically do about the situation; (4) motivational intentions or readiness, or what we are prepared to do and plan to do and why; and (5) a feeling state in the subject, such as when you feel happy or disappointed (p. 290). You learned to "bite your tongue" or to "count to ten" when feeling the emotion of anger, either from experience or more likely from parents or authority figures. Let's examine a few emotions that most persons feel or respond to in some way and see how persuaders use them to move us to action.

Fear

Fear is one of the most familiar emotions that we experience. Initially you learned to be afraid when you did something wrong and angered someone else—usually a parent—and were punished for the behavior. As time passed, you learned that other situations and events can also lead to negative outcomes, and you became fearful of a number of things—disease, injury, loss of property, or personal embarrassment to name a few. Nabi (2002) says that fear includes a threat to our physical or psychological self that is out of our control, and that it can change attitudes (p. 291–292).

Appeals to the emotion of fear have been one of the most researched issues in persuasion, but the conclusions of the research are often contradictory. Sometimes the fear appeal works powerfully, but at other times it boomerangs, especially if it is too strong to stomach or simply is unbelievable. Politicians have used fear appeals in negative television advertisements in campaign after campaign, and 2008 will probably not be any different. In the 2004 presidential campaign, President Bush implied that a vote for his opponent would lead to a loss of national security. Fear appeals are also common in marketing communication. For example, the insurance industry tells us to be afraid of financial loss. We are told that we need insurance for everything from floods to identity theft, the need for long-term medical care, and national disasters like Hurricane Katrina in 2005, which made New Orleans essentially uninhabitable and resulted in billions of dollars in insurance claims. Personal grooming ads emphasize the possible loss in prestige that comes from teeth that aren't white enough, underarm odor, or bad taste in clothing. And cause-related persuasion frequently uses fear appeals in campaigns advocating family values, safe sex, and national security. In most uses of fear appeals, the persuader must first convince us of the probability of the threat before offering us a means (usually a product or practice) of avoiding it and then demonstrating that the proposed solution will work. As receivers of fear appeals, you need to carefully examine the probability of the threat, the difficulty of taking the proposed actions to dodge the threat, and the evidence that these actions will prevent the problem.

Guilt

As we observed elsewhere, guilt is a powerful motivator in persuading others to vote, purchase, donate, or join. Guilt usually comes from a realization that we have violated some rule or code of conduct but can reduce the guilt by atonement or punishment. Borchers (2005) defines guilt as "a psychological feeling of discomfort that arises when order is violated" (p. 195). Guilt frequently arises out of some kind of interpersonal situation—we have wronged our parents, children, spouse, friends, or the community, and we must set things right. For example, the politician claims that we have under-funded education, and many poor kids are left behind, doomed to failure. We can atone for the mistake by having nationwide competence tests, eliminating tenure for teachers, and getting actively involved in our children's learning. If we missed an appointment, we can send flowers or an "I'm sorry" card. If we have engaged in unsafe sex, thus endangering our partner, we can engage in preventive actions in the future. The best way to prevent drug usage by teens is for parents to ask where the teen is going, who will be there, when they expect to come home, and whether adults will be present. That

FIGURE 7.10 This ad by the Partnership for a Drug Free America uses the avoidance of future guilt to persuade.

advice is part of a cause related campaign sponsored by the Partnership for a Drug Free America and is about avoiding guilt in the future. Its slogan is "Parents: The Anti-Drug."

Nabi (2002) notes that the causes of guilt vary greatly across religions and cultures. In some cultures, losing face is about the worst thing a person can do. In others, dishonoring one's elders is the big guilt button. Receivers need to recognize guilt appeals for what they are and then determine what they need to do to reduce their own sense of guilt.

Anger

We usually become angry when things don't go our way. When we face some obstacle that keeps us from reaching our goal or that harms us or loved ones, we become frustrated, and we want to strike out at those who make things difficult for us. Anger is also very powerful. Nabi (2002) noted that while anger generates high levels of energy, it sometimes leads to constructive problem solving and often prompts careful analysis of messages (p. 293). Take the sentence "What did he mean by saying that I was naïve?" You might get angry over being called naïve, but you seek to get down to the actual meaning of the accusation, which is a constructive use of your anger.

We see appeals to anger in politics and cause-related persuasion and in some types of marketing and advertising. A significant proportion of the population was fearful and angry enough following 9/11 that in 2003 that they supported President Bush's call to go to war in Iraq. The justification for the action was that Iraq had caused the disaster because it harbored terrorists, and we wanted to strike back to cure the problem. In hindsight, we probably needed more careful analysis of the situation and the facts by critical receivers. The "striking back" was enormously costly in human and economic terms and didn't result in fewer terrorist attacks. In fact, it may have led to an increase in the number of suicide bombers in Iraq and elsewhere and may have been used to recruit new members of terrorist organizations. Employees, stockholders, and retirees in the late 1990s became angry with CEOs who looted their company's resources and pension funds. Some of them went on a crusade to reform the Securities and Exchange Commission, and they succeeded. They used cause-related persuasion to recruit supporters and donors by appealing to the anger felt by those who were cheated by the crooked CEOs. In my state an organization called the Citizen's Utility Board (CUB) regularly gets donations by appealing to the anger felt by consumers when utility rates are arbitrarily raised. On an intrapersonal level, some persons are angry with the way they look, even if it's their own fault. A "Fatties" organization is now bringing suit against food manufacturers for not disclosing ingredient information that might lead overweight individuals to avoid the products (see Figure 7.11). We have recently seen persons in middle age go to orthodontists to have braces put on their crooked teeth. Perhaps they were angry with their parents, who didn't take care of the problem earlier—now they are willing to pay for the improvement themselves. So anger frequently serves as a motivator in persuasion. Other negative emotions include envy, hatred, and disgust (Nabi, 2002).

Pride

On a more positive note, persuaders appeal to pride to enact legislation, sell products, and prompt joining or donating. A feeling of pride usually includes taking credit for some positive outcome in our lives. As a result, people become expressive about their accomplishments and may make announcements about the good deeds. Sometimes this causes resentment in those who haven't achieved as much, so persuaders need to be careful about using appeals to pride. And cultural differences affect the emotion of pride. Nabi (2002) reports that collectivist cultures (such as China's) "respond more favorably to pride-based appeals" (p. 296) than do cultures that are more individualistically based (such as the United States).

We can find pride appeals in many persuasive contexts. Politicians tout the accomplishments of their administrations or programs. Cause-based pride appeals are intended to make the potential donors feel proud about making a donation to the good cause. And of course many products promise to make consumers feel proud when they use the brand to improve their appearance. For example, Neutrogena Skin Clearing Tint uses a pride appeal when the ads urge consumers to "rethink makeup . . . now, don't cover up. Clear up." The ads give the brand credibility by using the words "Dermatologist Recommended" together with the pictures of two young females who are presumed to use the product and who appear not to have acne or blemishes.

Happiness and Joy

Happiness and joy are obviously similar. Happiness is associated with a mood, and joy indicates a positive emotional response to events. For our purposes they are synonyms. Happy persons are positive about their future, confident, sharing, and trusting, and they seem to attract other persons (Nabi, 2002). We can all think of persuasive happiness appeals made by advertisers who link use of their brand with happy outcomes and satisfied consumers. Estee Lauder's Pleasures and Pleasures for Men ran a three-page fold-out ad in the May 2005 issue of *Cosmopolitan*. It had no copy aside from the name of the brand. Instead it showed nine pictures, seven of which focused on the members of a young family. The other two pictures were of cherry blossoms and a puppy. The implied conclusion was for consumers to "Use the brand and be as happy as these folks." Politicians promise better,

Obesity:

"~~Epidemic~~"

"~~Problem~~"

"~~Threat~~"

"~~Issue~~"

"Hype"

Americans have been force-fed a steady diet of obesity myths by the "food police," trial lawyers, and even our own government.

Learn the truth about obesity at:

ConsumerFreedom.com

The Center for Consumer Freedom is a nonprofit organization dedicated to protecting consumer choices and promoting common sense.

happier, sharing, and more trusting times if we enact their policies on the economy, the environment, and education. Cause-related advertising usually implies that support for a cause such as Save the Children will bring the joiner or donor a sense of well-being, self-respect, and happiness instead of a sense of guilt for ignoring the issue. Nabi (2002) also says that appeals to happiness frequently use humor in advertising because of its ability to distract audience attention and cause laughter (p. 296).

Other positive emotions that persuaders can invoke include relief, hope, compassion, and many others.

ATTITUDES: THE THIRD PROCESS PREMISE

In Chapter 4 we looked at how researchers use a variety of theories to explain attitudes. One unifying element among these theories is that attitudes can and do serve as the unstated major premises in persuasive enthymemes. We also noted that attitudes act as predispositions to behavior, so holding an attitude or a set of attitudes makes us ready to take action. However, while attitudes are sometimes excellent predictors of behavior, at other times they are not. Psychologists Martin Fishbein and Icek Ajzen (1975) now believe that a better predictor of behavior is what they call the *intention to behave*. When the person tells you how he or she intends to act, the person is prone to act that way. By articulating their intentions, they have already acted symbolically.

Psychologists Alice H. Egley and Shelley Chaiken (1993) define an attitude as "a psychological tendency that is expressed by evaluating a particular entity with some degree of favor or disfavor" (p. 1). The important word here is "tendency," by which they mean "an internal state that lasts for at least a short time" (p. 2). Since the attitude is internal (in our heads), we must infer it using "evaluative responses." Examples of evaluative responses include expressing "approval or disapproval, favor or disfavor, liking or disliking, approach or avoidance, attraction or aversion, or similar reactions" (p. 3).

Researchers into consumer behavior identified a social function served by attitudes. For instance, they asked whether family, friends, authority figures, or celebrity figures affect our attitudes toward a brand, candidate, or ideology. They concluded that socially significant persons do influence our attitudes (Schiffman & Kanuk, 1997), and note that mass media exposure correlates highly with the formation of consumer attitudes (pp. 260–262).

Advertising researcher S. Shavitt (1990) maintained that attitudes serve both social and utilitarian functions. In researching audience reactions to advertisements, he found that the social functions of attitudes in the ads tell us what persons responding to the ads were like and in all likelihood what sorts of appeals would prompt them to action. For example, the ad might claim that discriminating people prefer high-fiber diets to high-fat, low-carb Atkins' Diets that only temporarily take off pounds. If we want to be a discriminating and slimmer person, we adopt the eating habits of other discriminating and slim persons.

Utilitarian functions of attitudes stress the features and benefits of the product. An ad might claim that the Honda Prius gets up to 60 miles per gallon, and it is extremely quiet in the electrically powered mode. Two utilitarian elements operate here—mileage and quietness. This also fits with elements of the ELM model. For example, psychologists K. G. De Bono and R. Harnish (1988), R. E. Petty and D. T. Wegener (1998), and others found that for high self-monitoring individuals, (e.g., those who were usually very aware of why they were responding to an ad), an attractive source of persuasion usually triggers elaborate processing of the message. For low self-monitoring individuals (e.g., those who were barely aware of even responding to the ad), elaborate processing is more likely to occur only if an expert rather than an attractive source conveys the message. This makes sense. If you are a high self-monitoring person, you do not want to blunder simply because a celebrity recommends the product. That makes you seem impulsive in the eyes of others. So, you do serious investigation of the product in the central processing route. Low self-monitoring persons respect expertise more than advice from a celebrity, and they avoid looking foolish by relying on the recommendation of the expert.

We usually find attitude objects in the persuader's requests for action or offers of products, ideas, candidates, beliefs, and so on. For example, recently many Americans started flying the flag and displaying patriotic bumper stickers, yard signs, and other emblems with slogans like "United We Stand" or "These Colors Won't Run." These displays are in response to political persuasion emphasizing the value of patriotism. These attitude objects serve a social function because they announce the person's attitudes. This, in turn, causes alignment or identification with others who feel the same way and helps to foster interpersonal relations and influence. The attitude object of the flag, bumper sticker, or sign serves as part of the appeal, and we follow suit if we want to identify with them. The obverse is also true: If we want to distance ourselves from jingoistic patriotism, we won't follow the requested action and may even display a "Get Out of Iraq!" sign in our yard. This reduces the possibility of forming interpersonal relationships with super-patriots.

So attitudes have an important social function in that they can either foster or discourage social networking. Nelson (2001) notes that the social function of attitudes in organizations (especially businesses) can make or break the organization. And according to D. C. Schrader (1999), the social function of interpersonal influence is largely dependent on the goal complexity of appeals. In other words, if the persuader's advice is too complicated, we judge his or her attempts to influence us as unworkable, incompetent, or inappropriate. As a result, the social function of attitudes often affects persuasive outcomes.

To learn more about the importance of interpersonal influence on getting compliance from others, access InfoTrac College Edition, enter the words "interpersonal influence" in the search engine, and review a few of the many articles listed there.

Attitudes, Beliefs, and Opinions

As noted in Chapter 4, Rokeach (1968) pointed out that individual beliefs range from primitive and strongly held to those based on authority and not as strongly held. These belief sets cluster and form attitudes which fall into two categories: (1) attitudes toward objects or issues and (2) attitudes toward situations. Both predispose us to action, but they also might confuse us when they conflict with one

another. For example, when parents protest the presence of a student with AIDS in their children's school, attitudes toward the object (the infected student) and toward the situation (the possibility of infecting my own children) can either conflict or converge. When the two attitudes conflict, the parents sympathize with the victim, but they don't want their child infected.

Opinions resemble beliefs but are far more fickle, as opinion polls demonstrate—opinions can change overnight. We have opinions about politicians, what they say in campaigns, and their actions taken after assuming office. These opinions change, especially if the politician blunders, loses to Congress on an issue, or supports a corrupt friend. Usually the politician's errors lead to low voter ratings and sometimes rejection at the polls. But opinions are fickle and unpredictable. For example, during Bill Clinton's impeachment trial, his ratings in the polls actually went to an all-time high in spite of the sordid sex scandal. Why? Rokeach's theory helps explain the riddle. People had a highly negative attitude toward Clinton's sexual dalliance (attitude toward object). But they had highly positive feelings about other issues like the economy, low unemployment, budget surpluses, and a bullish stock market (attitude toward situation). These opinions conflicted with their feelings about the scandal, and the economy won out. A similar scenario played out for President George W. Bush on his plan to institute private investment accounts as part of the Social Security system. After he campaigned for the change in over half of the states, his ratings on the issue plummeted in the public opinion polls.

To learn more about the measurement of and uses that are made of measures of public opinion, go to InfoTrac College Edition, and enter the words "public opinion" in the search engine. Check a few of the more tantalizing items listed under the periodical titles.

Social psychologist P. Zimbardo and his colleagues (1976, 1991) note that attitudes are "either mental readiness or implicit predispositions that exert some general and consistent influence on a fairly large class of evaluative responses" (p. 20). A school of advertising research known by the acronym DAGMAR suggests that ad agencies ought to Define Advertising Goals for Measured Advertising Results (Colley, 1961). In other words, establishing positive attitudes toward a brand serves as the goal of advertising, not instant purchase behavior. The idea is that if consumers have an improved image of a product, they will probably buy it sometime in the future. Therefore, if the marketer can change their attitudes, purchase eventually follows. Unfortunately, this attitude–behavior link sometimes flip flops, perhaps because of intervening variables that also affect purchase behavior such as time of day, attractiveness of the offer, a store display, price, or background music. Even in experiments with these causes filtered out, attitude and behavior do not consistently link.

The Functions of Attitudes

Attitudes can have several functions. For example, they have a cognitive or knowledge function; we aren't born with attitudes, we must learn them. Consider our attitudes about being environmentally responsible. How did they come about? Probably we first learned about air and water pollution and the dangers that they bring. Then we learned about recycling and what it can achieve. Then we learned that endangered species may act as early warnings about what might ultimately happen to humans. Only after learning all of these things do we finally form an overall attitude toward environmental responsibility. Likewise, some advertisements also persuade by teaching. A mutual fund company advertises that it is "no load" and goes on to explain what that means—customers don't have to pay commissions when they make investments. Persuadees learn the value of this and form a positive attitude toward that company, and they decide to use the company when they make investments. The same learning operates in political or cause-related campaigns. For example, since the March of Dimes no longer supports polio research (the disease has been nearly eradicated), it must teach potential donors that now it supports research into premature births—the leading cause of infant

mortality. The receiver learns about the organization and its purposes and then forms an attitude toward it and decides whether or not to send a donation.

Attitudes also influence our emotions and feelings, and thus they have what has been termed an *affective function* or an emotional outcome. For instance, our attitudes about the development of hydrogen fuels affect how we feel about this new source of energy. If we equate hydrogen energy with the hydrogen bomb, we experience fear and may actively oppose its production. Some ads target the affective dimension, or emotions. For example, how did *The Sopranos* affect viewers' attitudes and emotions toward mob figures? Chris Seay, a Christian minister, worried about his wife's response when he rushed home from church activities to watch the nudity- and profanity-filled fourth season. He ultimately convinced her that the show was about "faith, forgiveness and family values." That nifty bit of persuasion got him out of his affective dilemma (Pinsky, 2002).

Finally, attitudes have a behavioral function in that they prepare us to take certain actions. Because we hold certain attitudes toward air and water pollution, we may choose to recycle, to not buy a gas guzzler, or only use biodegradable detergents. The behavioral function of attitudes affects what we do about these issues. Some ads aim at changing attitudes in order to prompt behavior change. Two goals of advertising are to create traffic in a store or to get consumers to try a brand. The advertiser offers huge discounts or special events such as the visit of a celebrity to create traffic. They may send a free sample or offer an attractive rebate with a purchase. Few people reject anything that is free or cheaper, so they give the brand a try. The marketer's hope is that visiting the store will prompt impulse purchases or that satisfaction with the performance of the brand will lead to brand loyalty and future purchases.

Attitudes and Intention

As we noted earlier, the work of Fishbein and Ajzen (1975) added the concept of **behavioral intention** to the research on attitude and behavior change. Here, a fairly consistent set of results emerges. Attitude change usually precedes what people say they intend to do. As noted above, when people articulate what they intend to do, they have already acted symbolically. Nonverbally, when the person clips or saves a coupon, he or she has already "bought" the brand. Likewise, the person who displays a bumper sticker in favor of a certain candidate will show up at the polls to vote for that candidate on election day. Knowing this, politicians urge people to display bumper stickers, buttons, and yard signs to guarantee their votes rather than trying to persuade others who may be undecided.

Attitudes and Interpersonal Communication/Persuasion

There are several other dimensions of attitude change and the subsequent behavior puzzle. One of these is the degree to which attitudes function as tools of interpersonal communication or persuasion, or both. In other words, do expressions of attitudes have more to do with fitting ourselves into a comfortable position with others than they do with our ultimate behavior? R. J. Eiser (1987), a critic of attitude research puts it this way: "One of the main shortcomings of many attitude theories is their emphasis on individualistic, intra-psychic factors to the relative neglect of the social and communicative context within which attitudes are acquired and expressed" (p. 2). In other words, we overtly express attitudes in order to get along with and identify with others.

Attitudes and Information Processing

The focus on human information processing in the ELM which serves as a unifying model throughout this book also relates to behavioral intentions. We can't look at attitudes and behavior without also looking at how audiences process such persuasive information. One of the first questions to ask is whether the audience even comprehends the message. In the central path they usually do

comprehend the message and may even research it. In the peripheral path they probably don't. For example, "cents off " coupons as persuasive information fit with several memory networks in our minds, such as whether we already use the brand, how often, and whether the coupons are valuable enough to justify clipping them. Peripheral cues may prompt behavior. For example, people will clip more coupons if there is a dotted line around the coupon and clip even more if there is a little scissors on the dotted line. And there are diversity issues to be concerned with in deciding whether or not to offer coupons. For example, Latinos tend not to clip coupons because they associate them with food stamps, a social stigma in their subculture. So if an advertiser is targeting Latinos, that advertiser should not use coupons but may want to emphasize the warranty or quality instead.

Research into how information is stored in our long-term memory (LTM) is fairly recent, and most researchers agree that information is usually stored in networks and in the form of key words, symbols, and relationships. A good organizing device for LTM is to make one's persuasion episodic in nature, probably due to the power of the narrative or story form. For example, we all have been late for an appointment and find ourselves stuck behind the slowest driver on the road, who also misses all the green stoplights. Imagine a television commercial to promote Compoz, an over-the-counter treatment for settling people's nerves. This episode could act as a script for the commercial. The ad opens with the character realizing that he or she has nearly missed a doctor's appointment. We see them rush out to the car, get in, and speed off, only to get behind the slowpoke. They glance nervously at the clock and begin having a silent "conversation" with the slow driver. They are about to commit road rage, but instead they take a Compoz tablet. The ad closes with the slow driver turning at the next intersection and the product's slogan, "For those nerve-racking occasions try Compoz." At the behavior stage of the ELM (voting, buying, joining, or donating), the critical episode is retrieved from long-term memory and provides persuadees with good "reasons" for taking action.

To learn more about what affects our long-term memory, access InfoTrac College Edition, and type the words "long-term memory" in the search engine. Browse some of the titles.

The ELM model has prompted a multitude of research insights into the process of persuasion since its introduction. Researchers S. Booth-Butterfield and J. Welbourne (2002) suggest that the model "has been instrumental in integrating the literature on source, message, receiver and context effects in persuasion and has also been a springboard for new research in this domain" (p. 155). Although people want to have "correct" attitudes, the degree to which they will elaborate on an issue varies from individuals and situations, but the following patterns remain clear.

1. A number of variables affect attitude change and can act as persuasive arguments, peripheral cues, or attitudinal positions.

2. When motivation or ability to elaborate decreases, peripheral cues become more important and carry the persuasive load. For example, persons who are uninterested in the implications of diversity will rely on stereotyping.

3. Conversely, as motivation or ability to elaborate on a claim increases, peripheral cues lose impact. For example, if our new boss is ethnically different from us, we devalue stereotypes.

4. The persuader affects consumers' motivation by encouraging or discouraging careful examination of the argument or claim. The persuader says, "April 15 is only a week away, so bone up on the new tax laws," instead of saying, "At your income level, you might as well use the short tax form 1040EZ and file online."

5. Issues and arguments flowing from the central processing path persist, predict actual behavior best, and seem resistant to competing persuasion. Persuasion using process premises is likely to follow the peripheral path, whereas persuasion using reasoned premises is likely to be processed in the central route. Petty and Cacioppo's (1986) chart in Figure 7.12 depicts various options and routes.

Notice that the various options in the ELM depend on whether you have the motivation to process a persuasive message. You must want to investigate a given product, candidate, or cause or the elaboration process is short-circuited. If they are motivated to process an offer, appeal, or claim, persuadees must also possess the ability to complete the processing. Thereafter, the nature of the attitude change depends on which path is followed. If the peripheral path is used, the attitude change will be weak, short-lived, and less likely to yield behavior. If the central processing path is used, attitude change will be potent, long-lived, and likely to lead to behavior.

Each path has its strengths and weaknesses. Most researchers agree that attitudes have something to do with behavior, that attitudes can be altered by persuasion, and that the suggested behavior usually follows a change in attitude. What does all this mean to us as persuadees who live in a world concerned with diversity and ethics? What can we do to uncover persuaders' intentions toward and beliefs about the diverse audiences? Being aware of attitudes helps us to pinpoint what persuaders think of us and others. Identifying the attitudes that persuaders assume we have makes us more critical receivers, and so we judge persuasive attempts as ethical or unethical. We also become conscious of our attitudes, and as a result, we anticipate how persuaders use them to get us to follow their advice. However, few situations involve a single attitude. Most situations involve several attitudes, which leads to a need for consistency among those attitudes.

CONSISTENCY: THE FOURTH PROCESS PREMISE

We looked at balance theory in Chapter 4. It posits that we feel comfortable when the world lives up to (or operates consistently with) our

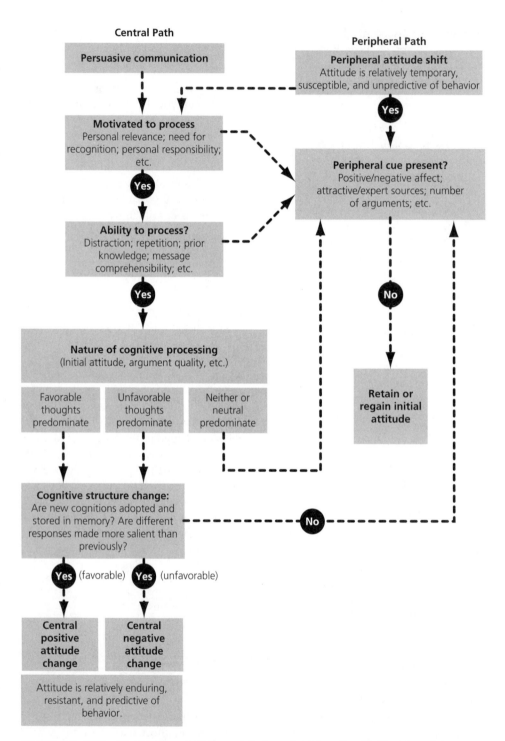

F I G U R E 7.12 Decision flow in Petty and Cacioppo's elaboration likelihood model.

BOX 7.3   Ten Lenses and the Diversity Channel

In his book entitled *The Ten Lenses: Your Guide to Living and Working in a Multicultural World* (2001), Mark A. Williams, author and founder of The Diversity Channel, (a diversity training company) discusses how human emotions vary in organizations and institutions. He describes and explains ten "lenses" or perceptual filters through which most of us view our diverse world. There are the *Assimilationists* who believe that all diversities should behave like regular Americans, and then there are the *Cultural Centrists* who believe that we must not tamper with the diversity of others. The *Meritocrats* believe that if you work hard enough and pull yourself up by your bootstraps, you will achieve your goals regardless of your race, ethnicity, or other aspects of diversity. The *Victim/Caretakers* believe that bias will forever hold down persons of diverse origins. The *Colorblind* believe in ignoring cultural differences and seeking the true value of any individual whose diversity differs from the majority. The *Elitists* believe that it is their destiny and their right

to be superior to others of varying diversities. The *Integrationists* believe that the best way to break down biases and stereotypes is to merge persons of various diversities in the workplace and elsewhere. The *Multiculturalists* want to celebrate our diversity—the more diversity we have the better things will be for everyone. *Seclusionists* want to distance and protect themselves and their families from persons of diverse cultures. And *Transcendentists* believe that race, gender, and ethnicity reflect our unified humanity. Where do you fit?

 Speculate on how these lenses might apply to human needs, emotions, and attitudes. How do you look at persons of other races, nationalities, genders, sexual preference, or ethnicities? If you want to explore Williams's work further, pick up his book and take his Ten Lenses Survey or or go online to www.thediversitychannel.com and explore its home page options.

---

perceptions or our predictions of it. When this doesn't happen, we try to change either ourselves or our interpretations of events to bring about a balanced state. Persuaders offer a means (usually a product, service, or action) to return to balance and psychological comfort. If you want to change attitudes toward health care, for instance, then try to create imbalance in health care users. You might say, "With an HMO, you can't go to the best surgeon."

We all seek out psychological equilibrium, so as receivers we need to identify what puts us into states of imbalance or inconsistency, thus making us vulnerable to persuasion. If psychological equilibrium is our goal, we need to feel comfortable and look for persuasion that reinforces attitudes. As Eiser (1987) pointed out, defining the "existing frame of reference" is a critical factor in predicting attitude shifts. Once we identify the receiver's current frame of reference, we create the kind of inconsistency that prompts psychological uneasiness, that leads to attitude change.

Cognitive Dissonance Theory

A problem with balance theory is that it doesn't relate to the degree of difference between the two people or the two instances judged. Instead it looks at the kinds of differences—positive or negative—that exist in the comparisons of persons or instances. In other words, the theory accounts for *qualitative* differences between judgments but it doesn't deal with *quantitative* differences. That may seem like a minor problem, but major differences might exist between persons or concepts regarding controversial topics such as abortion, school prayer, or patriotism, so it's important to determine how far persons and their issue positions are from one another on a topic. Leon Festinger's cognitive dissonance theory (1962) addressed this problem of quantitative and qualitative differences between persons and ideas.

Unlike balance theory, **cognitive dissonance theory** predicts that when we experience psychological tension, or dissonance, we try to reduce it in some way instead of totally resolving the tension. Tension reduction has a quantitative dimension.

We can change our attitudes a little, a moderate amount, a lot, or not at all. The tension caused by dissonance grows out of our psychological belief system, whereas balance theory relies more on logical inconsistencies. Festinger defined dissonance as a feeling resulting from the existence of two nonfitting or contrasting pieces of knowledge about the world. As in balance theory, there are times when things fit or go together and times when they do not. For Festinger, the opposite of dissonance, or "consonance," exists when two pieces of information do fit together, and hence reinforce one another. Some persons change dissonant cognitions by moving their beliefs closer to one another. Others rationalize the problem away or discredit the source of the information. Others reduce dissonance by selective perception, selective retention, or selective exposure—they choose not to receive or perceive the dissonance, they forget about it, or they choose not to be exposed to conflicting information.

Recently, dissonance theory helped explain the new sense of uneasiness affecting sexually active individuals who have multiple partners. Most of us know that the main causes of infection by the AIDS virus is unsafe sex practices, the sharing of needles among drug users, and sometimes from blood transfusions or accidental exposure to the blood of AIDS carriers. What can sexually active people do to reduce the uneasiness or dissonance they feel regarding their own sexually activity? They can:

1. Devalue their beliefs about the most effective methods of birth control and use condoms

2. Devalue AIDS information, telling themselves that this is just a scare tactic to cut down on the promiscuity of the younger generation

3. Selectively perceive the information and choose to believe that *their* sex partners don't have the AIDS virus

4. Try to forget the information about AIDS through the process of selective retention

5. Try to rationalize the problem away by believing that a cure for AIDS is just around the corner

6. Become celibate or have fewer partners

7. Do more than one of these things

Although Festinger mainly dealt with the notion of dissonance, it seems clear that we seek its opposite—consonance—to reinforce our existing attitudes. We listen to the candidates of our choice and avoid listening to their opponents. Conservatives read conservative newspapers, and liberal people read liberal ones. We seek information that confirms our position and reinforces our beliefs. Several actions build consonance in this way. We can:

1. Revalue our initial beliefs, making them stronger

2. Revalue the source of the information input by giving it more credibility than it deserves

3. Perceive the information as stronger than it actually is

4. Remember the most positive parts of the information and highlight them

5. Seek out even more supporting information

6. Do several of these things

Creating consonance strengthens and reinforces attitudes, increases credibility, and probably induces action. Persuaders probably use consonance at least as frequently as dissonance. They often want to reinforce people's opinions, attitudes, beliefs, or behavior.

In many cases, dissonance theory oversimplifies the human situation. Recently, researchers in communication, psychology, and sociology have looked at a variety of other factors that affect feelings of dissonance. W. Wood (2000) points out that social factors play a role in reducing dissonance. People want to fit in with significant reference groups and engage in normative behavior to do so. Internal states determine the outcome of persuasion as much as do the source's skill at designing the dissonance or consonance producing messages.

Sources of Dissonance

What causes you to feel imbalance or dissonance? Some are unique to you, but many of them are similar for large groups of people. These more universal factors are useful for persuaders because they are potent first premises in enthymemes. Descriptions of a few common ones follow.

Loss of Group Prestige.   This relates to the pride felt by members of a well-respected reference group, profession, or organization that has fallen on bad times and no longer is as highly respected. For instance, Martha Stewart was highly respected by many people who identified with her because they felt that they also had her class and good taste. They wanted to emulate her, to try her recipes, and to have a flower garden like hers. One of her fans said, "We put a copy of Martha Stewart's *Living* magazine on a coffee table. It's the prettiest thing in the living room." Another said, "We want a little of what she's got—a scant teaspoon in Marthaspeak—of her taste and talent" (Rowell, 2002, p. 16). After she suffered a financial scandal and served jail time, her sheen dimmed a bit. A former fan observed, "There's nothing in her magazine that even hints at her virtue" (Rowell, 2002, p. 16). Ultimately, however, Martha regained some of her previous sheen. The loss of group prestige affects small and large groups alike—from a fraternity or sorority to an entire profession such as lawyers or a region of the country such as the East Coast.

Economic Loss.   When we feel that our economic value is in danger of being reduced, we experience dissonance. We deal with the obvious dissonance of losing a job in a number of ways. After the dot-com bubble burst, many displaced workers chose to take early retirement, others returned to school or accepted jobs with much lower salaries, and others started their own businesses.

Loss of Personal Prestige.   Ads promoting hair restorers or weight reduction plans play on one's loss of personal prestige resulting from physical appearance. Being passed over for a promotion at work also leads to a loss of personal prestige. Other fears relating to loss of prestige include the loss of youth, the loss of health, and the lost of self-respect.

Uncertainty of Prediction.   Whenever we move, change schools, take a new job, or break up with a spouse or significant other, we feel uncomfortable because we can no longer predict probable outcomes. Products that promise to protect us from some negative circumstance (illness, job loss, financial difficulties) use the inability to predict as a "hook" to persuade us.

Sources of Consonance

On the other side of the coin, some appeals give receivers a sense of consonance, and reinforce beliefs, attitudes, or behaviors and activate receivers.

Reassurance of Security.   Today, police stations, airports, courthouses, schools, and other public buildings are protected with metal detectors and even armed guards. We want to feel secure in public places, and these preventatives provide that sense of security. Promises of job security are powerful persuaders for persons making career choices, and IRA and Keogh accounts offer retirement security.

Demonstration of Predictability.   Consonance happens when the world operates in predictable ways. Manufacturers rely on the appeal to predictability by offering guarantees or warranties. And everyone likes to know what to expect at work, at home, in the community, and so on.

The Use of Rewards.   Rewards or positive reinforcements increase feelings of consonance and the probability that a behavior will be repeated. Persuaders often use positive and complimentary statements to reinforce behavior. In his best-selling book *How to Win Friends and Influence People*, Dale Carnegie (1952) advised his readers to "try to figure out the other man's good points...and people will cherish your words and treasure them and repeat them over a lifetime" (p. 38). Carnegie put his finger on ways to make audiences feel good about themselves. This is still good advice for persuading audiences or influencing people. Successful supervisors seem adept at giving rewards rather than offering criticisms.

REVIEW AND CONCLUSION

We are searching for various kinds of unstated and widely held major premises that can serve in persuasive enthymemes. One of these kinds of major premises is the process or emotional premise, which appeals to our needs, emotions, attitudes, and the psychological processes of dissonance and consonance operating daily in each of us. We can see needs and wants operating in Maslow's hierarchy of needs, Packard's compelling human needs, and Feig's hot buttons. Although some of these models have been around for a long time, they still have applicability for us, as their many rejuvenations demonstrate.

A second kind of process premise involves our emotions. Persuaders target our emotional states and get at us through such things as fear, guilt, and anger or by appeals to more positive emotions such as happiness, joy, or pride. A third kind of process premise involves attitudes, beliefs, and opinions. If persuaders change our attitudes about fuel efficiency, they predispose us to buy fuel-efficient autos, furnaces, and water heaters. If persuaders want us to continue voting for a certain party, they reinforce our existing beliefs and attitudes about that party. Both of these persuasive types can be used with either attitudes toward objects and issues or attitudes toward situations. It may be important for persuaders to reinforce or change our behavioral intentions. Attitudes also impact important and not so important purchase, voting, joining, or donating decisions, as depicted in the ELM.

The fourth kind of process premise is the human desire for psychological consonance, in which we seek a world where our predictions are verified, and in which people we like approve of the same things we do. If we feel a lack of balance, or dissonance, we actively seek ways to bring our world into congruity by reducing psychological tensions. If we perceive balance or consonance to exist, we experience a sense of ease and can be easily motivated to continue to act as we have been. Persuaders try to create dissonance if they want us to change our behavior, and they create consonance if they want us to maintain our behavior. Process premises are important in the ways we persuade others and the ways in which we are persuaded.

KEY TERMS

When you have finished reading this chapter, you should be able to identify, explain, and give an example of the following words or concepts.

process or emotional premises	reassurance of worth	prepotency	attitudes
motivation research	ego gratification	basic needs	opinions
hidden needs	creative outlets	need for security	behavioral intention
compelling needs	love objects	belongingness or affiliation needs	consistency
hot buttons	sense of power or strength	love and esteem needs	cognitive dissonance theory
emotional security	need for roots	self-actualization needs	

APPLICATION OF ETHICS

It is finals week at a state university. A professor of communication gets an email from a student in one of his classes in which the student expresses a fear of failing the final exam. The two previous exams were so difficult that she was only able to get low "D" grades on them, and since the final counts double, she is in danger of failing the class. She tells the professor that she is already on probation and will be dismissed if she fails the class. Her parents have already given her an ultimatum—"get off probation or support yourself through the remaining two years of schooling!" By chance, the professor runs into the student in the library and tells her that he is not about to cater to students who don't study enough and chides her for even sending the email. She denies having sent the message and says that she suspects someone has stolen her password and sent a forgery to embarrass her. The professor convinces the manager of the university email system to track down the source of the message, and indeed it has not been sent from the student's computer but from the male teaching assistant for the class. The professor suspects that the teaching assistant wants to use the email to sexually harass the female student. There are emotional issues involved. Has the teaching assistant used a fear appeal? Is that ethical given the professor's suspicions? What should the professor do?

QUESTIONS FOR FURTHER THOUGHT

1. What is a process premise? Explain.

2. What is the difference between an attitude and a need? Give examples.

3. What did Maslow mean when he called his hierarchy of needs "prepotent"?

4. Which needs described by Packard are the most ego involving or personal in nature?

5. What is an example of the need for emotional security?

6. What is an example of how advertisers use the need for ego gratification?

7. What is an example of the need for a sense of power?

8. What emotions are being used when persuaders alert us to the possibility of job loss or identity theft?

9. What emotions are being used when a persuader tells us that we have been cheated by an auto repair shop?

10. What are three functions of an attitude?

11. What is the difference between an attitude and an opinion?

12. What is the difference between a behavior and a behavioral intention?

13. According to the ELM, which decision path will be used when purchasing ice cream?

14. According to the ELM, what happens if the audience isn't motivated to vote?

15. According to the ELM, what happens to a decision if the audience can't respond?

16. Using the elaboration likelihood model as depicted in Figure 7.12, explain the flow of information regarding a current issue.

17. What are some sources of dissonance?

18. What are some sources of consonance?

19. What ethical standards should we apply when using process or emotional appeals?

 For online activities, go to the *Persuasion* book companion website at http://communication.wadsworth.com/larson11.

8

Content or Logical Premises in Persuasion

LEARNING GOALS

After reading this chapter, you should be able to:

1. Give everyday examples such as ads or speeches that rely on logical versus emotional appeals.

2. Find everyday examples of each of the types of evidence discussed.

3. Explain the difference between the two types of analogy and when they might be appropriate.

4. Find everyday examples of the three types of syllogisms and explain them to the class.

5. Explain the three major elements and the three substantiating elements in the Toulmin model.

6. Identify examples of logical fallacies in ads, newspaper editorials, and letters to the editor in a newsweekly like *Time* or *Newsweek*.

7. Identify logical fallacies used in sensational publications like *The National Enquirer*—our nation's largest circulation "newspaper."

8. Explain the various types of reasoning (e.g., reasoning from symptoms).

Chapter 7 looked at premises based on psychological processes or emotions. Another type of premise frequently operating in enthymemes is based on people's ability to think logically or rationally. The elaboration likelihood model (ELM) suggests that this kind of persuasion uses the central information-processing route and entails considerable analysis and intellectual activity. Premises relying on logical and analytical abilities are called **content premises** because they don't rely on psychological processes and/or emotions as process premises do. Many content premises such as *causes have effects* are perceived as valid and true by large segments of the audience, so persuaders can use them as major premises in enthymemes. Some persuasion theorists call these premises **arguments** or *propositions* while marketers call them *offers*. In fact, argumentation scholars and professors Lunsford and Ruszkiewicz (2004) claim that everything is an argument, including stained glass windows, the presidential seal, and bumper stickers. Aristotle defined an argument as a statement supported by proof. The dictionary defines it as "a discussion in which disagreement is expressed for some point" (*American Heritage Dictionary*, 1985). Most theorists agree that argument contains a controversial claim which should be debatable and supported by evidence (Lunsford & Ruszkiewicz, 2004 p. 125). They make the case that an argument seeks to discover the truth in order to win conviction, while persuasion seeks to apply the known truth in order to prompt others to action. Whatever the label—premise, argument, proposition, offer or claim—this chapter looks at persuasion that uses the receiver's logical, reasoning, rational, and intellectual abilities.

For example, suppose I want to persuade you to support legalized marijuana. What would you consider good and sufficient reasons for supporting the idea? For some persons, there aren't any good (let alone sufficient) reasons for such a policy, so there would be no way to persuade those folks. For others, the policy seems so sensible on the face of it that you don't need to persuade them either. But what about those who neither approve nor disapprove—the undecided members of the audience? They require more information, evidence, discussion, and debate before taking a side. In other words, they are asking for good and sufficient reasons for supporting the proposition. You might tell them about how legalized marijuana reduced the rate of usage of stronger and more addictive drugs in Holland. You might discuss the revenues that could be generated by having the government tax marijuana just as it does with cigarettes. And you might point out that such a policy would remove criminal elements from the sale of the drug. The success or failure of any of these arguments, claims, or propositions relies on beliefs already held by the audience. They already believe that tax revenues are needed, and that criminal elements in any activity are undesirable. Those widely held beliefs serve as major or minor premises in persuasive enthymemes.

We have all encountered and learned logical patterns. Most of us believe, for example, that events have causes. When certain things occur other things invariably follow. Problems have causes but their removal resolves the problems. This pattern of rational and intellectual reasoning is called **cause–effect reasoning**. Huglen and Clark (2004) define it as "linking some cause and effect to prove their existence" (p. 23). This makes sense, because if you have no effect(s), there obviously would be no cause, and vice versa. The two have to exist together. For instance, a certain baseball team's pitching staff had experienced many training camp injuries. A logical effect of this cause would be that the team ends the season with a poor record. It's not necessary to convince anyone that injuries lead to losses. You just need to list the various injuries and rely on the cause–effect premise already at work in the audience's mind. As this example shows, the cause–effect pattern is a potent first premise in a persuasive enthymeme. Politicians and government officials, the courts, business, and advertisers all use cause–effect reasoning. Content premises persuade because they rely on widely held patterns of logical reasoning. Our goal in this chapter is to identify some of these patterns. Recognizing them will make you a more critical receiver.

WHAT IS PROOF?

Basically, content or logical premises consist of two elements—proof and reasoning. **Proof** is defined as enough evidence connected through reasoning to lead typical receivers to take or believe the persuader's advice. What may prove a point to fraternity members may not prove the same point to a university administrator. For example, one claim given to justify going to war in Iraq was that Iraq had chemical, biological, and nuclear weapons, and that these were a threat to stability in the region. What evidence would be needed to prove this claim? For some, satellite photos of supposed weapons sites sufficed. For others, physical evidence was needed—they wanted to see the actual weapons. Others required the actual weapons and evidence that Iraq intended to use them. This tells us that "proof" varies from person to person. Proof also varies from situation to situation. For example, some economists claimed that cutting the nation's budget deficit (the cause) would spur economic growth (the effect). Their evidence convinced some people but not others. When the economy improved after the deficit cuts, many of the doubters were convinced. They needed more proof than the original believers did, and the economy provided it. Other economists argued that cuts in the estate tax, taxes on dividends, and capitol gains would spur growth in the economy and thus reduce our budget deficits. The taxes were cut (the cause), but growth didn't follow (the effect).

Most contemporary theorists agree that proof is composed of two facets: **reasoning** and **evidence**. The dictionary definition of reasoning is "the use of reason especially to form conclusions, inferences, or judgments." Evidence is defined as "the data on which a conclusion or judgment may be based; something that furnishes proof" (*American Heritage Dictionary*, 1985). In the proper mix, these two elements lead persuadees to adopt or believe in the changes a persuader advocates. There are several ways to look at evidence and reasoning. First, by examining how persuaders operate, we can infer their motives and discover what they are up to. For example, suppose I want to persuade you that an unrequested kiss on the lips between a male and a female was not sexual harassment. Lunsford and Ruszkiewicz advise asking four questions: (1) Did something happen? (2) What is its nature? (3) What is its quality? and (4) What action should be taken? In this case there was an unrequested kiss on the lips, witnesses observed it, and the female objected to it. Usually, unwanted kisses on the lips are considered harassment. In this case the answer to the third question—what is its quality?—provides the proof: both participants were six years old. "Most people don't consider six year olds as sexually culpable" (p. 16–17).

Another way to look at evidence and reasoning is to investigate how specific the evidence is in relation to the reasoning it supports or the conclusion. Before the advent of electronic media, modern advertising, and contemporary propaganda, audiences were accustomed to receiving very specific and verifiable evidence. For example, if a person gave testimony to prove a point, it was critical to tell the audience why that person qualified to give the testimony. Audiences were also suspicious of some kinds of evidence such as analogies. Today, however, we accept the testimony of professional athletes when they endorse an investment plan even though they don't qualify as experts on finance. And we frequently do accept analogies as evidence, such as animated automobile tires depicted as having tigers' claws to grip the road.

Other kinds of premises and evidence convince us through the central information-processing channel. Politicians offer us evidence in support of a policy, and parents supply what they think are good reasons for not living with someone of the opposite gender unless married. Underlying these examples is the pattern of enough evidence with reasoning to result in proof.

To discover how proof operates in the law, access InfoTrac College Edition, type the word "proof" in the search engine, and select the burden of proof option(s). Read a few of the items listed.

TYPES OF EVIDENCE

Evidence varies in persuasive power depending on the context in which it is used. In some situations, for instance, statistics have a powerful effect; in other situations, pictorial evidence persuades; and in yet others, vicarious or retold experience convinces us. Experiential evidence relies on the assumption that people learn about and act on information gained indirectly, and this is why stories about the experiences of others are so persuasive. Advertisers use testimonials from both ordinary people and celebrities to endorse products, assuming that consumers vicariously absorb the experiences and buy the product. Demonstrations can also logically persuade us. This was the case in the O.J. Simpson trial when the supposed murder glove didn't fit. The defense argued, "If it does not fit, you must acquit" (Lunsford & Ruszkiewicz, p. 102).

But even when we do not learn from or become swayed by the experiences of others, our own experience is usually enough to cause us to change. The Lakota were aware of this. As a Lakota baby crawled close to the campfire, no one pulled it away with shouts of, "Hot! Stay away, baby! Hot!" as we would do in our culture. Instead, they watched the baby's progress very closely and allowed the baby to reach into the fire and touch a hot coal, burning itself mildly. They then quickly pulled the baby away and treated the burn. The experience persuaded the child to be careful with fire. Or suppose a professor explains to you her very stringent attendance policy for a television production class, but you take the policy with a grain of salt and fail the class, necessitating taking it over. You hear the same lecture on attendance on the first day of the class the next semester. If experience persuades, you won't miss a class.

There are three broad forms of evidence: (1) **direct experience**, (2) **dramatic or vicarious experience**, and (3) **rationally processed evidence**. The first two usually are processed via the peripheral information-processing route of the ELM without much forethought, whereas rationally processed evidence usually follows the central information-processing route. Direct experience demonstrates the major premise that actions have consequences. Dramatic evidence relies on the human tendency to structure our lives in narrative or story form. Rational evidence relies on our innate ability to reason using logic and evidence. In previous chapters, we looked at some theorists who present the case for dramatic evidence convincingly. Burke (1985), for example, discusses the power of dramatic or narrative evidence. Let us briefly examine these three broad categories of evidence in more depth.

Direct Experience

Most parents of more than one child tell of their one kid who always had to learn the hard way by experiencing the "actions have consequences" principle. Most of us learn the power of this principle after only a few experiences, but some seem never to catch on. Probably each of us has been in an auto accident, and as a result we have learned to call the police, family, and insurance agent, in that order. You also learned that even a minor accident can take up an inordinate amount of time, paperwork, and effort. You can probably identify some direct experiences in your life that provided a powerful form of evidence for you.

Dramatic or Vicarious Experience

All of us have learned or been persuaded by hearing about the experiences of others—that is, by vicarious experience. There are a variety of types of vicarious experience, most of them dramatic in nature.

Narratives. A good way to use dramatic evidence is through narrative. People have always been fascinated by stories, including myths, legends, and ballads, handed down in an oral/aural tradition. Literacy brought other forms of the narrative (plays, poetry, novels, and short stories). Technology has brought us still other forms such as movies, cartoons, video games, documentaries, talk shows, and broadcasts of athletic events—all having roots in storytelling. Evidence that is dramatic invites our vicarious involvement as it attempts to persuade us to a course of action. It relies on the human ability to project ourselves into the situation described by the persuader and to co-create proof. The results are powerful and long lasting.

In his book *People of the Lie: The Hope for Healing Human Evil*, noted author and psychotherapist M. Scott Peck (1983) related "The Case of Bobby and His Parents." The narrative began with Bobby, who had been admitted to the hospital emergency room the night before for depression. The admitting physician's notes read as follows:

Bobby's older brother Stuart, 16, committed suicide this past June, shooting himself in the head with his .22 caliber rifle. Bobby initially seemed to handle his sibling's death rather well. But from the beginning of school in September, his academic performance has been poor. Once a "B" student, he is now failing all his courses. By Thanksgiving he had become obviously depressed. His parents, who seem very concerned, tried to talk to him, but he has become more and more uncommunicative, particularly since Christmas. Although there is no previous record of antisocial behavior, yesterday Bobby stole a car by himself and crashed it (he had never driven before), and was apprehended by the police.... Because of his age, he was released into his parents' custody, and they were advised to seek immediate psychiatric evaluation for him (p. 48).

Peck went on to observe that, although Bobby appeared to be a typical fifteen-year-old, he stared at the floor and kept picking at several small sores on the back of his hand. When Peck asked Bobby if he felt nervous being in the hospital, he got no answer —"Bobby was really digging into that sore. Inwardly I winced at the damage he was doing to his flesh" (p. 48). After reassuring Bobby that the hospital was a safe place to be, Peck tried to draw Bobby out in conversation, but nothing seemed to work. Peck got "No reaction. Except that maybe he dug a little deeper into one of the sores on his forearm." Bobby admitted that he had hurt his parents by stealing the car; he said he knew that he had hurt them because they yelled at him. When asked what they yelled at him about, he replied, "I don't know." "Bobby was feverishly picking at his sores now and...I felt it would be best if I steered my questions to more neutral subjects" (p. 50). They discussed the family pet—a German shepherd whom Bobby took care of but didn't play with because she was his father's dog. Peck then turned the conversation to Christmas, asking what sorts of gifts Bobby had gotten.

BOBBY: Nothing much.

PECK: Your parents must have given you something.

What did they give you?

BOBBY: A gun.

PECK: A gun?

BOBBY: Yes.

PECK: What kind of a gun?

BOBBY: A twenty-two.

PECK: A twenty-two pistol.

BOBBY: No, a twenty-two rifle.

PECK: I understand that it was with a twenty-two rifle that your brother killed himself.

BOBBY: Yes.

PECK: Was that what you asked for for Christmas?

BOBBY: No.

PECK: What did you ask for?

BOBBY: A tennis racket.

PECK: But you got the gun instead?

BOBBY: Yes.

PECK: How did you feel, getting the same kind of gun that your brother had?

BOBBY: It wasn't the same kind of gun.

PECK: *(I began to feel better. Maybe I was just confused.)* I'm sorry, I thought they were the same kind of gun.

BOBBY: It wasn't the same kind of gun. It was the same gun.

PECK: You mean it was your brother's gun? *(I wanted to go home very badly now.)* You mean your parents gave you your brother's gun for Christmas—the one he shot himself with?

BOBBY: Yes.

PECK: How did it make you feel getting your brother's gun for Christmas?

BOBBY: I don't know.

PECK: *(I almost regretted the question: How could he know? How could he answer such a thing?)* No, I don't expect you could know (p. 52).

Peck then brought the parents in for counseling. However, they seemed unable to realize what message they had sent their remaining son by giving him his brother's suicide weapon. Bobby continued therapy until he was sent to live with a favorite aunt.

When I first read this dramatic example, I literally gasped as I learned about the Christmas gift, and I was totally dumbstruck to learn that it was *the* gun. When I read this dialogue aloud in class, I always hear gasps from around the room. Although the story was emotionally charged, we would be hard put to call it "illogical." In fact, it is probably totally logical to conclude that the parents' behavior was harmful, perhaps even evil. If the evidence is dramatic enough or emotional enough, persuadees will not ask for more.

Most great preachers, orators, and politicians are also great storytellers. They use the narrative to capture the audience's attention and to draw them into the topic. This effect is reinforced with other evidence, and more narratives might be worked in to keep the audience interested. Chances are, you have heard speeches or sermons in which narrative was skillfully used. Such speeches seem to have the most impact and to be remembered the longest. As a professor of mine once said, "The narrative will carry more persuasive freight than any other form of evidence."

Testimony. Testimony of a person who has seen, heard, and experienced events also is persuasive. The persuader might read aloud an eyewitness account or simply recount his or her personal experience. If the issue is unemployment, receivers might be swayed by hearing from people who are out of work. The humiliation of waiting in line for an unemployment check, the embarrassment of accepting government surplus foodstuffs, and other experiences of the unemployed will probably have dramatic persuasive power.

As receivers, we vicariously live through what the witness experienced when we hear direct testimony. Although eyewitness testimony is potent,

FIGURE 8.1 Witnesses see events or persons from their own point of view.

SOURCE: Reprinted by permission of John Jonik from *Psychology Today*.

studies have shown that it is often unreliable and even incorrect (Loftus, 1980). In many cases, as has been documented, persons have been wrongfully imprisoned on the basis of eyewitness testimony (Loftus, 1984). As Figure 8.1 illustrates, witnesses often see and hear what they want to see and hear, and give testimony from their idiosyncratic points of view.

As receivers, we need to carefully examine the testimony used to persuade us. We need to ask questions like these: Was the witness in a position to see what is claimed? Could the witness be mistaken in any way? Does the witness have a bias that might cloud his or her testimony? Might the witness have a motive for giving the testimony? Is the witness being paid for giving the testimony? What might he or she have to gain from testifying?

Anecdotes.   Anecdotes are short narratives that make a point in a hurry—maybe in only a sentence or two. For example, there is the anecdote of the optimist who was asked to describe his philosophy: "That's simple. I'm nostalgic about the future." Anecdotes are often funny and are frequently hypothetical, so they are quite different from actual testimony. The key thing about anecdotes is that, unlike testimony, we rarely take them as truth. Instead, we tend to process anecdotes as if they are the exclamation points of persuasion. Consider the anecdote about Abraham Lincoln being asked why he pardoned a deserter—he quipped, "I thought he could do us more good above the ground than under it" (Moore, 1909).

Participation and Demonstration. There are several other ways in which persuaders can dramatize evidence. At an antismoking presentation, for instance, audiovisual materials can show cancerous lung tissue. Smokers can participate by exhaling cigarette smoke through a clean white tissue and observing the nicotine stains left behind. Sometimes persuaders dramatize a point by using visual aids to demonstrate the problem and solution. The demonstrations that form the core of most direct marketing on television also use participation in that the viewer is repeatedly urged to call the 1-800 number and place an order. The viewer sees the greaseless grill, the guaranteed bass bait, or the shapely persons using the Bowflex, and imagines what it would be like to use the product.

Rationally Processed Evidence

Not all evidence is dramatic. Sometimes evidence appeals to our logical processes in nondramatic and intellectually oriented ways. For instance, newspaper editorials frequently use evidence that appeals to readers' logical processes, as do other persuasive messages such as advertising. Look at Figure 8.2. The Campbell Soup Company knows that persons concerned with health and nutrition are aware of the need to increase the amount of fiber in their diet. Most of the literature on this subject has recommended eating high-fiber foods such as whole wheat bread and bran cereals. Campbell's offers similar benefits. You can get fiber by eating Manhandler soups such as Bean with Bacon or Split Pea with Ham.

As you can see from these examples, the appeal to logical processes relies on a reasoning pattern such as "the past is a guide to the future" or "the cost is less than the benefit." What are some other logical patterns that persuaders often use?

To see how many kinds of evidence exist, access InfoTrac College Edition, type the word "evidence" in the search engine, and sample the references listed.

TYPES OF REASONING

Recall our definition of proof as "enough evidence connected with reasoning to lead an audience to believe or act on a persuader's advice." We now explore the second step in the process of logical persuasion: connecting the pieces of evidence using reasoning.

Several patterns of reasoning seem to be deeply ingrained in our culture. When people violate the accepted deep structure of logical reasoning, they are often labeled "off the wall" or "out in left field." Sometimes a logical deep structure is violated and humor results. Sometimes, such violations make a potential persuader sound like a lunatic. A letter to the editor of a local newspaper discussed removing nuisance deer from public parks in the area (Scott, 1989). He pointed out what it had cost to remove such deer from other parks, the taxes hunters pay on ammunition and guns, and how removal costs were cut at another park by allowing hunting at the park. So far, so good. He begins with what appears to be an inductive line of argument using **effect-to-cause reasoning**, which is defined as citing a set of effects and then concluding by identifying their cause. We anticipate that he is about to claim something like "Therefore, hunters are positive persons and deserve to hunt nuisance deer." But what does the author conclude? Take a look.

> If you were an animal, would you prefer to live ten years free, even if you died a slow death, or would you want to live it penned up, sleeping

FIGURE 8.2 This appeals to our logic. What rational argument does it present?

SOURCE: Used by permission of the Campbell Soup Company.

MADE OF THE FINEST FIBER

If you're like most people who eat right, you probably give high fiber high priority.

And like most people, when you think of fiber, you probably automatically think of bran cereals.

Well, there's another good source of dietary fiber you should know about. Delicious Campbell's Bean with Bacon Soup.

In fact, Campbell's has four soups that are high in fiber.

And you can see from the chart that follows exactly how each one measures up to bran cereals.

So now when you think of fiber, you don't have to think about

FIBER IN A SUGGESTED SERVING			
CAMPBELL'S SOUP		**BRAN CEREALS**	
Bean with Bacon	9g	100% Brans	11g
Split Pea with Ham	6g	40% Brans	6g
Green Pea	5g	Raisin Brans	5g
Low Sodium Green Pea	7g	Others	5–10g
This comparison includes soluble and insoluble fiber			

having it just at breakfast.

Instead, you can do your body good any time during the day. With a hot, hearty bowl of one of these Campbell's Soups.

You just might feel better for it—right to the very fiber of your being.

CAMPBELL'S SOUP IS GOOD FOOD

Campbell's has a full line of low sodium soups for those people who are on a salt-restricted diet or have a concern about sodium.

in your own manure? I think most Americans would want to be free. That's also the way God wanted it. That's why he said it is a good thing to be a hunter. For Jesus Christ is alive and well, but Bambi never was. (n. p.)

The conclusion is wacky. It seems unrelated to the evidence.

Remember that we are looking for content premises—logical patterns that serve as the first premises in enthymemes. The deeply ingrained logical preferences serve in this way. We believe and act on what we perceive to be logical arguments backed by good and sufficient evidence and well presented to us. Fishbein and Ajzen's (1975,

1980) theory of reasoned action (TRA) is one such deeply ingrained logical structure. The theory predicts that actions are the effects of behavioral intentions. Behavioral intentions, in turn, are the results of people's attitudes on issues and on the social norms that they hold in high esteem. For example, if we were trying to persuade people to stop buying SUVs and to consider purchasing one of the new hybrid automobiles, we might compare the hybrid's performance with the poor mileage of most SUVs, note that four-wheel drive isn't really necessary for most people's needs, and back that up with a quote: "Critics claim that 95% of SUVs never venture off-road" (Lunsford & Ruszkiewicz, p. 28). This might change peoples' attitude toward SUVs. Then we could point out that the hybrid owners are opinion leaders, tend to be better educated, to have better jobs, to earn more, and to be more socially conscious. According to TRA, if our audience believes that these traits are ones to be emulated, then the shift in attitudes toward SUVs and the audience's changing respect for hybrid users will lead to a behavioral intention—the audience will consider buying a hybrid instead of an SUV. Communication scholar S. Sutton (1998) points out, however, that intentions are subject to change over time and are provisional in nature. Several researchers have found the predictive power of behavioral intentions to be either weak or negative as more and more time passes. Let us now turn to some traditional forms of reasoning.

Cause-to-Effect Reasoning

We've seen that **cause-to-effect reasoning** is powerful in our culture; even our language depends on it. For example, we rarely say, "The ball was thrown, and the window was broken." Instead, we put the cause out front and let it "create" the effect. We say, "Johnny threw the ball and broke the window." This active-voice sentence tells us that Johnny caused the ball to fly through the air, resulting in the broken window. It gives us much more information: It tells us who did what.

Persuaders frequently use cause-to-effect reasoning to identify events, trends, or facts that have resulted in certain effects. They tell us that if a cause is present we can expect certain effects to follow. If the effects are bad and we want to do something about them, we usually try to remove the cause. For instance, if you are allergic to garlic and eat some food that has garlic in it, we can predict that you are going to have an allergic reaction. Or, if you are carrying too much credit card debt, you should get rid of all but one of your credit cards. This argument assumes that cutting up all but one credit card (cause) will reduce your ability to accumulate consumer debt (effect). Both these examples make perfect sense, and that is why cause-to-effect reasoning has such persuasive power.

There are three kinds of causal reasoning: (1) A cause is identified, and you seek out its effects; (2) An effect is identified, and you try to trace it back to its cause; and (3) A series of cause–effect relationships lead to a final effect (Lunsford & Ruszkiewicz, p. 207). Advertising frequently uses the first strategy, as in an ad for a cellulite-reducing complex. It identifies the cause—a weak skin support system—and its undesirable effect—cellulite. Regular use of the product strengthens the skin support system, thus removing the cause and its effects. In the second strategy, the effect is identified. We look at the effect—global warming—and try to identify its possible causes, such as the emission of carbon dioxide from the burning of fossil fuels. Or take the case of food poisoning. The poisoning followed a buffet lunch at which only those who became ill were found to have eaten the dishes that contained mayonnaise. Conclusion? They probably were ill from *Salmonella*, a kind of food poisoning that occurs when mayonnaise is not properly refrigerated. In the third strategy, we trace a series of cause-and-effect relationships—the persuader says sulfur dioxide emissions from power plants causes acid rain, which in turn kills plant life. Conclusion? A single cause might have several effects. Acid rain also kills plankton, which are food for fish and crustaceans, and it makes soil too acidic for farming. In law courts, establishing a motive for the crime is sometimes seen as the same thing as identifying its cause. The thief needed money for his surgery and so he robbed the store (Huglen & Clark, 2004).

B O X 8.1   Interactive Reasoning in Wonderland

 Go to www.cut-the-knot.org/LewisCarroll and explore the many logic games, conference announcements, interactive activities, and more. Lewis Carroll is of course most famous for his children's stories, such as "Through the Looking Glass" and "Alice in Wonderland," and his poetry, such as "Jabberwocky." However, few realize that

he was a professional logician and that he worked many elements of logic, reasoning, and fallacy throughout his fiction. A great example of illogical reasoning occurs when the Queen of Hearts insists that she must sentence Alice before, not after, the verdict. And the Cheshire cat is a whole different case.

Communication scholar C. Hitchcock (2001) puts cause-to-effect slightly differently. He argues that there are at least two types of effect: component effect and net effect. The causes of a **net effect** are cumulative and result from a number of component effects. **Component effects** are linked to a cause but may not be the only cause of the net effect. In other words, the initial component effect contributes to the overall effect, but there might be other causes. Global warming, for instance, has several effects in addition to carbon dioxide emitted from the burning of fossil fuels. It is also caused by the release of freon gases used in refrigerators and air conditioners. Again, this kind of reasoning is usually processed in the central route of the elaboration likelihood model.

To explore how others have viewed causation, access InfoTrac College Edition, and enter the word "causation" in the search engine. Read several of the over one hundred periodical articles.

Effect-to-Cause Reasoning

Another type of reasoning that is less frequently used (and sometimes flawed) is called effect-to-cause reasoning. Sources of food poisoning, for example, are identified this way. In another example, many auto accidents are attributed to the use of a cell phone while driving. There is a problem here with the possibility of an intervening cause—who the driver is talking to and about what. Suppose that further investigation shows that in a high

percentage of these accidents the drivers were arguing with their spouses about family matters. Is the cell phone the cause of the accidents or is the discussion of family problems the intervening cause?

Reasoning from Symptoms

Persuaders sometimes identify a series of symptoms or signs and then try to conclude something from them. For example, politicians cite how much worse things are now than they were when their opponent took office. Unemployment is up, and the stock and bond markets have been ravaged. Recent polls show that people have lost faith in their ability to control their own destinies. The hope is that the voters will blame the incumbent for the troubles. Many advertisements present receivers with a set of symptoms that indicate there is a real or potential problem for them. Receivers have lost their job, can't pay the bills, and are faced with foreclosure. They need to contact Harvey's Financial Advisor Inc. Interpersonal persuasion is frequently laced with reasoning from symptoms, especially when laying blame.

Criteria-to-Application Reasoning

Sometimes persuaders establish a reasonable set of criteria for purchasing a product, voting for a candidate, or supporting a cause and then offer their product, candidate, or cause as one that fits these criteria. For example, when a credit card company makes an offer to you, you probably have several criteria in mind that the card must meet before you

FIGURE 8.3 What is the figurative analogy here?

SOURCE: Reprinted by permission of Aaron Johnson.

will take the offer. There must be no annual fee. There must be free balance transfers and an introductory rate of 0.0% and a reasonable rate thereafter. The initial 0.0% must hold for at least a year, and the company must give you frequent traveler points on any airlines plus discounts on other travel services. Unless the card meets your criteria, you reject the offer. Remember the student who cut classes and flunked because of his absences, only to have to retake the class and maintain perfect attendance, thus earning a passing grade? Reasoning from criteria to application persuaded him.

Reasoning from Analogy or by Comparison

Sometimes persuaders use a figurative or real analogy as their logical reason for some conclusion. In this form of reasoning, the persuader analyzes and describes an issue, and an analogy is made comparing this issue with an example of a similar one or a figurative one. In a real-case analogy on the war in Iraq, opponents to the war compared it to the war in Vietnam because in both cases we were fighting an indigent population that was very different from us culturally, and both sets of terrain were not conducive to traditional warfare. The conclusion is that we should not invade Iraq. In the figurative analogy, the comparison is done through a figure of speech, usually a simile or a metaphor. Consider the following figurative analogy: "War is like a boxing match in which the opponents are evenly matched and there's no referee. Rarely does anyone throw a single knockout punch. It's slugging it out in round after round until you get the other guy on the ropes, and his managers admit defeat."

We also frequently see argument by comparison in advertising, with competing products compared in terms of cost, effectiveness, safety, and so on. For instance, the big battle over the light beer market largely relies on reasoning from comparison, with one brand claiming fewer calories and better taste than others. The same thing is seen in ads for low-tar and low-nicotine cigarettes. And the Energizer Rabbit uses comparison to make the point that the Energizer brand is much longer lasting than, say, Duracell.

Deductive Reasoning

A familiar form of appeal to logic is **deductive reasoning,** which is reasoning from the general to the specific. For example, in a legislative body a persuader might support a bill or a motion by saying something like, "The legislation before us is desperately needed to prevent the state budget from going into a deficit situation," and then providing the specifics. An editorial might begin, "Sycamore needs to pass this school bond referendum to save its extracurricular sports, its music and art programs, its newspaper, and its drama program," and then go on to describe the details. One of the problems with the deductive approach is that receivers who feel negatively about the persuader's general point may quickly lose interest and not pay attention to the specifics that are at the heart of the issue.

Inductive Reasoning

Inductive reasoning gets the specifics out on the table before bringing up the generalized conclusion. For example, in the school bond case, the persuader might begin this way:

> Many of you know that it costs over $60,000 just to run the athletic program. The budget for the marching band is over $12,000 for travel, instruction, and uniforms. I was surprised to learn that it cost over $2000 just to pay the royalties for the spring musical. We have cut and cut until there is nothing left to cut. The last referendum increase was fourteen years ago—inflation has risen over 200 percent since then. Unless we pass the referendum, the district now faces elimination of these valuable extracurricular programs.

With the specific evidence apparent, the generalization flows logically from it.

To see the variations in the use of reasoning, access InfoTrac College Edition, type the word "reasoning" in the search engine, and look at the article by Brian McGee on the argument from definition. You will see how reasoning was used to define "race" in the early twentieth century. Also check the various articles from the journal *Argumentation and Advocacy* and the item on the conditional syllogism and deductive reasoning.

MISUSES OF REASONING AND EVIDENCE

Of course, logical persuasion is vulnerable to intentional or unintentional misuse of either evidence or reasoning, or both. Let's look at some examples of the misuse of reasoning and evidence so that we can spot it when it occurs.

Statistics

One of the mainstays of logical persuasion is the use of **statistics.** We tend to believe statistics without questioning them. But we ought to ask several questions when statistical evidence is offered. First, "Is the sample from which the statistics are drawn a representative one?" In other words, is the sample selected in a way that might bias the results? Or is it a reliable representation of the larger population? We might want to know how the sample was selected. Perhaps the researchers took names from the phone directory. But not everyone has a telephone number listed, some people have several, and others only use cell phones for which there is no directory. Perhaps the subjects were approached at a shopping mall on campus and given a survey there. But, again, mall shoppers might not be representative of the population at large. Maybe the subjects were intercepted in front of the student union. Would we find any different results if we interviewed them in the morning rather than in the evening when most students are studying? These and other questions should be asked of any statistical proof used by the persuader. Another misuse of statistical evidence is the use of a single instance as an example of all instances. Thus, we hear of an enormously wealthy person who pays no taxes and are led to believe that other enormously wealthy persons pay no taxes. Still another misuse of statistics is biased sampling, which occurs when a nonrepresentative portion of the population is sampled. Responses from a sample drawn from subscribers to *Newsweek* will be very different from one drawn from subscribers to *Horticulture* or *The Organic Gardener*.

The mode of presentation can also misrepresent statistics. For example, the graph in Figure 8.4 was used to demonstrate the degree to which homosexuality exists in the general population. The shaded portion indicates persons who have had at least one homosexual encounter; the unshaded portion of the graph indicates heterosexual persons. The graph suggests that the proportion of the population that is homosexual is at least 50 percent when actual research indicates that it is far smaller—around 2 percent (Guttmacher, 1993). Clearly, the graph visually misrepresents the actual case and distorts the meaning of the statistics. What the graph fails to provide is information about the size of the sample in each segment.

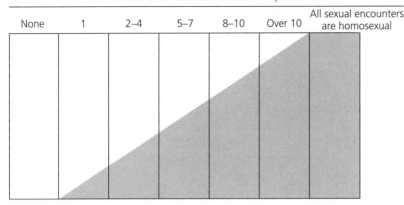

FIGURE 8.4 This graph is misleading because it implies that half the population is homosexual when the statistics being represented are much lower than that.

Testimony

One problem with the use of testimonials is that the person testifying might not be providing accurate information. Also, seemingly insignificant shifts in wording can lead witnesses to certain answers. Most of the time, we don't have the opportunity to cross-examine the person giving the testimonial. Instead, when we see or hear a person endorsing a product, a candidate, or an organization, we are forced to make up our minds right away about whether the person is qualified to give the testimonial. When testimonials are used to persuade, we need to ask whether the person giving the testimonial is an authority on the subject, and if so, how reliable he or she is. Was the person close enough to have witnessed the evidence he or she is testifying about? Is it possible that the person giving the testimonial is biased, and if so, in what direction? For example, in Chicago, a violinist was recently awarded nearly $30 million from METRA, the commuter train conglomerate. Her $500,000 violin got caught in the train doors, and when she tried to save it her leg was torn off. She testified at the trial, offering "dramatic detailed testimony...as she painfully recalled for jurors the winter day in 1995 when she became pinned against the doors of a commuter train and was dragged more than 360 feet before she fell under its wheels" (Deardorf & Finan, 1999, p. 1). Could her testimony have been biased? How much of it was used to build

sympathy and thus boost the size of the award? How well could you remember what happened if you were in that situation? Was she partially responsible for putting herself at risk? These and other questions are the kinds of issues to be raised when the testimonial is being offered as evidence.

As persuadees, we need to be alert to the ways in which testimonials can be distorted or misused. We know that in many cases the testimonial is being given only because the sponsor has paid the person to give it. So, the next time you see a sports personality endorsing a product, don't assume that he or she uses it on a daily basis. By law, they only have to have tried it one time. And try to determine the degree of authority the person has about the product.

COMMON FALLACIES USED IN PERSUASION

Webster's Collegiate Dictionary defines **fallacy** as "deceptive appearance...a false or mistaken idea...an often plausible argument using false or invalid inference." It is this last definition that concerns us here: believable arguments or premises that are based on invalid reasoning. Keep in mind that a logical fallacy is not necessarily false, but its process of inference is invalid. In spite of the fact that these fallacies have been identified for centuries, they still pop up frequently in advertisements, political persuasion, interpersonal persuasion, and other arenas. Briefly, here are some of the common fallacies we encounter almost daily.

Post Hoc, Ergo Propter Hoc

Post hoc, ergo propter hoc, commonly called **the "post hoc" fallacy**, derives from the Latin meaning "after this, therefore because of this." As the translation implies, because one event follows another, the first event is assumed to be the cause of the second. We constantly run into this fallacy in the world of advertising. After using the diet pill, Jane lost 40 pounds. Maybe she just got more exercise. Citizens might charge that the reason the school system is out of money is that the superintendent and school board wasted all the money from the referendum eight years ago on unneeded frills, but it is not necessarily so.

Ad Hominem

The Latin term **ad hominem**, meaning "to or at the person," refers to any attack against an individual instead of against her or his position on the issues. The purpose is to lead the audience to take certain actions simply because of an alleged character quirk or other flaw in the person presenting the opposite viewpoint. The cartoons in Figure 8.5 are good examples of the ad hominem argument being used against the faculty president of the policy-making body on a college campus. This tactic is not usually used in advertising because products, not people, are being promoted. However, it is frequently used in ideological persuasion such as in politics. Whenever attacks are made on a person's character instead of on his or her stand on issues, be aware that the ad hominem fallacy is probably at work. If persuaders have nothing to debate, they frequently resort to attacking the personality of the opponent.

Ad Populum

As its name implies, the **ad populum** fallacy relies on whatever happens to be popular at that time. It is aimed at or to the populace. There are

many historical examples of ad populum arguments—some important, some tragic, and some trivial. For example, consider just a few popular notions that justified themselves using the logic of the ad populum: Prohibition, the baby boom, rock 'n' roll, and suburbs in the 1950s. Appeals using the ad populum also abound in the worlds of fashion and popular culture—for example, wearing one's baseball cap backward or getting one's body pierced. Encouragement to "follow the crowd" clues us in to the ad populum fallacy in operation.

The Undistributed Middle

The fallacy of the **undistributed middle** can be defined as "inferring that because an individual, group, or philosophy shares some aspects or attributes with another, it shares all other aspects or attributes." It occurs in most cases of what we call "guilt by association"—for example, "Gut Malloy is a member of Tappa Kanna Bru fraternity, and fraternity boys are heavy drinkers, so he must be a heavy drinker, too." Common sense tells us that there is something missing here. The heart of the fallacy is in the phrase "fraternity boys are heavy drinkers," which is used to suggest that *all* fraternity members share *all* attributes beyond group membership. In other words, the argument assumes that heavy drinking is equally distributed among all members of fraternities when some are moderate drinkers or don't drink at all (Jensen, 1981).

Of course, this example is trivial, but persuaders use the undistributed middle principle to sway opinion and alter behavior in significant ways. For example, because someone serves on the school board, many critics assume that the person must favor all the board's decisions. This example appeared in a small-town newspaper recently:

> Consider these facts: The Japanese eat very little fat and suffer fewer heart attacks than the British or the Americans. On the other hand, the French eat a lot of fat and suffer

FIGURE 8.5 These cartoons use the ad hominem fallacy. They are aimed at the person, not the issue.

SOURCE: Reprinted by permission of Kevin Craver.

fewer heart attacks than the British or the Americans. The Italians drink excessive amounts of red wine and also suffer fewer heart attacks than the British or Americans. Therefore eat and drink what you like. It's speaking English that kills you ("Consider the Facts," 2002, p. 10).

This fallacy underlies any appeal suggesting that using a certain brand will make us like others who use it.

The Straw Man

The **straw man fallacy** sets up a weak, or "straw man," case that can be easily defeated. The persuader represents this case as the position of the other side in the debate, and then brings out key evidence and reasoning to defeat the bogus case, along with the opposition. Political persuasion is riddled with this tactic. For instance, candidate A might charge that candidate B's position on defense spending is reliance on conventional weapons. This is an easy position to demolish. Candidate A promptly shows how wrong the straw man position is by presenting impressive statistics and examples to the contrary. In the world of advertising, we occasionally see, read, or hear a straw man case. A good example is the TV ad in which the announcer says something like, "Some think this Chevy pickup truck can't climb this tough mountain carrying a Dodge pickup on its back." Then we see the Chevy climb the mountain with the Dodge on its back. Of course, if the Chevy couldn't do the job, they would never have aired the ad.

Most comparative advertising depends on the straw man fallacy. In the cola and burger wars, for instance, the opposition is often set up as a straw man waiting to be overcome by the advertiser's brand. The straw man fallacy is also commonly used in ideological arguments. Antiabortion advocates frequently argue that abortion is an inhumane form of birth control and should thus be outlawed. However, pro-choice advocates have never recommended abortion as a means of birth control—that claim is a straw man argument that will naturally be demolished by pro-life advocates.

Other Common Fallacies

Another type of fallacious reasoning uses partial or distorted facts (such as telling only one side of the story or quoting out of context). Other fallacies include substituting ridicule or humor for argument (such as depicting the opposition candidate as "a slow-dancing bureaucrat"), using prejudices or stereotypes, appealing to tradition, begging the question or evading the issue ("National health care is nothing less than socialism!"), using a *non sequitur* (a thought that doesn't logically follow from the preceding one), or creating a false dilemma ("either outlaw deficit spending or declare the country bankrupt") (Kahane, 1992; Thompson, 1971).

LOGICAL SYLLOGISMS

A form of logical argument that goes back to the ancients is called the syllogism. **Syllogisms** are forms of reasoning with three parts: a major premise, a minor premise and a conclusion. They typify content premise persuasion and can be of three types: conditional syllogisms, disjunctive syllogisms, and categorical syllogisms.

Conditional Syllogisms

Conditional syllogisms are defined as arguments using "If/Then" reasoning. Like other syllogisms, they have a major premise, a minor premise, and a conclusion. The major premise states a logical relationship that is presumed to exist in the world and that receivers are to accept. The minor premise states the existence of one element in the relationship, and the conclusion is then drawn between the relationship and the existence of one element in it. Here is a conditional syllogism in classical form:

> If the U.S. government can't control terrorism with the present laws, then we need to give it new laws that are tough enough to stop terrorism (major premise). The World Trade Center bombings and the events of 9/11 are proof that the government can't control terrorism with the present laws (minor premise). Therefore, we need to give the government tougher laws to stop terrorism (conclusion).

The first element, or the "If" part in the major premise, is called the antecedent, and the second element is called the consequent. Affirming the antecedent, which we did in the minor premise by referring to the attacks, we can draw a valid conclusion that tougher laws are needed.

Note that the syllogism is valid, but the premises are not necessarily true. **Validity** refers to how well the syllogism conforms to the general rules of reasoning, and not to the true or false nature of the premises. The other valid way of affirming a part of the conditional syllogism is to deny the existence of the element in the major premise. Using the same example, we could state, "Since 9/11, there have been no major terrorist acts in the United States (minor premise). Therefore, there is no need for new laws (conclusion)."

Advertisers frequently make perfectly valid arguments using false premises. A good example is this statement on a package of Trilene fishing line: "If you are seeking a world record, you should use one of the pound tests coded in the chart at right." You can detect the "if...then..." format in the sentence. We all know that using the right line—Trilene—won't assure anyone of a world record fish, but receivers tend to accept it as logical and buy the line.

There are two valid ways to draw a conclusion in a conditional syllogism. First, we can affirm the "if" part of the major premise and accept the "then" part of the major premise. For example, if we affirm the first portion of the premise ("If you are seeking...") we can affirm the second half about using Trilene line. The other valid combination begins by stating something about the first part of the initial premise. For example, we might say, "Smaller fish taste better," and then reject the advice on using Trilene line. A related but invalid procedure is to deny the antecedent and conclude that the consequent has also been denied. In the Trilene example we might state, "You don't want a lunker," and conclude that therefore you shouldn't use Trilene. The fallacy becomes apparent immediately—you might still want to use Trilene for another reason—perhaps because of its warranty. In a related but also invalid procedure, suppose in the terrorism example we had denied the consequent in the minor premise by saying, "We have not given enough tough new powers to the U.S. government," and then concluded, "Therefore, the U.S. government will not be able to control terrorism." The fallacy is less apparent but is still there—the lack of tough laws doesn't necessarily indicate an inability to control terrorism. Again, there could be intervening causes.

Although invalid, this form of syllogism is frequently used in advertisements. For instance, a romance is "saved" by a certain mouthwash or shampoo. Be alert to this trap. Persuaders can use a logically valid syllogism to camouflage untrue premises. Ask yourself whether the premises are true and whether the argument is valid. The conditional syllogism is similar to the cause–effect linkage described earlier.

To get a better idea of how conditional syllogisms can be used, access InfoTrac College Edition, and type the words "conditional syllogism" in the search engine. Then read the items on the various strategies for using syllogisms and on the order of information in them.

Disjunctive Syllogisms

The **disjunctive syllogism** uses an "Either/Or" format. Consider this major premise of a disjunctive syllogism: "Either we reduce the deficit or we increase taxes." The premise is usually accompanied by some proof or evidence in the minor premise, and the conclusion is then drawn. For example, a school board threatens, "Either we vote to increase property taxes or you lose all extracurricular activities." The voters would provide the minor premise of the syllogism through their votes—if they vote to increase taxes, the board denies the need to eliminate the activities. A second valid conclusion comes about if the voters vote down the tax increase and the board eliminates the activities.

This strategy works if the issue is clear-cut. However, few situations have a clear "either/or" dichotomy, even in extreme cases such as the Terry Scheivo case in 2005. She had been in a comatose state for several years, and her husband wanted to remove her feeding and water tubes, but her parents objected and the issue went into the courts. Ultimately the U.S. Congress voted on the right to life aspects of the case. The central issue revolved around the disjunctive syllogism "Either she is alive or she is dead." The real question should have been "Will she ever recover?" This argument would still exemplify a disjunctive syllogism—either she will recover or she will not—but the controversy would not have been as extreme.

B O X 8.2   **The Logic of Cultural Transformation**

 In his book *Communication and Cultural Transformation: Cultural Diversity, Globalization and Cultural Convergence*, Stephan Dahl (2000) draws a distinction between "high culture" (the opera or symphony, art museums, live theatre) and mass or popular culture (MTV, sports events, newspapers), which emerged in the mid-nineteenth century. He argues that it is popular culture that really is affected by diversity issues. Some of the diversity issues he lists include social groupings, language, nonverbal communication, values, concepts of time and space, perception, and national character. For example, he maintains that in Western culture time is thought of as linear, while in Eastern cultures time is thought of as being circular in nature. Or take our nonverbal signal for "A-Okay," which is the thumb and forefinger forming the letter O. In other cultures or subcultures, the same signal has sexual implications. What kinds of differences in persuasive meaning might follow from these ways of viewing time and space? Various nonverbal gestures? Which of his other diversity issues can you see operating in your everyday life? You may want to view a copy of Dahl's book and other of his publications at www.stephweb.com/capstone/1.htm.

Strict either/or logic cannot take into account other belief systems or more than two alternatives in a situation. Examine persuasion framed in the either/or mode to search for other alternatives or belief systems under which the disjunctive model will not work.

Categorical Syllogisms

Categorical syllogisms deal with parts and wholes, or sets and subsets, of events in which the major and minor premises both involve membership or nonmembership in one of two categories. The conclusion relates the clusters of both premises into a new finding or result, as shown in the following classic categorical syllogism:

> All men are included in the class of mortal beings (major premise). Socrates is included in the class of men (minor premise). Therefore, Socrates is a mortal being (conclusion).

Although this example is frequently used to demonstrate the categorical syllogism, it is not one that you will find many opportunities to use. Its format, however, is frequently seen, read, or heard in various kinds of persuasion. Take, for example, the U.S. Marines' recruiting slogan: "We're looking for a few good men." The implied categorical syllogism is as follows: All U.S. Marines are included in the class of good men (major premise). You are a

good man (minor premise). Therefore, you should become a Marine (conclusion).

Because you are a member of one category, it is assumed that you must or should be a member of another. IBM used this technique when it ran a two-page public relations ad that features two pairs of baby booties, one pink and one blue, and the question "Guess which one will grow up to be the engineer?" The question implies a cultural gender stereotype—women are poor at math and science. One underlying premise concerns engineers. It is "Persons encouraged to excel in math and science are likely to become engineers" (major premise). The next step is "Males are encouraged to excel in math and science" (minor premise). Thus we infer that "Males are likely to become engineers" (conclusion). On another level, the ad creates good public relations by implying that "Good companies encourage women to excel" (major premise); "IBM encourages women to excel" (minor premise): "IBM is therefore a good company" (conclusion). Although the first syllogism is valid (and probably true as well), the second is invalid. IBM uses the illusion of a valid syllogism to make its case that good companies encourage women to excel, but simply doing that does not necessarily guarantee that a company is "good." For other examples of cultural biases see Box 8.2, where nonverbal patterns and different ways of considering time and space are part of the cultural stereotype involved in the syllogism.

THE TOULMIN FORMAT

Most of us do not encounter persuasion that is overtly syllogistic. Instead, the syllogism often is the underlying structure in persuasive arguments. British philosopher Stephen Toulmin (1964) developed a model that identifies the kinds of logical persuasion we encounter in everyday events. According to Toulmin, any argument aimed at our logical reasoning processes is divided into three basic parts: the claim, the data, and the warrant.

Basic Elements

The **claim** is the proposition that the persuader hopes will be believed, adopted, or followed. Claims usually need to be supported by **data**, the second part of the model, which is simply evidence. Data give the receivers reasons for following the advice of the claim. The **warrant** is the reason the data support the claim; it explains the relationship between them. These three elements become clear as we examine persuasion at work. If there is reason to believe that receivers will accept the claim on its face, there is no need for the persuader to continue. However, if the persuader expects receivers to doubt the claim, then data must be presented. If the data are accepted or rejected outright, again there is no need to proceed. However, if the persuader anticipates some doubt about the claim now supported by data, then it will be necessary to present a warrant that explains the reasoning by which the data support the claim. This pattern of moving the logical argument from claim to data to warrant, and the resulting three kinds of responses (agree, disagree, and uncertain), are typical of almost every reasoned argument in the everyday marketplace of ideas. Figure 8.6 uses the claim that the United States must become a "globo-cop" to show how the flow of argument goes in the **Toulmin system**. Trace the stages of argument in the figure.

Substantiating Elements

Toulmin's system has a number of secondary terms. For example, a claim may be modified by a **qualifier**—usually a simple word or phrase such as "In most cases" or "Probably" or "It is likely that." Conceding that the claim is not necessarily universal qualifies or limits the claim. In our globo-cop example, the persuader might alter the claim to state, "In most cases, the United States should become an international peacekeeper in world crises." Qualifiers limit the claim, thus allowing for the possibility that this is not a simple case of the either/or argument.

Another minor term in the model is the **reservation**, defined as a statement that specifies the conditions under which the warrant is valid. The reservation features words like "unless" or "only if there is a reason to believe that." In the globo-cop case, suppose the warrant stated, "Except in the case of revolutions, the United States is the only remaining superpower capable of establishing and maintaining world stability." Another reservation is expressed with the word "Unless," in which case the warrant might state, "Unless the United States is not the only remaining superpower capable of establishing and maintaining world stability . . ."

Both persuaders and persuadees often overlook the use of the reservation to cite circumstances in which the claim should not be accepted. They assume that both parties begin from the same point, from the same frame of reference. We must begin at the same point or make allowances (such as reservations) to make real progress in any persuasive transaction. Coupled with the qualifier, the reservation allows for great flexibility in persuasion because both encourage dialogue; both provide the persuadee with an opportunity to object or agree to part but not all of the persuasion.

Advertisers are clever with the use of qualifiers. For example, the label on Cascade dishwasher detergent says that it will make your dishes, not spotless, but "virtually spotless." Who can say whether one spot or three spots or twelve qualifies as being "virtually spotless"? Thus, we need to be aware of two problems connected with qualifiers and reservations: (1) their absence, which can lock us into one course of action or belief; and (2) the use of vague qualifiers, which allows persuaders to wriggle out of any commitment to a product,

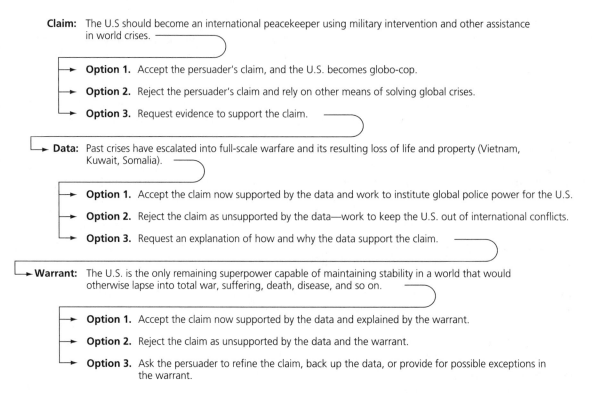

Claim: The U.S should become an international peacekeeper using military intervention and other assistance in world crises.

    Option 1. Accept the persuader's claim, and the U.S. becomes globo-cop.

    Option 2. Reject the persuader's claim and rely on other means of solving global crises.

    Option 3. Request evidence to support the claim.

Data: Past crises have escalated into full-scale warfare and its resulting loss of life and property (Vietnam, Kuwait, Somalia).

    Option 1. Accept the claim now supported by the data and work to institute global police power for the U.S.

    Option 2. Reject the claim as unsupported by the data—work to keep the U.S. out of international conflicts.

    Option 3. Request an explanation of how and why the data support the claim.

Warrant: The U.S. is the only remaining superpower capable of maintaining stability in a world that would otherwise lapse into total war, suffering, death, disease, and so on.

    Option 1. Accept the claim now supported by the data and explained by the warrant.

    Option 2. Reject the claim as unsupported by the data and the warrant.

    Option 3. Ask the persuader to refine the claim, back up the data, or provide for possible exceptions in the warrant.

F I G U R E 8.6 Toulmin's basic elements of an argument, applied to the example of U.S. intervention in world crises.

action, person, or idea. Persuaders may still try to interpret the qualifiers to their advantage, but it is more difficult when more details are given.

The final element in Toulmin's system for showing the tactics of argument is the **backing** for the warrant, which is information that establishes the credibility of the reasoning or connection between data and claim.

We can now see that the tactics of persuasion are not usually simple syllogisms. Instead, persuaders make claims that persuadees can respond to by (1) accepting them outright, (2) rejecting them outright, or (3) asking for proof. Persuaders then can provide data, which receivers can accept, reject, or question. If the persuadee continues to request more proof, the persuader ultimately must provide the warrant, or reason, for linking the proof to the

request. Given enough time, three other elements may enter into the persuasive appeal: the qualifier, the reservation, and the backing. What matters is that persuadees be aware, critical, and systematic as they are exposed to persuasion. Toulmin's system provides us with a simple tool that operates well with many kinds of persuasion.

Evidence on Evidence

Recently, Reynolds and Reynolds (2002) generated a list of facts we know about the uses of evidence:

1. Evidence is cognitively processed. In other words, people must process evidence in the central route of the ELM.

2. Evidence must seem legitimate in the eyes of the persuadee. In other words, the persuadee needs to view the evidence as authentic, high quality, and unbiased.

3. Evidence is evaluated by the audience. This evaluation of evidence leads to overall message evaluation, which, in turn, leads to post-message beliefs. It then follows that these post-message beliefs will lead to some sort of action.

In conclusion, evidence is probably most effective when it encourages audience participation. Earlier, we noted that persuaders are most effective in using emotionally oriented evidence when they present audiences with a dramatic scene or setting and then ask members to empathize. By using their imaginations, members of the audience co-create the proof—they incorporate the proof into their own frames of reference. In using intellectually oriented evidence, effective persuaders present claims and perhaps data to support them. They hope that warrants will be provided by the audience, but the audience members are still participating in their own persuasion when they begin to co-create a proof, even if they do not provide their own warrants. Finally, effective persuaders highlight the evidence—either as part of a narrative or in some form of analogy.

REVIEW AND CONCLUSION

Content or logical premises don't rely on the internal states of persuaders, as do process or emotional premises. Instead, they rely more on universally agreed on norms or rules. Evidence tends to be either dramatically oriented, intellectually oriented, or experiential/participative in nature. Users of dramatic evidence lead persuadees to a "logical" conclusion by creating a dramatic scene and then inviting the audience to join in the drama. Persuadees thus "prove" the validity of the premise to themselves. Users of intellectually

oriented evidence lead their persuadees to "logical" conclusions by presenting them with a set of data in support of a certain claim or content premise. The persuadees provide the connection between these data and the claim in the form of a warrant. And experiential or participative evidence may prove to be the most persuasive because of persuadees' personal involvement with the evidence. All three types of evidence rely on self-persuasion on the part of the persuadee. Persuadees participate in some way in their own persuasion, whether the evidence is intellectual, dramatic, or experiential/participative. When we engage in self-persuasion, even if it runs counter to our own beliefs, the effect of the participation is powerful.

The traditional syllogism usually forms the skeletal structure of arguments or content premises. Within this structure, the tactics or particular arguments or premises are represented by claims supported by data. Claims and data are linked through warrants.

Finally, of the types of evidence available to the persuader, several seem more important than others. Most important, probably, are those that support the three major linkages: cause–effect, symptoms, and comparisons. Also, evidence that provides a perspective for the audience is probably more effective than evidence that does not. We focused on two particularly effective methods of providing this perspective: the use of analogy, which provides a comparative perspective, and the use of narrative, which has the same ability to provide a perspective within a dramatic frame of reference. Both are also "artistic" in the sense that neither merely presents information; rather, both depict evidence in dramatic or visual formats. In sum, we are most effectively persuaded by experiences—real, vicarious, or imagined. Successful persuaders try to shape content premises—their linkages, claims, data, and warrants—in terms of the audience's experience. If persuaders invite audiences to participate in drawing conclusions, audiences will share in their own persuasion.

KEY TERMS

When you have finished reading this chapter, you should be able to identify, explain, and give an example of the following words or concepts.

content premises	participation and demonstration	deductive reasoning,	disjunctive syllogisms
arguments		inductive reasoning	categorical syllogisms
cause–effect reasoning	effect-to-cause reasoning	statistics	claim
proof	cause-to-effect reasoning	fallacy	data
reasoning		the "post hoc" fallacy	warrant
evidence	net effect	ad hominem	Toulmin system
direct experience	component effects	ad populum	qualifier
dramatic or vicarious experience	reasoning from symptoms	undistributed middle	reservation
rationally processed evidence	criteria-to-application reasoning	straw man fallacy	backing
narratives	reasoning from analogy or by comparison	syllogisms	
		conditional syllogisms	
		validity	

APPLICATION OF ETHICS

Two logical opposites in decision making are (1) conflict of interests and (2) compatibility of interests. In conflicts of interest, a person in a position to have inside information might be able to influence decisions so that s/he might personally benefit, as in the case of most corporate scandals. When compatibility of interests exists, persons with an inside position and information make decisions that benefit both themselves and all others with the same interests. For example, a company is having production problems that may lead to layoffs. The CEO decides to bring in efficiency experts to analyze the problem. They do so and cut costs, returning the company to profitability, and removing the layoff option. Apply both of the options to the following example: A CEO at a major automobile corporation sees the prices for energy rising at increasing rates and a resulting drop in sales of SUVs. The executive has several choices: Provide incentives for buying SUVs (e.g., "Now you can buy an SUV at employee discount rates). Another option is to develop hybrid models, which will result in higher costs of the vehicles because of the research and development needed. Another option is to "cook the books," which will jack up the stock value, at which point the CEO can sell off his stock at a profit. Which option should the CEO choose?

QUESTIONS FOR FURTHER THOUGHT

1. What are the three types of syllogisms discussed in this chapter? Give examples of each from advertisements, political speeches, or some other source of persuasion.

2. Define proof. What constitutes adequate proof for you? Does it change from issue to issue? If so, in what ways?

3. Review some magazine commentary concerning a particular issue, and attempt to identify the data offered. What kinds of evidence are they? Are they dramatic? If so, in what ways? If not, are they persuasive? Why or why not? What is the underlying syllogistic structure inherent in the discussions of the issue?

4. What is the difference between intellectually oriented evidence and emotionally oriented evidence? Give examples and explain how they differ.

5. Give examples from your own experience of (a) opinion, (b) attitudes, (c) beliefs, and (d) values that affect behavior. Give examples that do not affect behavior. How do they differ?

6. Why was "The Case of Bobby and His Parents" so persuasive? Was logic involved? Was the example an illogical one to prove the point Peck wanted to make?

7. What is the difference between a figurative and a literal analogy? Which is being used when a political campaign is compared to a horse race?

8. What are some of the ways in which statistics can be misused? Give examples.

9. What are some of the ways in which testimony can be misused? Give examples.

10. What is a post hoc fallacy? Give an example.

11. What is an ad hominem fallacy? Give an example.

12. How has the ad hominem been used in recent elections?

13. What are some contemporary examples of the ad populum being used in advertising?

14. How does the undistributed middle fallacy operate? Give examples.

15. How does the straw man fallacy operate? Give examples.

16. What is the false dilemma fallacy? How does it operate? Give examples.

17. How does the ELM help to explain the differences between content and process premises?

 For online activities, go to the *Persuasion* book companion website at http://communication.wadsworth.com/larson11.

9

Cultural Premises in Persuasion

LEARNING GOALS

After reading this chapter, you should be able to:

1. Identify and explain what cultural patterns are.

2. Recognize how you are affected by cultural training and societal pressures.

3. Recognize in persuasive messages the cultural myths of the wisdom of the rustic, the possibility of success, the coming of a messiah, conspiracy, the value of challenge, and the myth of the eternal return.

4. Identify, explain, and give examples of Reich's cultural parables in advertisements, editorials, or political speeches.

5. Identify messages that appeal to the myths of the man's man and the woman's woman.

6. Discuss image and charisma as cultural premises and explain their three central elements.

7. Identify Redding and Steele's core American values, giving contemporary examples of each.

We are all prisoners of our own culture, and as a result, we often overlook patterns of behavior that influence us and by which we are persuaded. Anyone who has visited another culture (even a similar or related culture) immediately becomes aware of significant differences between our patterns of behavior and those of the foreign culture. Not only are values, languages, and customs different, but hundreds of little things are also different, such as bus passengers lining up in orderly fashion in England, whereas Americans usually crowd around the bus door. In the United States, skiers line up in orderly fashion to wait their turn to use the lift, but in France, locals walk over others' skis to get ahead in the line. In a more significant example of cultural differences, one-third of the world's people eat using knife, fork, and spoon; another third eat with chopsticks; and the rest use their fingers

I visited several formerly communist countries in Eastern Europe in the 1990s, and quickly understood the immense difference between hard currency and soft currency. Hard currency has real worth, but soft currency is widely overvalued, so people don't want to accept it. The hotel I stayed at in Prague refused to accept soft Czech currency but was more than willing to accept hard currencies like the U.S. dollar or the German Mark. It has been that way for so many years that it has become a cultural habit in Czechoslovakia to trade currency on the black market even though trading at above the official rates has been outlawed there

for more than 50 years. I was told the best exchange rate in Czechoslovakia could be gotten from any priest. That's something that would never occur to someone from America.

In Eastern European countries at that time, most people carried a net shopping bag just in case they found something available to buy. In fact, the slang term for such a shopping bag was a "perhaps." People at that time didn't buy something because they needed it, but because it was available. Usually store shelves were nearly empty of any goods, and as a result hoarding was common—an idea that would rarely cross an American's mind.

Although many aspects of any given culture are relatively permanent, cultures are also subject to constant change. In the United States and elsewhere, for example, the constant influx of different ethnic groups and minorities is reflected in the culture in a variety of ways, and diversity and multiculturalism are apparent everywhere. For instance, in our supermarkets the shelves are always loaded, which astounds many foreigners from Eastern Europe. In addition, you will usually find ingredients for foreign dishes that weren't available just a decade ago. So increasing diversity is changing our shopping options. Many schools have sought the help of translators and interpreters to assist them in communicating with the immigrant parents of their newest students. In such small things we can see the continual changes in U.S. culture.

B O X 9.1 People of the Deer

Consider the following instance of cultural patterning. Suppose you are a member of a tribe whose sole food supply is caribou. When the animals make their fall migration south, the tribe kills enough to supply it with food until spring, when the animals migrate north to follow their food supply. The custom is to kill and preserve these deer in a period of a week or two. You have just finished the fall hunt, only to discover that you face a severe winter without having killed enough caribou to last until the spring migration north. Death is certain without sufficient supplies of protein and fat. You attend a council of elders called by the chief to address the crisis and to solicit input and ideas. What would you do? For many years, students in my persuasion classes have brainstormed solutions to this problem and come up with the following suggestions, usually in this approximate order:

- Follow the deer and kill more of them, thus increasing the supply.
- Seek an alternative food supply—we can eat berries or fish or birds.
- Send a band of the young and healthy to get help.

- Ration food to make it last longer.
- Eat all the parts of the caribou—skin, horns, everything—to increase the supply.
- Send some of the people away to another place where food is more plentiful and thus decrease demand.
- Kill some members of the tribe to decrease demand.
- Kill the most useless persons—the old first, and the very young next to decrease demand.
- Resort to cannibalism; let's eat those we kill.

The most practical solutions emerge first, and then the ideas become increasingly desperate. The actual tribe does nothing. They eat the food at their regular rates, knowing that it will not last through the winter. Then they sit and wait for death. They accept the situation, whereas Americans try to find solutions for all problems, even though some are probably insoluble. In all the years of using this example not a single one of my students has suggested doing nothing. Do you think it is good to be solution oriented? Why or why not?

To better understand the wide-reaching impact cultural diversity has on our lives, access InfoTrac College Edition, and type the words "multiculturalism" or "cultural diversity" in the search engine. Explore the many articles that address various aspects of this phenomenon.

CULTURAL PATTERNS

Cultural patterns are defined as the "socially transmitted values, beliefs, institutions, behavioral patterns, and all other products and thought patterns of a society" (*American Heritage Dictionary*, 1985). These are instilled in us from early childhood through our language, the myths and the tales we hear, and our observations of the behavior of those around us. These become cultural patterns, or the activities, beliefs, and values that typify a culture. British

passengers wait in orderly lines for a bus or subway whereas we crowd around the door. In Japan professional "packers" stuff as many persons as possible into their subways. Most persons from the U.S. would view that as unacceptable. Cultural training or patterning is the basis for some of the widely held premises we have discussed in earlier chapters.

The cultural preferences, myths, and values we embrace can all serve as major premises in enthymemes. Persuasion that builds on cultural premises occurs at a low level of awareness and is usually processed in the peripheral information-processing channel of the ELM. Thus, we often react subconsciously to various stimuli based on our cultural training. Robert Cialdini (2001) calls these reactions *fixed action patterns* or *shortcuts*, which are automatic and instantaneous. Cialdini observes that "you and I exist in an extraordinarily complicated environment, easily the most rapidly moving and complex that has ever existed on this planet. To deal with it, we need shortcuts.... As the stimuli saturating our lives continue to grow more intricate and variable, we will have to depend increasingly on our shortcuts to handle them all" (p. 7). And cultural patterning and cultural premises are just such shortcuts to being persuaded.

Another cultural pattern for most Americans is the value of individualism. We like the idea of pulling ourselves up by the bootstraps. There is a flip side to this individualism, as Robert Bellah and his associates (1985) pointed out in *Habits of the Heart: Individualism and Commitment in American Life*. Bellah and his colleagues did in-depth interviews with more than 200 Americans from various walks of life, and described the core American values and beliefs as "habits of the heart." Key among them was the value of the individual. Bellah and his coauthors point out:

> The central problem of our book concerned the American individualism that Tocqueville described with a mixture of admiration and anxiety. It seems to us it is individualism and not equality, as Tocqueville thought, that has marched inexorably throughout our history. We are concerned that this individualism may have grown cancerous (p. viii).

What they meant by "cancerous" is that individualism has become *me-ism*, with emphasis on the individual and not the community, thus drawing people into themselves and forgetting others. Many other observers have echoed this theme. Recall that the initial student responses to the dilemma of too few caribou are positive and action oriented, reflecting the good side of the American value of individualism. The middle responses are more reflective of a sense of community and cooperation, but the last three reflect the bad or cancerous side of American individualism. How do we identify these patterns of cultural values? Where do they come from? How do persuaders appeal to them?

To see how these premises relate to persuasion in general, we look first at how we get them—through cultural training and societal pressure. Then we look at two kinds of cultural premises: (1) **cultural images and myths**, which are defined

as real or imagined narratives that illustrate a society's values, and (2) our value system, which is defined as the hierarchical network of beliefs and values that typify a culture. Bear in mind that a value is an idea of the good or the desirable that we use as a standard for judging people's actions or motivations. Examples of American values are honesty, justice, beauty, efficiency, safety, and progress. Because our value system is a major source of persuasive leverage, you may be interested in discovering how persuaders link proposals and arguments to such values. Cultural training forms the core of our values, which then become rules for governing ourselves. Persuaders appeal to and believe these premises and expect their audiences to do so too.

CULTURAL IMAGES AND MYTHS

Every culture has its own myths and heroic figures that do things valued by the culture, and many of these myths are borrowed from other cultures, particularly European cultures. An ancient example that Greek society developed centuries ago was a series of myths surrounding the sin of pride. We have similar beliefs. You know that the overly proud student won't be elected or chosen as team captain. The more humble person will be picked. What are some of the myths or legends or images underlying American culture and society, and how do persuaders use them? Can these images be changed, and if so, how? Are they being changed at present, and if so, how? Stereotypes and proverbs are indicators of cultural myths. Let us consider a few.

The Wisdom of the Rustic

One of the legends in American lore that has great persuasive appeal is the wisdom of the rustic. No matter how devious the opposition, the simple commonsense wisdom of the backwoods hero or heroine wins out. Numerous folktales rely on this rustic image, including the Daniel Boone tales and many Abraham Lincoln stories about his humble beginnings and meager education. We believe in humble beginnings, and we believe that difficulty teaches even the most uneducated to be wise and worldly. Thus, politicians throughout American history have emphasized their humble origins. For example, Ronald Reagan emphasized his humble origin in Dixon, Illinois, and Bill Clinton let it be known that he was born in a small house in Hope, Arkansas. Neither President Bush emphasized that they came from privileged origins. If the politician cannot claim humble beginnings, he or she finds some substitute, usually hardship or suffering such as being a P.O.W. or suffering from some disability. Products are frequently marketed using a rustic as the spokesperson. Wilfred Brimley, for instance, serves as a rustic when he endorses the value of good old-fashioned Quaker Oats, and the smiling Quaker man on the package reinforces the image.

Even as we value the simple, commonsense rustic, our culture tends to devalue the intellectual or the educated. Persuaders often use this reverse side of our faith in the wisdom of the rustic: The intellectual is the brunt of jokes, and the rustic wins out over the smart guy.

Access InfoTrac College Edition, and type the words "cultural myths" in the search engine. Look at Carl Stepp's review of "Slick Spins and Fractured Facts: How Cultural Myths Distort the News," by Caryl Rivers, which deals with how cultural myths put various kinds of "spin" on news events. If you find this review interesting, you can retrieve the entire item or read Rivers' book.

The Possibility of Success

The **possibility of success** myth is best seen in the numerous novels by Horatio Alger, written for boys in the nineteenth century. The protagonist of these novels was invariably a young man who, through hard work, sincerity, honesty, law-abiding behavior, and faith in the future, was able to make good. He might even rise to the top and own his own company, have a beautiful wife, live a fine life, and be able to do good for others. The possibility of success myth appealed to immigrants, the poor, and the downtrodden. They passed it on to their

children, admonishing them to work hard to achieve success. The myth has been generalized to include women and minorities, and has great appeal for new groups of immigrants. These new immigrants, particularly those from Third World countries, often share living quarters to save money or go into business for themselves, and all members are expected to help provide for the family. The myth of possible success is as alive today as it was when immigrants came mainly from Europe. Again, this myth was observed by Tocqueville (1965):

> No Americans are devoid of a yearning desire to rise.... All are constantly seeking to acquire property, power, and reputation.... What chiefly diverts the men of democracies from lofty ambition is not the scantiness of their fortunes, but the vehemence of the exertions they daily make to improve them.... The same observation is applicable to the sons of such men...their parents were humble; they have grown up amidst feelings and notions which they cannot afterwards easily get rid of..." (pp. 156–158).

You may recognize your grandparents in this description if they or their parents emigrated to the United States. You may also see yourself in it.

Naturally, we are receptive to persuasion that promises the possibility of success. That's why you decided to go to college. Products and services are marketed promising success for the entire family. Politicians promise a bright future for voters who support a commonsense approach to problems. The possibility of success myth is probably what led many investors to buy Internet stocks in the late 1990s. After all, the entire human race seemed to be going online, and marketing would never be the same again. When the dot-com bubble burst in 2002, the possibility of success myth went out the window for a time. Still, whether it is a pyramid marketing scheme, the lottery, or a weight-loss club, the carrot is always the same—try and you will succeed.

To learn more about the Horatio Alger novels and the possibility of success, access InfoTrac College Edition, and type the words "Horatio

Alger" in the search engine. Explore the link to the Horatio Alger Society. Try the "Pluck and Luck," "Tattered Tom," or "Ragged Dick" novels.

The Coming of a Messiah

A cultural myth related to the possibility of success myth is the **coming of a messiah**. Whenever our society is approaching disaster or is already in a terrible mess—economic, religious, or political— or we are in a period of great uncertainty and pessimism or when things are chaotic, confusing, and frightening, we believe someone or something will save us. We want to be rescued from the chaos and danger by some great leader who projects a sense of confidence and who can turn things around. Many past leaders filled this role. For example, Abraham Lincoln emerged from semi-obscurity to save the Union. Franklin Roosevelt emerged to lead the United States out of the Great Depression and to victory in WWII. Ronald Reagan delivered us from 18 percent interest rates and unbelievable inflation. And George W. Bush was depicted as the leader who would help us win the war on terrorism. The future will no doubt bring us other problems, and you can rest assured that there will be someone who will emerge in the role of a messiah. What makes us so receptive to the messianic? First, we are action oriented, as we noted earlier, and we want our saviors to be doers. Second, we want their solutions to be simple and practical.

The Presence of Conspiracy

Another cultural premise is the belief that when we face enormous, almost overwhelming problems, the only plausible explanation is that a powerful group must be behind them. This pattern is called the **paranoid style** and is defined as using conspiracies as explanations for otherwise unanswerable dilemmas (Hofsteder, 1963). Probably the best examples are the various conspiracy theories concerning the assassination of J.F.K. Many other conspiracy arguments have recurred throughout our history such as those about the Masons and Knights Templar, conspiracies that lent credence to the recent novel and film *The DaVinci Code* or Papal Conspiracy theories. Most recently, the conspiracy argument was used to explain the Oklahoma City bombing and the terrorism of our times. Some people believe that militia groups are presently conspiring to overthrow the government, and a few feel that the government is already in the hands of international conspirators. Many people believe there is an anti-U.S. conspiracy between Al Qaeda and rogue nations like Iran and North Korea. A conspiracy theory regarding terrorism apparently prompted the Bush administration to illegally wiretap phone calls to American citizens without obtaining a warrant, even when such warrants are granted as a matter of course. This in turn led to a conspiracy theory regarding the administration's disregard of constitutional rights

When it comes to persuasive communication, and if Hofstadter is right, we can expect to hear conspiracy offered as an explanation for problems any time three factors are operating for the audience members:

1. They have something of value to lose—power, property, or privilege.
2. They feel in danger of losing this power or property, or they have already lost some of it.
3. They see themselves as helpless to prevent the loss.

It is easy to see how belief in a conspiracy could give rise to a messiah as well. Only a messiah can defeat evil conspirators and save us. One of the dangers of this myth is that it invites mass hysteria and the rise of charismatic leaders, who seem to be heroes but who may be just the opposite.

The Value of Challenge

The myth of **the value of challenge** is fairly simple and parallels tribal tests of strength and character. It suggests that a kind of wisdom can be gained only through rigorous testing and that some rite of passage or initiation gives us power, character, and knowledge. You are probably now going through such a test in attending college. People say that going to college is more a test of endurance than training for a specific job. By graduating, you show that you can meet a challenge and handle it, that you have matured, and that you have learned how to learn. Job training comes after that. Boot camp offers another example of belief in the value of overcoming difficulty and meeting challenges. The Outward Bound program rests on the value of challenge myth. It says the most problematic children will be restored to good behavior if they get through a mountain-climbing expedition, a rafting trip down the Colorado River, or a wilderness canoe trip. Even corporate America believes in this concept and often sends its executives on such Outward Bound experiences to shape them up and build unity.

Political persuaders frequently offer voters a dramatic challenge to be met by their election. For instance, John Kennedy said that with his election a torch had been passed to a new generation and that the light from the torch would "light the world." George W. Bush promised to rise to the challenge to win the war on terrorism and return security to America. Product appeals frequently present consumers with a challenge. "Use the Soloflex machine regularly and lose 20 pounds in 30 days!" and "Get your MBA at Olivet College by attending one Saturday a month!" both rely on the value of challenge.

The value of challenge suggests that suffering could be good, or that nothing was ever accomplished without pain. Second, the myth suggests that suffering begets maturity, humility, and wisdom. Individuals learn and grow as they meet challenges and surmount them. Finally, all great leaders became so because they were tested and found equal to the challenge. Thus, defeats and failures are just tests that prepare you for the future. As you begin to catalog the persuasion aimed at you, you will find the value of challenge used frequently, whether for products, candidates, or ideologies (see Figure 9.1).

 Access InfoTrac College Edition, enter the words "meeting challenges" in the search

engine, and explore some of the ways this myth is used to persuade various constituencies.

The Eternal Return

Mercia Eliade (1971), a French professor of history, identified a historical myth persistent not only in Western culture but in other cultures as well. He called it **the myth of the eternal return**, and defined it as a rejection of concrete historical time or things that actually happened, accompanied by a yearning for and reenactment of a "periodical return to the mythical time of the beginning of things, to the 'Great Time.'" American culture embraces this myth, perhaps because our beginnings are so recent. America was conceived as a "second Eden," a chance to start anew with no historical baggage to clutter up its purpose. Many immigrants of the past and present want this chance to start over.

According to the myth of the eternal return, there was a time when things were perfect and harmonious, when events could be shaped or molded as they were meant to be. This time of creation is usually associated with a specific geographical center where things are assumed to have begun. In the United States, this center is probably Philadelphia, where the Continental Congress signed the Declaration of Independence and where the Liberty Bell is housed. Another potential symbolic center is Washington, DC, where our great historical documents are enshrined in the National Archives. At the creation there were great heroes (George Washington, Benjamin Franklin, Paul Revere, John Hancock, and others) and there were villains (King George, the colonial governors, Redcoats, and Tories). After suffering indignities, the heroes enacted some critical feat that was redemptive, and it released them and the people from their former enslavement and permitted them to create the "Great Time" or the "Golden Age." The Boston Tea Party is a familiar example.

Included in the myth is the notion that society has lost sight of its archetypal beginning and must find its way back if we are to rid ourselves of the corruption and confusion that have developed since

FIGURE 9.1 The U.S. Army's "Be All You Can Be" campaign exemplified the persuasiveness of the value of challenge myth, especially for women in this advertisement. The new slogan is "Join the Army of One," which also hints at challenge.

SOURCE: Army photograph courtesy of U.S. Government, as represented by the Secretary of the Army.

then. We usually accomplish this through reenactments of the original feat in a ritual, usually held at the center where everything began. This periodic return to the origins of our beliefs reestablishes our values for us and redeems the culture. The ritual freezes us in a mystical time that has power to transform us. As Eliade noted, "Time, too, like space is neither homogeneous nor continuous. On

FIGURE 9.2 This ad by Danner boots appeals to the myth of the eternal return with its reference to a "Golden Age" when men were men and their boots stood the test of time.

SOURCE: Reprinted by permission of Danner Shoe Manufacturing Co.

the one hand there are the intervals of a sacred time, the time of festivals and on the other hand there is profane time, ordinary temporal duration" (Beane & Doty, 1975, p. 33). We believe in and talk about the cyclical nature of things in the two types of time. For example, when we say, "What goes around comes around," we mean, "This will come back to haunt you," "What ye sow, so shall ye reap," or "History repeats itself." We have a reverence for certain sacred times like historical holidays, ritualistic meals such as Thanksgiving or Passover, and national rites such as the inaugural address, the oath of office, or the State of the Union Address.

BOX 9.2   Interactive Program for Anti-Drug Campaign

 Go to www.mediacampaign.org and you will find a multi-mediated program sponsored by the National Youth Anti-drug Media Campaign. There you can search over 35 television commercials, 55 radio commercials, 80 print ads, 25 banner ads, and several screen savers all targeted at diverse audiences and ethnicities and in several languages. In addition, you can explore various news stories and informational essays about drugs, and their short-term and long-term effects, the campaign's partnership with the NFL and other sports organizations, and much more. Be sure to go to the www.freevibe.com and wwwdrugstory.org links from the main page. You will learn about how cultural values are appealed to in a number of ways by exploring the many facets of this campaign.

Commercial persuaders are aware of the importance of sacred time. They have invented special sales on historical holidays—a "Hatchet Days Sale" on Washington's birthday, an "Independence Day Sale" on the Fourth of July, and, in recent years, a "Super Bowl Sale" in mid-January. And every four years, the Olympics provides numerous instances of sacred time being celebrated. At the same time, we disdain persons who waste time, who are just passing the time, or who are "couch potatoes" living through profane time. Recessions are profane times, as are losing seasons for athletic teams. Politicians are skilled at challenging us to return to an earlier time to reestablish and renew ourselves. Not only is this apparent in their speeches, but also in the inaugural ceremonies themselves, which are acts of renewal that promise to return us to the untainted past.

In ideological campaigns and mass movements, the return-and-renewal theme is also persistent. Martin Luther King, Jr., used it in his "I Have a Dream" speech. We hear strains of the myth but referring to profane times in the pro-life, antiabortion movement. One pro-life leader said, "People are going to look back on this era the way they look back on Nazi Germany. They'll say 'Thank God there were a few sane people'" ("America's Abortion Dilemma," 1985, p. 21). This profane time was echoed by a "moral majority" leader who said of abortion, "This criminal activity . . . sets us back to the Stone Age" (p. 22).

Even in product ads we can detect appeals to the new beginnings or to the return and renewal

myth. NEC Corporation says, "The new information age is built on the merging of computers and communication . . . you deserve no less. NEC, the way it will be." Mercedes-Benz reminds us, "This Year, as for Ninety-nine Years, the Automobiles of Mercedes-Benz are Like no Other Cars in the World." This myth of the eternal return is a powerful tool that persuaders use in a variety of circumstances. It is reflected in a set of cultural myths or parables described next.

REICH'S CULTURAL PARABLES

In his book *Tales of a New America*, Robert Reich (1987) contends that the future appears chaotic for a variety of reasons: rapidly advancing technology, rising expectations for prosperity throughout the world, and general confusion about where we are headed as a nation. Reich and his Harvard colleagues have identified what they call basic *cultural parables* for the United States. These parables convey

lessons about the how and why of life through metaphor, (that) may be a basic human trait, a universal characteristic of our intermittently rational, deeply emotional, meaning-seeking species. In America the vehicles of public myth include the biographies of famous citizens, popular fiction, films, and music, feature stories about people who do good things. They anchor our political understandings. What gives them force is their capacity to make sense of, and bring coherence to, common experience. The lessons ring true, even if the illustration is fanciful (p. 7).

Reich's work often echoes what has been emphasized earlier in our study of persuasion: Human beings are fascinated with and driven by the power of the dramatic.

Reich's parables are manifest in the following story about a man named George, the son of immigrant parents who worked hard to provide a good home. He did well in school and worked long hours to bring home a few dollars for the family. He was good in sports although he didn't have much time to participate. He never picked a fight, but on one occasion he did step in to stop the town bully and banker's son, Albert Wade, from beating up on the smallest kid in class. He let Albert have the first swing and then decked him with a single punch. George went off to fight in Europe in World War II and saved his squad by single-handedly destroying a machine gun nest, but he was too humble to wear or display the medal he received for bravery. After the war, he returned to his hometown, married his childhood sweetheart, and built a successful construction business. He gave his spare time to good causes and lived modestly. George kept to himself until his old nemesis, Albert Wade, inherited his father's bank and began to squander the depositors' savings by making shady loans to his buddies and buying himself into the office of mayor. The only person to stand up and challenge the corrupt election was George. Then Wade's bank refused to loan any money on houses built by George. In a showdown town meeting, one of Wade's corrupt councilmen finally broke down under George's accusatory gaze and spilled the beans on Wade, who ended up in jail while George went back to his modest life. It is *the* American morality play, according to Reich.

This brief story has been told over and over again in many versions, including Horatio Alger novels, and biographies of famous Americans. It contains Reich's basic cultural parables that have remained current for generations. As you read about these parables, look for the similarities between them and cultural myths.

The Mob at the Gates

The basic idea in this parable is that America stands alone as the last, best hope for a good, moral, and affluent life in a world filled with perilous possibilities and awesome problems. This parable creates an "us versus them" mentality or mind-set. The **mob at the gates** may be drug traffickers, illegal aliens, terrorists; or it may be environmental polluters, the militia movement, or foreign or slave labor that can provide goods at lower prices than American companies charge. The mob may also be the greedy corporate executives who exploit workers through insider trading, outrageous salaries and perks, and outright cheating. The mob may be secular humanists, minorities, and do-gooders. Those who see themselves as heroes may defy the mob at the gates on some issue, such as foreign competition, but on other issues, the mob may be acceptable for one side but not for the other. For instance, liberals see illegal aliens as less threatening than conservatives do.

Reich (1987) cites several persuasive events of central importance to our nation that rested on the mob at the gates parable. One is the "rotten apple" metaphor. Several rotten leaders or countries can ruin the "whole barrel" of free nations. The rotten apples at the top of corporate America have ruined the trust and confidence so essential for a healthy and growing economy. We also have seen this myth applied to George W. Bush's "rogue nations" that form an "axis of evil" that condones, supports, and even trains terrorists. Note how the language used frames the issues for us. "Rogue" nations don't play by the "rules," defined by Bush as American ways of behaving, and the "axis of evil" is reminiscent of the German, Italian, and Japanese "Axis" of World War II, thus equating those nations with fascist tyrannies.

Advertisers base many of their ads for products on this parable. Millions of germs are lying in wait to infect you, but if you use Listerine mouthwash, you'll knock them for a loop. Hordes of mosquitoes will ruin your picnic unless you are vigilant enough to spray the area with long-lasting Raid insect fog. The mob myth is a natural for ideological campaigns as well. For example, the secular humanists are supposedly tainting America's moral fiber, so it is absolutely essential to join the Born Again group. And, of course, politicians use the image in a variety of ways: The mob may be the other party, the homeless, or tax-and-spend politicians. Not to worry—the "good guys" will save the day.

The Triumphant Individual

The **triumphant individual** parable has as its subject the humble person who works hard, takes risks but has faith in him- or herself, and eventually reaches or even exceeds goals of fame, honor, and financial success. It is the story of the self-made man or woman who demonstrates what hard work and determination, combined with a gutsy approach to problems and a spunky style, can do. Usually, the individual is a loner (sometimes even a maverick) who is willing to challenge the establishment and try to do something on a shoestring.

A modern example is Bill Gates, the inventor of Microsoft, and now a major philanthropist. Another is Steven Jobs, who invented the Apple computer and built the Apple empire, beginning in his garage. Both Gates and Jobs were self-reliant and hardworking, and they believed in themselves. Another example from the fairly recent past is Lee Iacocca, the maverick at Ford who bucked the odds and the office politics, and finally persuaded the company to bring out its most successful product ever—the Mustang. He took over the nearly bankrupt Chrysler Corporation and turned the company around, paying off a $1.2-billion government bailout loan early; innovating with front wheel drive, the minivan, driver and passenger airbags, customer rebates, a 70,000-mile warranty, and the convertible.

The triumphant individual myth strikes the same chord as several cultural myths mentioned earlier, such as the wisdom of the rustic. We frequently see the triumphant individual in a variety of persuasive arenas. In politics, self-made men or women are the ones to put your money on. They made it this far on guts and a belief in themselves, and as a result, they will come out winners on election day as well. A good example is Senator John McCain who was a tortured P.O.W. during the Vietnam War and was finally returned to his home state of Arizona where he triumphed and became a senator. Some speculate that he may run for the presidency in 2008. Companies that are willing to take risks on new technologies also are a kind of triumphant individual.

The Benevolent Community

The myth or parable of **the benevolent community** reflects the essential goodness of people and their willingness to help out the other guy in time of need. An ad for Miller beer portrayed this myth in action. A small town in Wisconsin was struck by a tornado that demolished several homes, businesses, and nearby farms. But the men and women of surrounding communities joined forces and within two weeks had nearly rebuilt all that had been destroyed. Of course, at the end of a hard day of raising walls and rafters, they enjoyed drinking the sponsor's product. During devastating floods and storms, students, neighbors, and others volunteer to fill sand bags, build levies, and help out the victims. And the hurricane-ravaged Gulf states received billions of dollars in relief from donations by ordinary citizens of the "benevolent community." Though recent events have soured our trust in CEOs, corporate America regularly enhances its image after various disasters by advertising that it has donated money and products to the victims, and thus the corporation becomes part of the benevolent community. The U.S. Marines are a part of the benevolent community with their annual Toys for Tots campaign around the holidays. We find this cultural parable recurring throughout our history in struggles like abolition, women's suffrage, the civil rights movement, past and current anti-war movements, and pro-life or pro-choice demonstrations. As Reich notes, "The story celebrates America's tradition of civic improvement, philanthropy, and local boosterism" (p. 10). Persuaders will continue to use the lesson of this parable to market products, candidates, and ideologies.

Rot at the Top

The **rot at the top** parable or myth has conspiratorial aspects and revolves around a number of sub-themes such as corruption, a lack of morals or ethics, decadence, greed, and the malevolence of persons in high places. Like the presence of conspiracy myth, it seems to follow a cyclical pattern, which Reich calls "cycles of righteous fulmination." First, we trust the elite, but then we find them lacking in trust or goodwill, and finally, we end up unseating them and "throwing the rascals out!" Reich traces the myth to the Founding Fathers' sensitivity to the abuse of power experienced under King George and his colonial governors. Abuses of power by elites who buy their positions of power with money and favors (as did Albert Wade) or who have been corrupted by power always exist.

Our history features numerous and varied types of rot at the top, but Reich believes that the myth usually has one of two main targets: political corruption or economic exploitation. Politically, we have seen it in Teapot Dome in the 1920s, Watergate in the 1970s, the Iran–Contra scandals of the 1980s, sex scandals in the 1990s, and, most recently, the fiscal scandals in corporate America. We often hear that big business has exploited the common man, and we still see Wall Street scandals based on insider trading by "stock market jackals" and "corporate barracudas." All of these are examples of rot at the top. The lesson of this myth is simple: Power corrupts; privilege perverts.

Writer Michael Parenti (1994) identifies several other myths that are fairly self-explanatory. "You can't fight city hall," "our leaders know best," "you can't legislate morality," and "all politicians are the same" (p. 2–13) are all examples. Communication scholar D. Hahn (1998) identified several other political myths, such as the myth of progress, the myth of youth, and the myth of love and openness (p. 128–129).

Go to InfoTrac College Edition, enter the words "corporate scandal" in either the subject or the key word search engine, and read a few of the titles listed. See if they incorporate elements of the rot-at-the-top cultural myth.

THE MAN'S MAN AND THE WOMAN'S WOMAN

Another popular cultural myth for many Americans is that for a male to be a success, he must be a macho **man's man**. Schools, family, and television tell children that important males are those who do macho things: compete in manly activities, use colognes with names like "Iron," get involved in sports, talk tough, own guns, and drive SUVs. They never show their emotions, and they die with their boots on. In contrast, the ideal **woman's woman** is soft spoken, kind, and nurturing but also practical and competent. She may work, but she is also the perfect wife and mother and is always immaculately groomed. However, she may also be vain, rarely has meaningful thoughts, and never wastes time talking about serious things.

These myths, of course, affect the way we treat our children, valuing certain things they do and devaluing others. Until recently, it was unfeminine for females to engage in any sport except tennis, golf, gymnastics, figure skating, or swimming. On the other side of the coin, it was not masculine for males to take up gourmet cooking, needlepoint, or flower gardening (vegetables were okay). Further, males weren't very nurturing or emotional, and they talked about important things like jobs, the economy, cars, and sports.

However, this myth of the distinctions between the sexes is obviously changing. High schools and colleges boast women's field hockey, basketball, boxing, and softball teams. Female executives are featured in ads for business hotels, and female pilots are shown using deodorant. At the same time, men are now expected to contribute their fair share of housework. Old myths do not die easily, however, and we still see many examples of the stereotypical macho man and the perfectly feminine woman. Beer ads feature retired athletes engaged in a man's world, bragging to one another over beers or testifying to the effectiveness of potency enhancers. One look at any current magazine shows advertisers pitching their products at people who buy into these images of men and women.

Although gender-bound and stereotypical representations of men and women are changing, these images still have persuasive power and are still used to advertise products and promote ideas. Despite reductions in gender differences in job and political candidacy and in gender-related language use, the old stereotypes are still potent persuaders. The major change in attitude toward gender-related issues has occurred in young, college-educated, upper-middle-class, nonminority populations. But the far greater proportion of our population still seems to buy into the man's man and woman's woman myths. We still see ads for SUVs, assault weapons, and chain saws, and we continue to see ads for Victoria's Secret (sort of a prudish but sexy name), *Elle* magazine, and beauty products. All of these examples continue to promote gender stereotypes. Try counting the number of features or ads in a single issue of a magazine like *Elle* or *Marie Claire* devoted to the woman's woman. Consider a few of the following feature titles from the cover of a single issue of *Cosmopolitan*: "Super Sensual Sex—Touch Him Tricks," "A Man's Body Craves Certain Strokes, Caresses and Pressure. Here's Your Hands-On Guide," or "28 Romantic Rituals to Do With Your Man," or "Try This Simple Trick and Get What You Want." They all promote gender stereotypes. The woman's woman is not only good at work and home, but she is also skilled at lovemaking. They are just a few appeals to the woman's woman myth we encounter every day.

Persuaders will adapt as Americans shift their values regarding gender and other human characteristics, such as age, single parenthood, and economic status, but their persuasion will reflect the premises that the audience believes. Persuasion is more often a reflection of a culture's values than a shaper of them (see Figures 9.3 and 9.4)

There is a broad literature on gender stereotypes. Explore it by accessing InfoTrac College Edition and entering the words "gender stereotypes" in the subject search engine. Browse the periodical selections.

IMAGE AS A CULTURAL PREMISE

Sometimes persuaders are successful because of their **image or charisma**. Somehow they seem to have a special presence, and they command the public's attention. We believe them because their presentations are convincing and dynamic, or because they have a reputation for being truthful or knowledgeable. As we noted earlier, Aristotle called this kind of credibility *ethos*, or ethical proof. More recently, researchers have worked at identifying exactly what causes or creates high ethos in some persons and low ethos in others. One research technique is to have audiences rate speakers on a variety of scales that have sets of opposing adjectives at either end. For example, the scales may have words like "fast/slow." On one end of the scale is the number 1 and on the other end is the number 5. Other word pairs include strong/weak, hot/cool, or active/inactive. Researchers see where the ratings cluster and infer that those items with positive loadings are important to credibility, image, charisma or *ethos*. The choices tend to cluster around the three traits or dimensions of source credibility: expertise, trustworthiness or sincerity, and dynamism or charisma. Together, they accounted for more persuasive success than all the rest of the dimensions. For example, the dynamism ratings were associated with words like "active," "fast," "hot," and "strong." Let us explore these dimensions of source credibility more fully.

Expertise

The **expertise** dimension of source credibility means that highly credible sources are perceived as having knowledge and experience regarding the topic they address and therefore are credible. This makes sense because we tend to put more store in ideas and advice that come from experts than in those that come from nonexperts. To whom would you go for advice on gourmet cooking—Emeril or the cook at the local cafe? The clustering of words such as "competent," "experienced," and "professional" related to the expertise dimension and have been verified by experiments in which a variety of groups listened to the same audio tape of a speaker giving the same

FIGURE 9.3 Here are examples of the myth of the "man's man" done tongue in cheek.

SOURCE: *Making It* copyright 1988 Keith Robinson. All rights reserved. Reprinted by permission of Making It Productions.

FIGURE 9.4 The myth of the man's man has always revolved around sexual potency, as can be seen in this Big Stinky cartoon.
SOURCE: Reprinted by permission of Nick Jeffries.

speech. The speaker was introduced to some of the groups as the surgeon general while to others the speaker was introduced as a college senior. The listeners found the "expert" much more credible than the nonexpert. Many advertisements use expert testimony from doctors, financial advisors, and scientists because they are deemed to be credible, and consumers feel that they can rely on these experts' advice. Over 35 years ago, researchers reported that three believability factors emerging from audience-generated words describing credible sources were safety, qualification, and dynamism (Berlo, Lemmert, & Davis, 1969). Qualification is similar to expertise. This dimension seems to be one of the more stable factors in determining whether we believe someone.

Trustworthiness or Sincerity

Another dimension that recurs in studies of image, credibility, or charisma is **trustworthiness** or sincerity. Early persuasion researchers at Yale first identified this factor in their studies, concluding that the credibility of any source is tied to "trust and confidence" (Hovland, Janis, & Kelley, 1953). This dimension emerged in numerous other studies over the years, and has sometimes been called "safety" or "personal integrity" (Baudhin & Davis, 1972).

An interesting indicator of trustworthiness occurs in situations in which a biased source testifies against his or her own self-interest or bias. This may give us a clue to what is really involved in the trust dimension. Psychology researchers Herbert Kelman and Carl Hovland (1953) wanted to know who would be believed in the following situation: A message promoting the need for stiffer penalties for juvenile delinquents that was attributed in one case to a juvenile court judge and in another case to a reformed drug-pushing juvenile delinquent. The audience believed the judge because of his expertise in dealing with juvenile cases, but their belief in the delinquent came from their trust that his sincere testimony was obviously against the speaker's image.

Trust or sincerity requires us to analyze speakers' motives or hidden agendas. The etymology of the word *sincerity* gives us some insights. It comes from the Latin *sincerus*, which literally means "without wax." This referred to a practice of unethical pillar carvers, who used wax to cover up blemishes in an otherwise perfect pillar that had been ruined by the carver's mistakes. Only after decades of weathering did the wax fall out and reveal the deception. So a sincere person was without wax or not camouflaged.

Audiences believe speakers who are sincere and trustworthy. These speakers maintain good eye contact, don't shift back and forth on their feet, and lack a tremor in their voices. Or audiences judge sincerity from speakers' reputations—offices they have held, accomplishments, and what others say about them. Trustworthiness has been repeatedly demonstrated in research studies as a key component of credibility. Although its effects vary from situation to situation, receivers believe persons they trust, whether because of their reputation, delivery, or motivation.

Dynamism

A final dimension of credibility that has been demonstrated through experimental research is not as easy to define or even describe. This factor has been labeled **dynamism**, **charisma**, or **image** by various researchers. It is the degree to which the audience admires and identifies with the source's attractiveness, power, forcefulness, and energy. The following word pairs have been used in testing for the dynamism factor: "aggressive/meek," "emphatic/hesitant," "frank/reserved," "bold/passive," "energetic/tired," and "fast/slow." The ratings clustered around the first word in each pair.

Dynamism equates with charisma, and although it is influenced by a speaker's attractiveness, unattractive persons can be charismatic or dynamic. Dynamic speakers don't necessarily move about or wave their arms to give off dynamism cues. They simply seem to take up a lot of psychological space. They enter a room and people expect them to be in charge. Their voices seem to be assured and confident. They are eloquent and sometimes border on being poetic. They seem to know just what to say in tough or even tragic moments, and the audience lingers on their words. Dynamic persuaders populate important and crisis events across American history.

Researchers have investigated other dimensions of source credibility. A tall speaker, for example, is generally more likely to be believed than a short one. Timid or shy and reserved persons are likely to have low credibility, whereas authoritative and self-assured ones have high credibility. Bossy and egotistical persuaders lose credibility, whereas pleasant and warm persuaders do not. These and many other dimensions of source credibility interact and affect the three fundamental dimensions of credibility—trust/sincerity, expertise, and dynamism/potency.

These elements of source credibility are not shared by all cultures. In cultures in which the *baksheesh* (bribe) is the order of the day, people actually are admired for being untrustworthy. The popularity of haggling over prices in bazaars is based on insincerity, not sincerity. So credibility has cultural differences, too.

THE AMERICAN VALUE SYSTEM

The myths and parables we have examined are actually fantasy forms of deep and enduring values held by most Americans. They are expressed in myths in order to simplify them. For example, Americans have a belief or value that all persons are to be treated equally and that in the eyes of the law, they are equal. This value has been debated for more than two centuries in the context of such issues as slavery, women's suffrage, civil rights, desegregation, and affirmative action. It is acted out or dramatized in the possibility of success myth. We see the myth portrayed in print and TV ads. For example, a recent print ad for the DuPont Chemical Company featured a man who was still able to play basketball even though he had lost both legs in Vietnam. This was thanks to DuPont, who sold the raw materials for making the artificial limbs that enable the man to succeed in the world of amateur sports (see Figure 9.5).

One of the early speech communication studies that explored American core values was conducted by Edward Steele and W. Charles Redding (1962). They looked at the communication used in several presidential election campaigns and tried to extract core and secondary values. Their work has been replicated numerous times since then with very similar outcomes, suggesting that these core American values have great durability and persistence. These values are frequently articulated by the media as the values that relate to various social issues (Kosicki, 2002). You will be able to see them if you look around. The following are descriptions of the core values observed by Steele and Redding and since verified by other communication researchers.

Puritan and Pioneer Morality

The **Puritan and pioneer morality** value is our tendency to cast the world into categories of right and wrong, good and evil, ethical and unethical, and so forth. Although we tend to think of this value as outdated, it has merely been reworded. Persons on the political right and left frequently make judgments based on it. The advocates and foes of marijuana laws and of legal abortion both call on moral values such as just/unjust, right/ wrong, and moral/immoral to make their cases. The injustice of terrorism, whether perpetrated against us or against others, is viewed as morally inexcusable, and the resulting loss of innocent lives

leads Americans and others to see it as having major moral dimensions. The decision by the Bush administration in 2004 not to fund new stem cell research was viewed by both sides as a morality issue. For those who favored the research, Bush's decision was bad because stem cell research might have provided cures for many diseases like diabetes and cancer. For those on the other side there was the good of not harming embryos that hypothetically could become living persons.

The Value of the Individual

This value ranks the rights and welfare of the individual above those of the government or other groups. It is encapsulated in many of our historical documents—the Declaration of Independence, the Constitution, the Emancipation Proclamation, and others. All politicians claim to be interested in the **value of the individual**, and our laws ensure and protect individual rights over all others. Further, each person has the right to succeed or fail on his or her own. Although no one is an island, no one is tied to the will of the majority either. In the world of advertising, most products are marketed with the individual in mind. Cosmetics, according to this value, are made "especially for you," and Burger King lets you "Have It Your Way." In politics and government the real power of a democracy lies within each individual. Most good causes target the individual recipient of aid and the individual donor as individuals who are "making a difference."

Achievement and Success

Achievement and success entails the accumulation of education, power, status, wealth, and property. During the anti–Vietnam War years, many young Americans rejected these values, favoring communal living and refusing to dress up for job interviews. Many of those same young people are now the upwardly mobile, achievement-oriented, and graying muppies (mature urban professionals). Many of these former renegades now evaluate others by the symbols or emblems of success they own— whether a BMW or Mercedes-Benz, a Rolex watch

For Bill Demby, the difference means getting another shot.

When Bill Demby was in Vietnam, he used to dream of coming home and playing a little basketball with the guys.

A dream that all but died when he lost both his legs to a Viet Cong rocket.

But then, a group of researchers discovered that a remarkable DuPont plastic could help make artificial limbs that were more resilient, more flexible, more like life itself.

Thanks to these efforts, Bill Demby is back. And some say, he hasn't lost a step.

At DuPont, we make the things that make a difference.

Better things for better living.

REG. U.S. PAT & TM OFF

FIGURE 9.5 This ad enhances DuPont's ethos by implying that the company is responsible for Bill Demby's "getting another shot" at an active life.

SOURCE: DuPont Company photograph. Used by permission of DuPont.

or Mont Blanc pen. Persuaders frequently appeal to our need for achievement or success. Most military recruitment advertisements and slogans promise that by starting a career in the Army, Navy, Air Force, Marines, or Coast Guard you will be able to climb the ladder to success faster. If you read the *Wall Street*

Journal, success and status will be yours. First impressions count, so be sure to "dress for success" by shopping at Nordstroms, and don't wear pierced jewelry to the interview. Self-help books and programs will help you to be an achiever and will contribute to your success. The achievement and success value, like the cultural myths, seems to ebb and flow with time. Thus, self-improvement will continue to be marketed even when the values of achievement and success seem most dormant.

Change and Progress

The **change and progress** value is typified by the belief that change of almost any kind will lead to progress and that progress is inherently good for us. This is the appeal of any product that is "new" or "new and improved." Product life cycle theory, which you may have studied in a marketing class, almost dictates that change and progress in the form of improvement must recur repeatedly to delay a decline of brand sales. From a legal point, the producer of a laundry product, for example, can claim that its product is "new and improved" merely by changing the color of the "beads of bleach" in it or by slightly altering the ratio of ingredients or offering a new pouring spout. General Electric once had as its slogan "At GE, Progress Is Our Most Important Product." The word *new* is one of the most powerful words in advertising. Indeed, many changes obviously have been beneficial, such as the downsizing of the American automobile and the increase in its fuel efficiency. And few would disagree on the value of the new generations of home and business computers, or digital audio and video, or many new medical technologies. The Internet has made an enormous quantity of information on any and every topic available to almost everyone as well as making communication with people all over the globe instantaneous. At the same time, certain products and brands have built-in obsolescence. The new and improved Whirlpool dryer may just have a new coating on its tumbler. But every year manufacturers bring out new models of their product or brands that really aren't changed that much. Nonetheless, the value of change and progress continues to be a powerful first premise in

many enthymemes we encounter. If you don't change and make progress, you are falling behind in life.

Ethical Equality

The **ethical equality** value reflects the belief that all persons ought to be treated equally. They should have an equal opportunity to get an education, to work and be paid a fair wage, to live where they choose, and to hold political office. But we all know that, although this value may be laudable, the reality is that not everyone is born equal, nor do they all have an equal opportunity for jobs, education, or decent housing. Nonetheless, since the nation's founding, through the abolition, women's suffrage, civil rights, and other movements, attempts to create a situation of equality have been a part of the American cultural landscape. The words from the Declaration of Independence, "All men are created equal," best illustrate the power of this value.

Effort and Optimism

The **effort and optimism** value expresses the belief that even the most unattainable goals can be reached if one just works hard enough and "keeps smilin'." The myths of the triumphant individual and the possibility of success are examples of these values in action. And in today's business world, it is important to be a "striver" or a "self-starter." Nuggets of folk wisdom such as "Every cloud must have a silver lining," "If at first you don't succeed, try, try again," "Keep on the sunny side," and "Lighten up" serve as cultural metaphors of the value we place on effort and optimism. And phrases such as "a hard worker" and "the eternal optimist" reflect how we much we believe in the value of effort and optimism. If you don't let the world get you down and keep plugging away, things will work out. This value motivates many of our life decisions.

Efficiency, Practicality, and Pragmatism

The **efficiency, practicality, and pragmatism** value is based on our need for solutions. The key question often asked of any piece of legislation is

"Will it work?" whether it be a new set of tax revisions, a new cabinet office such as the Office of Homeland Security, or new immigration statutes. This value extends to other parts of our lives, too. Years ago, my family was among the first purchasers of a microwave oven, which cost $400 then. Before making the purchase, we wanted to know whether a microwave oven would be energy efficient, practical, and handy, and not merely another fad. And of course, we now know that they are energy efficient, handy and practical, but now they are available for less than $100. On another issue, we want to be certain that an advanced education will lead to a rewarding job. We are fascinated by questions of efficiency—fuel efficiency in our cars, energy efficiency in our appliances, and efficiency of movement on the production line. And we go for practical solutions, whether it is the most efficient way to lose weight, to get in good shape, or to be able to buy one's first home. In other words, we value what is quick, workable, and practical.

Even though these values were cataloged more than 40 years ago, they still have a great deal of relevance. And the fact that they are held in high regard by liberals and conservatives speaks for their credibility and for the conviction that they are indeed "core" American values. Our culture is effective in instilling these values in nearly all its members; radicals, moderates, and reactionaries may believe in the same values, but they tend to apply them quite differently. The power of a social system or culture to train its members is immense—even though people do not often realize it, they react to the dictates deeply ingrained in them. Does this mean that values remain essentially static and cannot be changed? Not necessarily. It means only that they are so deeply ingrained in a culture that its members often forget how strong they are. They are probably processed in the peripheral channel of the ELM.

Access InfoTrac College Edition, and enter the words "American values" in the key word search engine, and examine a few of the many articles devoted to the topic. How closely do they resemble the Redding and Steele list of core values?

REVIEW AND CONCLUSION

By this time, you know that the world of the persuadee in a diverse and interactive information age is not a simple one. There are so many things to be aware of: the persuader's self-revelation in the language used and their style, the internal or process premises operating within each of us, and the interactive rules for content premises. In addition, societal and cultural predispositions for persuasion can and do act as premises in persuasive arguments. Persuaders instinctively appeal to values that rely on the societal training in the target audience. On separate levels, this training has an effect on each of us—in the cultural myths or images to which we respond, in the sets of values we consciously articulate. And in an evermore diverse world, both persuaders and receivers need to be aware that the cultural premises of today may not be the only way to see the world.

KEY TERMS

When you have finished reading this chapter, you should be able to identify, explain, and give an example of each of the following terms or concepts.

cultural patterns	the wisdom of the rustic	coming of a messiah	the value of challenge
cultural images and myths	possibility of success	presence of conspiracy	the myth of the eternal return
		paranoid style	

mob at the gates	woman's woman	image	change and progress
triumphant individual	image or charisma	Puritan and pioneer morality	ethical equality
the benevolent community	expertise	value of the individual	effort and optimism
rot at the top	trustworthiness	achievement and success	efficiency, practicality, and pragmatism
man's man	dynamism		
	charisma		

APPLICATION OF ETHICS

Dr. L. teaches a course in "Research Methods in Mass Communication" which is a difficult course for most communication majors, especially the quantitative topics like inferential statistics. A female student who is a member of a minority has been absent from classes frequently and has done poorly on all the tests. Dr. L. calls her in to discuss the problem and discovers that she is a single mother who is putting herself through school by holding down several part-time jobs. She is getting good grades in all her other communication courses and expects to graduate at the end of the semester. Furthermore, she has been promised an excellent job as an anchor newsperson and in all likelihood will never need to know statistics or research methods. The Affirmative Action Office has issued a memo stating that students who are members of a protected minority (including females) should be given special consideration and help. What should Dr. L. do? (1) Give the student a D- grade so she can graduate. (2) Give the student an Incomplete to be made up when the semester is over. (3) Give the student a failing grade. (4) Offer to give the student private tutoring in statistics—something Dr. L has not done before and is not doing for other students in a similar situation.

QUESTIONS FOR FURTHER THOUGHT

1. What are the three types of culturally or socially learned predispositions for persuasion? Give examples of each from your own experience.

2. How does a culture or society train its members? Give examples from your own experience.

3. How do you rank the core values mentioned in this chapter? How do you put them into practice? Are there other values in your value system not mentioned here? What are they? Are they restatements of the core values? If so, how? If not, how do they differ?

4. Considering today's headlines, is there a mob at the gates presently? Explain.

5. To what degree can you identify a benevolent community in your life? Explain.

6. In the popular Harrison Ford film *Patriot Games*, there clearly is rot at the top. At what critical moment does the "narrator" of the film discover the "rot"? What does he do about it?

7. Explain the ethos of the hosts of the various TV talk shows. How does each host's ethos differ from the others'—for example, does Jay Leno seem more or less sincere, expert, or dynamic than David Letterman?

8. How have the core values described by Steele and Redding operated on your campus? In your own life?

9. How have American values changed since September 11, 2001? What examples can you give?

10. The slogan "These Colors Don't Run" that appeared in many places following the events of 9/11 clearly articulate an American value. What is it?

 For online activities, go to the *Persuasion* book companion website at http://communication.wadsworth.com/larson11.

12

Becoming a Persuader

LEARNING GOALS

After reading this chapter, you should be able to:

1. Conduct an analysis of a hypothetical audience using demographics and identifying their needs.

2. Organize the same speech via the three formats of space, topic, and chronology.

3. Identify, explain, and give examples of stock issues used in considering a policy issue such as randomly assigned registration dates being debated on campus.

4. Give a speech using the motivated sequence format and exhibiting good delivery techniques and persuasive language.

5. Explain how you can improve your own credibility.

6. Identify various forms of proof statement in the mass media.

7. Explain the critical effects that the choice of channel can have on persuasion.

Thus far, we have focused on receiver skills: how to be a critical, responsible, and ethical consumer of persuasion. However, sometimes, we must become persuaders. Luckily, we can apply the knowledge we gained in our role as persuadee to our occasional role as persuader. We can use tactics of intensification/downplaying; we can mold our persuasion using process, content, cultural, and nonverbal premises; and we can apply our knowledge of what is ethical in persuasion.

As a persuader, you'll take your first steps in preparing your message by learning about your audience and shaping your message. Here, considerations such as patterns of organization, kinds of proof, and styling of messages will be important. Also, you must choose how to go about delivering your message, which includes choosing the channel as well as thinking about your voice and posture, making eye contact, and so on. Finally, you want to be aware of some common persuasive tactics. Throughout this entire process, you need to ask whether what you are doing is ethical in terms of the models presented by Richard Johannesen in Chapter 2. Sometimes, you need to ask questions about the lasting, larger issues in life. One such question is, "Is what I am being persuasive about likely to have a more negative or more positive effect on my listener's lives? For that matter, will it make for a better or worse world?" Being an ethical persuader means being part of a community in which your persuasion has a positive effect on relationships in that community. Your persuasion must not undermine the idea of community.

AUDIENCE ANALYSIS: KNOWING YOUR AUDIENCE

It is easy to assert that persuaders should know as much as possible about their audience, but it is not always so easy to prescribe specific ways you can get to know them. One of the best ways is to listen to them when they persuade, because they will likely use tactics that would be persuasive to them. For example, I often use narratives and examples to get you to take my advice. If you want to persuade me, fill your message with narratives and examples. I also look at my audience's patterns of processing information in terms of the elaboration likelihood model (ELM). I want to use the central information-processing route when that is appropriate, and I want to allow the audience to use the peripheral information-processing route when that is called for.

In other words, you will need to do some **audience analysis**, which is defined as learning as much as possible about your projected audience— their ages, their majors, the gender split in the

FIGURE 12.1 If you were preparing to speak in an informal situation such as this, how would you do your audience analysis?

audience, and many other things. Study audience members, observe them, listen to them, and analyze what they say and how they say it. When your parents try to persuade, how do they go about it? What kinds of evidence do they use? Some people, for example, are most easily persuaded when they think they are the ones who came up with the idea for change. It is best to give such persons several alternatives and let them make the choice. Then they "own" the idea or innovation. Others are most satisfied with a decision if they see that significant others have made or are making the same or similar decisions. Best-selling author Robert Cialdini (2001) calls this tool of influence "social proof," which means viewing a behavior or decision as correct "to the degree that we see others performing it" (p. 100).

But is it ethical for the persuader to use social proof to win the day? It depends on the issue, the costs, and the potential benefits of following the decision or action. It is far more important for us as persuadees (sensing that a persuader is using social proof to convince us) to ask ourselves whether we should decide or act simply because others have acted in a certain way. Sometimes the masses are wrong, and we need to forge a different path. Thus, the ethical issue reverts back to where it should be— with receivers of persuasion. It is certainly true that

persuaders *ought* to be ethical, but unfortunately that is not always the case. We need to be on guard and not be fooled by affinity appeals such that we follow the advice of persons who only seem to be like us. Recognizing ethical and unethical appeals aimed at us as persuadees also helps us to practice ethical persuasion when we are in the persuader's role.

To learn how important knowing your audience is, access InfoTrac College Edition, and type the words "social proof" in the subject search engine. Examine the items published in *Direct Marketing.* Then type in the words "audience analysis" in the key word search engine. Explore the many ways being used to analyze the invisible audience going to locations on the Web.

AUDIENCE DEMOGRAPHICS

When persuasion is aimed at larger audiences, persuaders can use demographics to analyze the audience. **Demographics** describes people in quantifiable terms of their shared attributes—their likes, dislikes, and habits, as well as age, gender, education, religious beliefs (if any), and income.

If you subscribe to *Outdoor Life, Field and Stream*, and *Sports Illustrated*, you likely differ from the person who subscribes to *The Atlantic Monthly, Horticulture, Organic Gardening*, and *Bon Appétit*. Both of you would be good bets for catalogs featuring outdoor clothing. Probably neither of you is interested in rock music or MTV. Your affiliations (church, fraternal, or community groups) are another demographic index.

Some marketing firms specialize in doing demographic research. Between their databases, census data, state government records such as driver's and fishing licenses, returned warranty cards, and many other sources, all of us have been identified demographically. What do you think about having all that information about you available to anybody wanting to sell you something? Is it ethical for the government, publishers, and others to sell that information?

Most of us don't do this kind of in-depth and elaborate analysis of a potential audience, but we can do a lot even with limited time and resources. For example, suppose you plan to make a presentation to the athletic board of your college or university. You want the board to ban smoking in the football stadium during home games. This will be a controversial proposal, and it could have unintended effects such as a campus-wide ban on smoking. You need to find out who the board members are, what they do for a living, and where they live. How have they voted or acted in the past? What kinds of past funding have they used? What kinds of alternatives have they allowed? Why? Most of that kind of information will be a part of the public record and easily found in their minutes, quotes in the student newspaper, and so forth. What demographic factors should you look at in preparing a formal persuasive presentation?

Audience factors that make a critical difference vary with the goal of your presentation. Age is important if you are discussing tax planning for retirement, but not if your topic is recycling. Gender is important for discussing screening for cervical cancer but not for a presentation about flu shots. Level of income, political affiliations, and many other factors may be more relevant in some situations than others. The board has both male and female students, faculty, athletes, administrators, and alumni on it; they vary in background, and one of them is the athletic director. Which of the following will you want to explore about your audience?

- *Average age.* Will it matter how many are over fifty or under eighteen? Probably. The older ones may see the proposal as just another "do-gooder" idea. The younger ones could see it as another infringement on student rights.

- *Income.* Will it matter if they are well-to-do or struggling to get by? Probably not, but smoking has become an expensive habit. So it could.

- *Gender.* The board is made up of both genders, so that will probably not be an important factor.

- *Religion.* This factor is one you can probably ignore. However, if your proposal was to have board approval for pregnancy counseling, it clearly would be important.

- *Family size.* Will it matter if your audience members have two or five children? Probably, because most parents discourage their children from smoking.

- *Political party.* In this case, political affiliation would have little bearing, unless the state has been aggressively pursuing no-smoking regulations.

- *Occupation.* Will the board members' occupations affect their willingness to consider the proposal? Probably. If the nonstudent board members are white-collar workers, they might know how smoking regulations are resented by some in the workplace. Some persons are well aware of the dangers of secondhand smoke, so knowing how many board members are nonsmokers will be important.

- *How many of them smoke or smoked at one time?* This will be a key factor. Smokers usually resent being told when and where they can indulge. Former smokers usually know how repulsive the smell and mess caused by smokers are and usually object to smoking in their presence.

B O X 12.1 Interactive Audience Analysis

We are all aware of the presence of email spam. Why do you think some spammers pick on you and others don't? How do they know to what you might respond? To get an idea of how detailed audience analysis has become in the interactive age, type the words "audience analysis" into the search engine at www.imediaconnection.com/consumer. How might you use sites like these when you need to do audience analysis?

How will you find out this information? Perhaps you could distribute a questionnaire designed to get other demographic information and include a question about their smoking and drinking habits. This will of course require that you allow enough time before the presentation for you to gather data. Do you think the athletic director will be concerned about loss of ticket and concession income if smokers boycott the games? After all, the stadium seats are often filled by townspeople and other adults who are more likely to be smokers.

Once you know the key demographic factors for your group/topic/context, the next stage is to explore them. The public relations people at your school can provide information about where board members live, and this can cue you as to their income and age. For example, some students live in fraternity or sorority houses while others live in dorms or apartments, and many live at home and have families of their own. Nonstudent members could live in town or commute from the suburbs. If the board has turned down past requests from students versus faculty versus administrators, you need to know why. Sometimes, merely talking to one or two typical members of a group before you attempt to persuade can be helpful in getting to know the audience. Any characteristics they share as a group can be useful in shaping your message for that audience. Would it be ethical for you to do demographic research for your presentation? Why or why not?

Determining Audience Needs

Some audience touchstones are emotional, some logical, some cultural, and some nonverbal. We can do some fairly sophisticated analysis of our target to determine **audience needs**. We might focus on the responsibility of the university to protect the health of students, faculty, and visitors to sell our idea. Or we could talk about the need of university decision makers to constantly keep up to date with social and environmental issues. Most of the "hot buttons" that help persuade others can be traced back to emotions, memories, and experiences that are common to large percentages of the population.

All audiences have some sets of shared experiences. Everyone remembers taking their first test to get a driver's license. Most of you remember your first visit to the campus where you now go to school and not knowing where the various buildings were located. Stored memories can be persuasive building blocks. What might be some of these stored experiences for the members of the governing board? Those who smoke or have smoked may remember their first cigarette. Former smokers will remember how difficult it was to finally quit. Some board members may remember not being particularly bothered by smoking when outdoors. Others will recall moving to a different seat to avoid smokers. The next time you need to persuade someone, try to list the experiences he or she likely has had and determine whether any can be tied into your message.

Tony Schwartz (1973) identified what he called the "task-oriented" approach to persuading, which is also useful for audience analysis. To use it, ask yourself whether your goal fits with the athletic board's authority to enact your proposal. Try to find out the state of mind of your audience—the board, the sales force, or the job interviewer. What is their likely mood? Will they be relaxed? Will they have doubts? Take these things into account, and design your message accordingly.

Once you know something about your target group and how its members feel about your topic, you can shape the message. People are more likely to recall messages that are well organized, so you need to consider the various forms of organization available to you.

FORMS OF ORGANIZATION

There are a number of ways to organize messages to make sure they are memorable and persuasive. We will look at five such formats here: (1) the **topic format**, (2) the **space format**, (3) the **chronological format**, (4) the **stock-issues format**, and (5) the **motivated sequence format**. For the first three of these formats, we will use the following example: A student group on my campus wanted to bring a highly successful filmmaker (a former student) back to school as a guest speaker to discuss the challenges of film production. The speaker was willing to donate his honorarium to the sponsoring student group to be used for field trips, travel to national conferences, and funding for a career day.

Organization by Topic

Organizing by topic is most useful when the message you want to convey covers several topics or issues. Here is a list of topics the student group might present in the filmmaker example:

- His fame and success as a reason to bring him to campus
- The kind of role model he would provide
- The special opportunity to preview his latest film
- The degree to which he is in demand on the speaking circuit
- His generosity in donating his fee to the student group in the department
- The other benefits to be derived from his presence on campus: publicity for the school,

the added programming made possible by his donation, and the career counseling he might be able to give to aspiring student filmmakers

By presenting these topics with supporting evidence, you give the student government a variety of good reasons to fund the speaker. The topic format is a good choice when presenting specific reasons for some suggested action.

Organization by Space

Organizing by space is a good choice when you want to compare your topic to some larger picture. In the filmmaker example, you might compare the relative cost of the desired speaker to that of speakers invited by other groups. The filmmaker's fee might be only a quarter of that asked by another student group for a less well-known speaker. Further, his fee might represent only 5 percent of the total guest speaker budget for the semester. And your student group may be only one of more than 20 similar groups in the university, so the fee is not out of line. In the spatial format, you might draw several pie graphs. In one, you could visually depict your speaker's fee as one-twentieth of the pie and label the remainder "Other Speaker Fees." Another graph might show your five percent share as only a fraction of the funds allocated to other student groups. In all these examples, you are using space as an organizing principle.

Organization by Chronology

Sometimes, the essential message in persuasive communication is best relayed by taking the audience through the issues in historical sequence or organizing by chronology. You might relate the filmmaker's career as follows:

1. In 1975, he became a major in our department and took his first media classes there.

2. Two years later, he transferred to the USC film school. But he still values the basics of filmmaking he learned while he was with us.

3. He made his first picture as an independent writer/producer a year later.

4. It was released the next June, and as a minor summer hit, it recaptured the initial investment plus a small profit.

5. Later that year, the film got several "honorable mentions" at film festivals, and he then signed a contract to make pictures for one of the largest film studios.

6. In the next few years, he turned out several moneymakers and prize winners.

7. Then, in 1982, he made his first blockbuster, *and* went on to win the Oscar for directing.

8. He is now one of the best-known writer/producers in Hollywood.

As a result of these facts, the committee backed the proposal and provided funding.

Organization by Stock Issues

The **stock-issues** organizational format is most useful for persuaders who are proposing a change in policy. The name "stock issues" refers to the fact that there are three universal (stock) issues that must be addressed when major policy changes are considered. They are sort of like the stock characters in melodrama: the villain, the hero, the heroine, the hero's helper, and so on. Any time there is a policy change under consideration the stock issues will be discussed. These stock issues are the **need for change**, a **plan to solve the need**, and your proof statements showing that the **plan meets the need** or removes the problem(s) you have raised and recognized. We frequently see stock issues used as content premises in the world of politics and business, and in other policy-making forums as well.

As a persuader attempting to bring about a change in policy, you need to begin by demonstrating a strong need for altering the status quo. You have the **burden of proof**. (As a receiver, you should also be aware of the stock issues. Any time you are the target of persuasion focused on policy change, identify which side of the debate is suggesting change. That will tell you who has the burden of proof.) Establish the need for change by citing symptoms of the problem. You should

research specific instances that demonstrate to the audience that they are suffering something, are losing something, or are in danger of losing it. In terms of the FUD model mentioned in Chapter 4, you need to create fear, uncertainty, and/or doubt. Tie the symptoms to a cause that, if removed and replaced, will solve the problem. For instance, you might state that there is a need to protect fans at university athletic events from the unpleasantness and health hazards of secondhand smoke. Next present a reasonable alternative to the status quo—the plan or the new policy. You are suggesting a ban on cigarette smoking within all the campus stadiums. Finally, show how that "plan meets need." One way to do this is to show that the plan has been successful in other places. Perhaps a no-smoking policy has been adopted at a neighboring venue with great success. Another way is to point to relevant historical events that prove your point, such as the repeal of Prohibition and the resulting positive effects on the economy in the Great Depression. This is arguing from precedent. Still another way is to use expert testimony to the effect that the plan for change has a reasonable chance of succeeding.

At each stage in the stock-issues organization, expect a rebuttal. In some cases, it will be openly stated, as in a policy debate within your student government. If you are giving a speech covering all three stock issues—need, plan, and plan meets need—anticipate such rebuttals and be ready to counter them. You might also short-circuit anticipated rebuttals by presenting a two-sided message stating the anticipated rebuttals and answering them then and there, depriving the opposition of an opportunity to impress the audience with its rebuttal.

Organization by the Motivated Sequence

Another organizational pattern, one that resembles the stock-issues approach, is the motivated sequence format, suggested by communication scholars Alan Monroe, Douglas Ehninger, and Bruce Gronbeck (1982). This format uses five steps to get persuadees to attend to the message, to feel a need to follow the persuader's advice, and, most importantly, to take action related to the advice. The motivated sequence is a good pattern to use in sales, recruitment, politics, and many other contexts.

The first step—the attention step—aims at capturing the attention of the audience. You could begin your message with a question, a startling statistic, or a fear appeal. Or you could use a quotation, a joke, or an anecdote—a brief incident or cliché that makes the point. A good example of the anecdote relates to the umpire who was asked if he called strikes and balls the way he saw them or the way they were. He responded, "They ain't nothing until I calls 'em." Other approaches are to make an important announcement in the first few moments of the message, begin with a narrative or story, or use a visual aid. The audience may process the attention gaining emotionally or in the peripheral channel of the ELM, but you want listeners to process more of your claims centrally.

In the second step of the motivated sequence, you try to convince the audience that they are losing something, are about to lose something, or could be gaining something but aren't. This is the need step (as in the stock issues approach), and it can be tied to the attention-getter.

Steps 3 and 4 are the visualization and satisfaction steps. Here you give examples, data, testimony, or some other form of proof to induce the audience to visualize what life will be like for them if they follow your advice—for instance, if they invest part of their student loan in student housing to build up a nest egg for the future. Or you might take the opposite tack pointing out what life will be like if they don't invest in the rooming house and instead graduate with the burden of student loans at government imposed high rates of interest. And they will graduate without the experience of having been in business for themselves, and, most importantly, without a nest egg to build their future on. Following this visualization step, you can then offer some way to satisfy the positive need or to avoid some negative consequences— for example, showing them how easy getting a student loan is and how little is needed for a down payment on income property.

Finally, the persuader needs to give a definite, specific, and realistic action step. It probably will do little to no good to ask audience members to alter their attitudes on the topic. Asking for change is different from providing good reasons for changing an attitude. And attitudes are fickle, and it is hard to know whether an audience has really changed. It is far better to give the audience specific things to do, such as flossing to avoid tooth decay, saving energy by turning down the thermostat, making real estate a wise investment, graduating with no debt and a handsome nest egg, or earning good grades. In one research study, people given a booklet with specific action steps to cut electricity consumption registered less use of electricity on their meters in the following two weeks than did those not given the specific action steps (Cantola, Syme, and Campbell, 1985). If you want the audience to write to their elected representative, it is a good idea to have a petition on hand that members can sign or to announce the phone number and email address of the legislator's local office and perhaps a sample email or note. After all, phoning or emailing is much easier than writing a letter, especially if you have to start by finding an address.

A related model for making a persuasive appeal is called the **AIDA** approach—short for attention, interest, desire, action. In this model, as in the motivated sequence, the first step is to capture the audience's attention using any of the tactics cited earlier. In the second step, the persuader's goal is to heighten the audience's interest in his or her topic or proposal. This might be done using a satisfaction or a visualization process, as in the motivated sequence. Or the persuader might tell how many persons have already tried the product or procedure and found it to be useful, or point out unforeseen problems with continuing the present practice.

Once attention and interest have been gained, the next task is to create a desire in persuadees to purchase the product or service, vote for the candidate, or follow the advice. In product-related persuasion, this usually is done by providing some product benefit or product promise. For example, Chrysler advertised built-in air bags for the front seat and side doors. The obvious benefit of this feature was that it could save lives in an accident. In its action step, Chrysler asked the customer to go to the nearest Chrysler dealer to learn more about the air bag and to take a test drive.

Rank's Desire-Stimulating Model

Hugh Rank (1982), whose intensify/downplay model was introduced in Chapter 1, has offered a simple four-part model for creating desire. His techniques are not a method of organizing a presentation. Instead, his techniques and examples relate to product promotion, but they can be used in other kinds of persuasion and in all of the forms of organization discussed in the preceding section. Rank says that persuaders can use four kinds of desire-stimulating tactics with this model (see Figure 12.2). First, they can promise the audience's security or protection by demonstrating that their advice will allow the audience to **keep a good** they already have but might be in danger of losing. He calls the opposite **getting a good**. Politicians frequently point out all the funding they have brought to their districts and then claim that their reelection will mean keeping this good. The other approach to motivating persons via various kinds of "good" is to point out that, although they are not going to lose something they already have, they are not taking advantage of an available good. It might be an inexpensive online account for buying and selling stocks and mutual funds or something as simple as Jell-O's no-bake cheesecake. If audience members have not tried the new good, telling them about it might motivate them to acquire it.

A third desire-stimulating tactic relates to **avoiding a bad** or preventing an uncomfortable symptoms or feelings. Persuaders promise that by following their advice people can either avoid a bad, get rid of a bad, or experience relief from it. A fourth approach is **getting rid of a bad**. For example, you probably would consider reducing credit card debt a good thing to do. Rank called these approaches the "prevention" and "relief" appeals. Advertisers often promise that their

To keep a "good" (protection)	To get rid of a "bad" (relief)
To get a "good" (acquisition)	To avoid a "bad" (prevention)

FIGURE 12.2 Rank's model for ways to create desire in audiences.

products will prevent the embarrassments of bad breath, body odor, or dandruff or will provide relief from headaches, heartburn, flyaway hair, or acne. Such "scare and sell" approaches can also be used in non-product persuasion. For example, a persuader can promise that by passing the school bond referendum we can "avoid" losing athletic and music programs and other extracurricular activities. More recently, school districts have been reassuring students and parents that their school buildings are safe because of the presence of security devices and personnel. The idea is that these precautions will prevent killings such as occurred in Littleton, Colorado, in 1999 and demonstrate that the school board is responsible and credible.

FORMS OF PROOF

People want good reasons for changing their attitudes, beliefs, and decisions. The proofs required for taking action steps, even good ones, are even more demanding. Let's look at the forms of proof available to persuaders and discuss how you can use them to prompt audiences to change attitudes or take action.

Statistical Evidence

Sometimes the most effective proof or support is **statistical evidence**. For instance, an important goal of some car buyers is to get good gas mileage. In this case, EPA data will probably persuade them to choose a car model more effectively than will a salesperson's reassurances that the car is a real gas saver. Statistics persuade best when they are simple and easy to understand. When you decide to use statistics, make them clear, and provide a reference point for the numbers. For instance, if you are warning persuaders about the severity of the national debt, make it real to them. Tell them that interest on the debt amounts to $1800 per year for every man, woman, and child in the country and that the average family has to pay taxes from January 1 until March 15 to work off its share of the interest on the debt.

Narratives and Anecdotes

Earlier, we noted the power of drama, stories, and jokes. **Narratives** make examples come alive and make them easy to recall and relate to. The story of a person rising from rags to riches probably persuades more people than any set of statistics does. An effective narrative I use tells about the success of the Cabela family and its widely distributed outdoors catalog and several retail outlets. Mr. Cabela began in the 1950s by purchasing hand-tied trout flies from Japan at a fraction of a penny each. He advertised them in newspapers in trout country using an initial offer of "Five Hand-Tied Trout Flies— Only $.25!!! Free Shipping and Handling," and he got some orders. But the venture didn't really take off until he changed his ad to read, "Five Hand-tied Trout Flies—Absolutely Free!!! Shipping and Handling—Only $.25." The example persuaded several advertising clients to include the word "Free!!" in their ads. Earlier we gave an example of an anecdote with the umpire.

To discover the power of the narrative and statistical evidence, access InfoTrac College Edition, and type the word "persuasion" in the search engine. Select the persuasion/rhetoric periodicals option, and find the article titled "Persuasive Effects of Story and Statistical Evidence." There you will find the details of an interesting research study on the topic implied by the title.

Testimony

We usually suspect people who attempt to persuade us using only their own feelings or opinions. This is why the testimony of another person is valuable. Of course expert testimony is the best kind, but even unqualified testimony has influence. Testimonials act as a kind of social proof, to use Cialdini's term.

Visual Evidence

Walk into a department store where a salesperson or a videotape is demonstrating a food processor or a pasta machine, and you will see the power of visual evidence. The many television offers for various cooking gadgets also testify to the power of the demonstration. Ron Popeil has made millions of dollars using the technique, beginning with his Pocket Fisherman and continuing with his Ronco glass and bottle cutter and various other unlikely kitchen devices. Much of the information offered in the demonstration is processed in the peripheral channel of the ELM. Visual persuasion also can be used—and misused—in political news coverage and advertising (Simons, 2001). You probably have presentational skills that can use computerized visual aids like PowerPoint.

Of course, actual demonstrations of products are not always feasible, but persuaders can develop various kinds of visual evidence (such as graphs or charts) to help the audience understand the problem. Visuals should be large enough that everyone can see them. They should also be simple, because complex charts will only confuse the audience. For example, a student promoting a trip to Jamaica sponsored by the student association effectively used travel posters, large pictures of local cuisine, easily seen cutouts of sandy beaches, and other images of tropical life to motivate her audience.

Keep visual evidence unobtrusive. For instance, it may be better to use drawings of how to fend off an attacking dog than to bring your dog to class and have it pretend to attack you while you demonstrate how to fend it off. Plan to use graphs, charts, and informational handouts in your presentation, but hold the handouts until the end or they will get all of the audience's attention.

You will find three very interesting articles about the use of visual evidence by accessing InfoTrac College Edition and typing "persuasion" in the search engine. Select the persuasion/rhetoric periodicals option, and explore the articles you find there, as well as related subjects. Then enter the words "visual evidence" in the key word search engine. There you will find some fascinating articles on the uses and power of visual evidence.

Comparison and Contrast

Sometimes it is difficult to put problems in perspective. People tend to see issues from single viewpoints and judge them inaccurately. For instance, how big is the problem of disposing of your old cell phone batteries in landfills? How does it compare with the problem of the disposal of auto or flashlight batteries? It is a little hard to know, so persuaders should provide something with which to compare or contrast their point about cell phone battery disposal, like comparing the quantity of pollution from one discarded cell phone battery compared with one discarded flashlight battery. As another example, it doesn't help the audience much to know that OPEC decided to increase crude oil production by 550,000 barrels per day. It will be more meaningful to mention that this is an increase of 20 percent over previous production levels. Or tell your audience that the increased production will reduce the price of a gallon of gas by as much as 25¢—that will mean even more to them than the number of barrels of oil. Or compare the gas mileage of the new gasoline/electric-powered hybrids with that of other fuel-efficient car models.

BUILDING YOUR CREDIBILITY

All the evidence in the world, organized perfectly and delivered well, will not persuade if listeners do not trust the persuader. In matters such as persuading the boss to give us a raise, **credibility** is a key factor. What makes some people credible and others not? How can we build our own credibility before and during persuasion?

In Chapter 1 and elsewhere, we discussed the idea of credibility using Aristotle's ideas about the reputation of the speaker, the speaker's delivery during the speech, and the audience's response to the speaker's image. In more modern times, ethos or credibility has translated into several dimensions. We roughly equate reputation with the known expertise of the speaker. For example, when in research studies an identical speech is attributed to experts in some cases and to novices in others, the "expert's" speech is always rated as more persuasive than the "novice's." Effective delivery is related to sincerity, dynamism, and charisma. We don't believe speakers who cannot maintain eye contact, and tall speakers have more persuasive potential than do short ones. Further, speakers with an animated delivery persuade more effectively than do speakers who are frozen at the podium. Exciting language usually helps make the speech more credible, and a well-groomed speaker is more credible than an unkempt one. Most of these points seem obvious, yet they are overlooked daily by sales reps, politicians, spouses, teachers, students, and parents. Here are some examples from everyday life in which the elements of credibility can be used.

Trust

We trust people for many reasons. We trust them because they have been trustworthy in the past, because they have made direct eye contact, and because they have a calm voice. We also try to give off **trust** cues. We look at our persuadees directly; we try to sound sincere; we remind our audience of our past record for trust; and we refer to times when it would have been easy to break that trust. You might, for example, remind your boss of the many times when she was out of town and you could have slacked off but didn't. Or you might remind your parents of the many opportunities you had to party but studied instead. All these devices help build credibility.

Expertise

How do we know whether someone is a true expert on something? Generally, we look for **expertise** in past success at a task. If a person was a good treasurer for the fraternity or sorority, he or she will probably be a good treasurer for the student government. You can also signal expertise by being well prepared and by demonstrating knowledge about the topic. Being willing to engage in Q and A sessions when you have finished speaking communicates expertise. Even if you do not have direct expertise on a given topic, you can "borrow" it by referring to known experts in your presentation. It is always useful and ethical to refer to your sources' background so receivers can judge the credibility of their testimony.

Dynamism

Dynamism is an elusive quality. It is sometimes related to physical appearance, in that attractive people tend to hold attention better than less attractive persons. Attractiveness or charisma probably cannot be developed much. However, many people who aren't particularly attractive are nonetheless persuasive and dynamic. Dynamic speakers seem to take up a lot of psychic space—they have stage presence. You can project a dynamic image in several ways. One is to speak with authority—project your voice, maintain appropriate volume, and choose words that indicate certainty. Try speaking a little more rapidly than you do in normal conversations. Good posture and good grooming also signal dynamism, as do appropriate gestures, facial expressions, and eye contact.

WORDING YOUR MESSAGE

Stylistic speeches and exciting language choices persuade better than dull speeches. How do persuaders develop style in their presentations? What kinds of factors make some speeches, advertisements, or other persuasion memorable while other presentations are quickly forgotten or even ignored?

Varied Vocabulary

Most of us need to improve our vocabularies. You should try to rewrite your speeches using word variety to make them livelier, flashier, more dramatic, or more humorous. It helps to develop an interest in puns and other wordplay, as they can help you get the attention and earn the goodwill of your audience. Study the eloquence of great speakers from the past. Pay attention to the language used in government news releases, by politicians, and in advertisements. Try to learn a new word a day and use the thesaurus feature on your computer.

Figures of Speech, Alliteration, and Assonance

Enhance your style by using appropriate **figures of speech** at the right time. We discussed several in Chapters 5 and 6. Metaphors and similes help your audience visualize a point. The audience ties the information to the metaphorical structure and then remembers the information better as a result. Alliteration—the repetition of consonant sounds—and assonance—the repetition of vowel sounds—also enliven style. Both create a kind of internal rhythm in the message, which makes it more lively and memorable. We see both alliteration and assonance in "A portable phone system? Gee! No, GTE." Both devices help improve your style.

Vivid Language

Choose **vivid language** to catch your audience's interest. Although vividness can be overdone, it is more frequently overlooked in favor of dull and uninteresting language. Which of the following is more vivid?

> I'm offended by your representation of lutefisk. It is not rubbery!

Lutefisk may be "a rubbery and repulsive ethnic dish" to the socially deprived, but to the properly initiated, it is the nearest thing to ambrosia this earth has ever produced.

Vivid and colorful language helps make a persuasive presentation memorable and effective. Developing your vocabulary arms you with more vivid and persuasive language. Familiarize yourself with famous quotations, which you can find by a subject search on any Internet search engine. Just enter the words "famous quotations" and you will find what you're looking for. There are also websites dedicated to listing quotations by category.

Concise Language

Go over your presentation and pretend you are paying 50 cents per word to send it by telegraph. Then see how much excess baggage you can cut. You can come up with more **concise language** that way. Straightforward statements are usually most effective. Make your major point as a concise assertion or frame it in a provoking question. Then follow up with elaboration. If you try to say everything in the opening sentence, you will confuse your audience. The use of concise language also will help build your credibility and will improve the organization of your presentation.

Parallel Structure

Parallel structure uses similar or even identical wording or sentence structure to make a presentation memorable. For example, in a speech to the American Legion, former president Bill Clinton once said, "I am not the only American whose life has been made better by your continuing service here at home. From baseball to Boy Scouts; from keeping veterans hospitals open to keeping kids off drugs; from addressing homelessness to preventing child abuse to instilling a deep sense of patriotism

into still another generation of Americans, a grateful nation owes you a debt of gratitude." His repeated use of the "from...to..." format provides parallel structure and symmetry in the speech. The idea behind parallel structure is to build audience expectations. For example Cicero once said, "Ask not what your country can do for you: rather ask what you can do for your country." President John Kennedy used almost exactly the same words in his inaugural speech in 1960.

Imagery

Imagery appeals to our senses. Perhaps you can't bring the smell, taste, touch, sight, or sound of something to the audience, but you can use words that conjure up sensuous memories. It might be of a "tall, cool glass of chilled beer dripping with beads of perspiration" or the "fragrant smell of Mom's pot roast, ready to fall apart, with its juices making a savory gravy that starts your mouth watering." A famous salesman once said "Don't try to sell the steak; sell the sizzle." Think about the sensory experiences your audience has had that you can evoke. A good way to develop this skill is to take a given product and try to restate its appeals in terms of the various senses. For instance, Campbell's soups are "Mmm, Mmm, Good." How might they be described using the other senses?

Humor

The use of **humor** in persuasion is an obvious stylistic asset if handled properly, and can build credibility as well. But a word of warning is necessary here: If a persuader uses humor that is inappropriate, in bad taste, or just plain unfunny, it will likely backfire. If you are going to use humor in your persuasion, test it out with friends and relatives. How can you develop humorous examples, comparisons, anecdotes, and stories? People who regularly engage in public speaking usually have a ready supply of humorous material with which to embellish their speeches. They develop the humorous aspects as they work up other materials for their speeches. Humor sometimes relies on the breaking

FIGURE 12.3 The trapeze artists seen in the cartoon face broken expectation, which accounts for the humor in the cartoon, together with the surprised looks on their faces.
SOURCE: Used with permission of Doug Walker.

of expectations as can be seen in Figure 12.3. If you can never remember a story or joke, keep a file of stories or jokes or just punch lines. When you need the material, the file will trigger your memory. Late night television can provide you with humorous examples, as can your daily newspaper, *Reader's Digest*, and friends who frequently tell jokes. Don't forget the Internet. Just enter your subject and the word "humor," and have some fun while building a successful and entertaining presentation. You can also use visual humor such as cartoons, perhaps by using PowerPoint.

DELIVERING YOUR MESSAGE

Usually, we think of delivery as relating just to the source or speaker. But other factors can affect the delivery of your message, including the channel and the means of audience involvement. Persuaders often overlook these. In the following section, we will look at all these factors.

The Persuader

Among the factors that persuaders adjust before and during delivery are their posture, eye contact, body movement and gesture, articulation, dress, grooming, and vocal quality. Other factors under the speaker's control are the use of visual aids and other nonverbal cues. Some persuaders are so nervous that they cannot stop pacing back and forth. And when they do stop, they stand ramrod stiff, looking

as if they might freeze into statues. Other speakers are so relaxed that they seem uninterested in their own messages. They slouch over the podium or slide down into their chairs during a meeting. What does the posture of the speaker in Figure 12.4 suggest?

Clearly, posture can signal the audience that you are either nervous or too relaxed. Observe persuaders in differing contexts—interviews, speeches, arguments—and you will see that the effective ones avoid both extremes. The ideal posture lies somewhere in between. You should be alert and erect, and your shoulders should not tense or slump. Your posture should communicate confidence.

You will be more believable if you maintain eye contact with your audience. You don't need to look at everyone individually (unless you are speaking to only one person). Instead, look at various areas in the room. Politicians look directly into the TV camera and so seem to make eye contact with each viewer. In meetings, establish eye contact with as many participants as possible.

Body movement and gestures liven up a speech, as long as they don't distract. Using gestures during a speech keeps audience attention. However, it is a mistake to over-rehearse gestures, body movements, and facial expressions. These nonverbal elements in delivery must appear natural, not staged, to have a positive effect. We all use gestures every day without thinking about them. Let your natural impulses guide you in your use of gestures in formal and interpersonal exchanges. Nothing can add more to your message than a

FIGURE 12.4 Posture is important in giving a persuasive message. Is this speaker's posture appropriate for the formal situation seen here?

natural gesture, movement, or facial expression (Scheflen, 1964).

Articulation and vocal quality also affect your delivery. Everyone has heard people who pronounce words incorrectly; as a result, the audience focuses on the error and not on the message. Successful persuaders work on articulation, pronunciation, and vocal quality. Listening to yourself on tape will help you pinpoint your mistakes and focus on your vocal quality. Some persons, especially females, think that a breathy or "thin" voice makes them sound sexier, but just the opposite is true. If you are interested in persuading others, spend some time working on your voice and your articulation.

The Channel

Choosing the correct channel for sending your message is another key element in delivery. In one rural political campaign for the U.S. House of Representatives on which I worked, the candidates put most of their money into billboard space—which was rather surprising in this media age. In this case, however, the candidate's district was large, stretching nearly half the length of the state, and no single TV network reached all of it. Using

TV would have meant having to pay a triple load to get a single message across. But because the district was so large, all residents had to drive to shop, do business, socialize, worship, and farm. Thus, the billboard was the one channel that could touch nearly all voters in the district.

Recent presidents have returned to using radio for regular weekly persuasive talks. Why is radio such an appropriate channel for political persuasion? It is estimated that Americans listen to the radio an average of four hours a day, and more than half listen at work, especially females (Russell & Lane, 1999). People also listen to the radio while they are doing something else—driving, reading, commuting, exercising, and so on. By choosing the relatively inexpensive medium of daytime radio, politicians can reach people they otherwise might not, and at a reasonable price. Cable television has some of the same advantages of reach and low cost.

On a more personal level, ask yourself what is the best way to inform your boss that you will look for another job if you don't get a raise or promotion. Perhaps tapping the grapevine might be best, or sending a straightforward memo, or asking her to be a reference so she will not get an

---

B O X 12.2   **Honoring Diversity in Public Speaking**

Lenora Billings-Harris is an internationally known public speaker working on diversity issues with Fortune 500 companies, and she offers the following advice for public speakers wanting to be diversity conscious. First, select your language carefully. One ill-chosen word can undo you in an instant. For example, saying "Hey guys..." in a mixed gender group can offend some. Pointing to your "flip chart" can offend any Filipinos in the audience—refer to your easel instead. Research your audience first—who will be there? Be careful about using humor even if it is self-deprecating. Whenever possible use people's names, especially during question and answer sessions; and don't refer to someone as "the tall guy in the back." If you do refer to ethnicity make sure that you've got the right word. Some Latinos resent being referred to as "Hispanic" since that term groups together persons from Cuba, Mexico, Latin and South America, and Puerto Rico. (The word was invented by the U.S. Census Bureau more than 35 years ago to categorize people who spoke only Spanish.) One way around this potential trap is to use the words "Americans of (blank) heritage." The same goes for the word "Oriental," which refers to rugs, a certain cusine, and certain styles of furniture. When speaking of people, use the adjective "Asian." If a member of the audience uses a potentially insensitive word, don't call attention to it in public unless it is truly offensive; instead talk to the person privately after the presentation. If the word is truly offensive, point that out by saying something like, "Most persons consider that usage offensive and using it reduces your credibility." Billings-Harris notes some potentially offensive usages and offers acceptable alternatives. Use "outcasts" instead of "black sheep." Refer to occupations in nongendered ways—"postal workers" not "postmen." Can you think of other examples of embracing diversity in your public speaking? For further study, go to @www.sideroad.com/PublicSpeaking/politicalcorrectness, and explore not only the work of Billings-Harris but the many interesting links on public speaking.

---

out-of-the-blue inquiry about you from another firm. In general, start by listing all the potential channels that could be used to send your message. Then try to match them with your audience. If your audience uses a particular channel over others, then that is probably a good one to use.

Sometimes, persuaders encourage audience participation, which can increase audience energy and activity. Get your audience involved by asking direct questions and addressing people by name. Or leave a sentence incomplete and let listeners finish it. One speaker got audience involvement right away by asking everyone to stand up before he even began his speech. He then asked them to become aware of the muscles they were using in their feet, ankles, calves, and thighs at that moment and tied this awareness to his topic—the need to develop communication awareness on the job. One word of caution: Don't distribute any printed material until the end of the speech. Audiences start reading right away, and you will lose them.

COMMON TACTICS OF PERSUASION

There are some persuasive tactics that are used frequently and even are emphasized in public speaking and sales short courses. Let's consider some of the more common ones.

The Foot in the Door or Door in the Face

Robert Cialdini (2001) describes several persuasive tactics, including the foot-in-the-door and the door-in-the face techniques. The **foot-in-the-door** technique relies on getting a potential customer, joiner, donor, or convert to make a small initial commitment that starts what will become a long-term relationship resulting in ever larger sales, contributions, and commitments. To illustrate, some time ago I signed a protest petition from the Citizens' Utility Board (CUB), which promised to use the petition to prevent price increases by Illinois utilities—Commonwealth Edison, Ameritech phone services, and the gas company, for example. Soon after, I received a newsletter explaining that CUB had stopped one of the utilities from instituting a 15 percent price increase. But the battle was not over, because the utility was appealing. Could I donate $50, $25, or even $10 to help carry on the fight. I donated $10. Next, a letter from CUB informed me of another victory, but warned that the other utilities were suing CUB, and asked that I become a full-fledged dues-paying member of the organization for only $25. My signature on the petition was merely a foot in the door, and I continue to receive requests for donations.

In the retail field, this technique might mean getting a prospective retailer to agree to carry one item in a product line. That commitment becomes the foot in the door to the retailer's finally agreeing to carry the entire product line. As Cialdini puts it, "You can use small commitments to manipulate a person's self-image; you can turn citizens into 'public servants,' prospects into 'customers,' prisoners into 'collaborators'" (p. 67). Cialdini relates how the same technique is used by the highly successful Amway Corporation. Staff members are asked to set specific sales goals and then write them down: "There is something magical about writing things down. So set a goal and write it down. When you reach that goal, set another and write that down. You'll be off and running" (p. 71). The written commitment somehow translates into motivation and action.

The **door-in-the-face** tactic is what a persuader uses when turned down on a request for a significant commitment, and then settles for an initial small commitment or engages in what Cialdini calls the **rejection-then-retreat** strategy. In other words, if a salesperson tries to get the prospect to go for the top-of-the-line or "loaded" version of the brand but is rejected, he or she can always retreat by offering a stripped-down version of the brand. Cialdini attributes the effectiveness of this strategy to feelings of responsibility and satisfaction on the part of customers, joiners, or donors. By agreeing to the lower commitment, they can feel as if they are in control of the

situation and have "dictated" the deal. This satisfaction makes them happier with their decisions. A related persuasive approach is to "sell up" after retreating to a position of concession. Thus, once you've signed the contract to buy the new car, a good salesperson will offer you the extras—the undercoating and soundproofing, the extended warranty, the upholstery fabric protection, and so on.

Others have suggested similar tactics using somewhat different terms. The following are some tactics suggested by Drs. William Howell and Ernest Bormann (1988). They may overlap with some of the other techniques discussed previously. Examine your world of persuasion for examples of these tactics in action.

The Yes-Yes Technique

A common tactic in sales and other persuasive appeals is called **yes-yes**. The source attempts to get the target group or person to respond positively to several parts of the appeal, withholding the key request until last. Having agreed to most parts of the appeal, the persuadee is likely to say yes to the key and final request. For example, suppose you are trying to sell a lawn service. You might ask the homeowner, "You would like to have a beautiful lawn, wouldn't you?" The answer is going to be yes. Then you ask, "And you'd like to get rid of the weeds?" Another yes is likely. "And wouldn't it be nice if these things could be effort free?" A yes answer is likely again. Now that the homeowner has accepted all your points in favor of the service, it is nearly impossible to respond with a no to "Then you'll want to sign up for our lawn service, won't you?" By accepting the yes pattern, the buyer accedes to your final request.

The same technique is useful in a meeting in which a persuader gets the participants to agree to all but the final point in favor of, say, a change in work schedules. They agree that flexibility is good, that more free time for workers is good, and so on. They are then likely to agree that the change is a good one.

The Tactic of Asking Not "If" but "Which"

It is easier to make a choice between two alternatives than from among many. This is the strategy behind the **"don't ask if, ask which"** persuasive tactic. I learned as a parent of young children that the worst thing to ask on Saturday mornings was, "What would you like Dad to make for breakfast today?" It was better to say, "Which would you like for breakfast today—Dad's blueberry pancakes or Dad's blueberry coffee-cake?" The same thing applies in persuasion. Don't ask your audience to choose from too many options; ask them to choose from only a few or only two—"Would you rather have us undercoat your new car, or do you want to take it elsewhere?" or "Would you rather meet on your promotion this week or next?" or "Do you want guns or butter?" Although this tactic can be manipulative, and hence can be used unethically, it has the distinct advantage and value of forcing some decision or action when buyers, voters, or others are stubbornly trying to avoid it.

A Question for a Question

A tactic some people use to throw others off guard is to respond to a request with a question. For example, if asked, "Wouldn't you like to sign up for our lawn service," they say, "Why do you think I would want to do that?" or "What gave you that idea?" You can use this tactic, too. Responding with a question, or asking the person to repeat or elaborate on the question, also gives you time to think. **Answering a question with a question** puts the ball back in the other person's court. People who question you sometimes are trying to discredit or annoy you. Turn the tables—answer with another question. Suppose a prospect for advertising services asks, "Who else has used your services? Maybe I could check with them before deciding to go with your agency." A good response is, "I can bring you written testimonials about how successful we are in generating qualified leads. Or I can give you names and phone numbers for local businesses that might be slightly different than yours, and you can call. Or I can do both. Which would you prefer?"

The Partial Commitment

The **partial commitment** tactic resembles the door-in-the-face or rejection-then-retreat strategy but uses acts instead of words to lead the prospect to the final request. Once you are partially committed, you are a good prospect for full commitment. Evangelists often close their pitches by asking people in the tent or auditorium to bow their heads and close their eyes for prayer. This gets a partial commitment from the audience. The preacher then asks the Lord to enter the hearts of all and asks those who want God to come into their lives to raise their hands. The final request may then be, "Those of you with your hands up come to the front and be saved."

We see this tactic elsewhere, too. Trying a sample of a product represents a partial commitment, as does clipping a coupon. The smart auto salesperson won't ask you to sign a sales agreement right off the bat. Instead, he or she will suggest that you look around and see whether you find anything that appeals to you and then suggests that you take it for a test drive. Merely by looking around, you are partially committing to the sales pitch, and the test drive is usually the clincher.

Of course, other kinds of commitment are used to persuade. When a politician asks you to sign a petition to put his or her name on the ballot, your signature is a form of partial commitment to that politician. A favorite way to generate "qualified leads" in the marketing of some products is to run a sweepstakes. Anyone who submits an entry for the free version of the product has already made a partial commitment to buy it and thus is a good sales lead to follow up.

Planting

Memory responds best, it seems, to messages that have sensory data as raw material. The tactic of **planting** uses one or more of the five senses to open a channel to the audience's memory of how they experienced the product, idea, or candidate. This kind of memory is almost certainly processed in the peripheral information-processing channel.

Restaurant ads often appeal to several senses, and not just the sense of taste. They describe the "crisp and crunchy garden salad" to appeal to the sense of touch. They offer "sizzling hot steaks seared on a grill" to appeal to the sense of hearing. They describe the "thick red tomato sauce" to appeal to the sense of vision and use the words "a steaming fragrance of garlic and spices" to appeal to the sense of smell.

In a classic case of invoking the sense of touch in an ad campaign, Charmin was successfully marketed as an uncommonly soft toilet tissue in TV ads because the grocer, a Mr. Whipple, was always caught squeezing the packages when he thought no one was looking. An ad for an automobile may have someone slam the door so audience members hear the solid "thunk" and mentally compare it with experiential memories of the rattles of their own five-year-old cars. Tie persuasion to senses via planting, and the audience will recall your message better and longer.

The IOU

Sometimes called the reciprocity tactic, the **IOU technique** gets listeners to feel they owe you something. For instance, the insurance salesperson spends several hours doing a complex assets–and–debts analysis to prove to the prospect that he or she needs more insurance. The sales rep then spends several more hours explaining the figures to the spouse, perhaps taking the couple out to lunch or dinner. By the end of all the special treatment, the couple may feel that they really ought to buy something even though they may not need it or cannot afford it. They respond to the obligation—the IOU—that was created by the salesperson's effort.

After observing how reciprocity works in various cultures, Cialdini (2001) notes that the need to reciprocate—the IOU—transcends "great cultural differences, long distances, acute famine, many years, and self interest" (p. 21). Persuaders find this tactic useful when it is hard to make a first contact with buyers, voters, or joiners. You can place your audience in your debt by giving them free samples or offers of help. As a listener, you may want to remember that "There's no such thing as a free lunch."

REVIEW AND CONCLUSION

We all have to persuade at some point. To be effective, we need to analyze the audience before planning how our format will affect the message. We must develop our forms of support and our use of language as we think about which will be most persuasive. We must also control factors in delivery. We need to use source factors, such as posture, eye contact, and dress. Channel factors are subject to our control as well. Receiver factors can be used to get the target group involved in its own persuasion. As you are called on to persuade, use these skills in preparing. Rely on the audience analysis and demographics that the receiver-oriented approach teaches—listen to your audience. Get messages out of them, not into them.

KEY TERMS

After reading this chapter you should be able to identify, explain, and give an example of the following key terms.

audience analysis	topic format	stock-issues format	stock-issues
demographics	space format	motivated sequence format	need for change
audience needs	chronological format		plan to solve the need

plan meets the need

burden of proof

motivated sequence
format

AIDA

keep a good

get a good

avoid a bad

get rid of a bad

statistical evidence

narratives

testimony

visual evidence

comparison and
contrast

credibility

trust

expertise

dynamism

figures of speech

vivid language

concise language

parallel structure

imagery

humor

foot-in-the-door

door-in-the-face

rejection-then-retreat

yes-yes

"don't ask if, ask
which"

answering a question
with a question

partial commitment

planting

IOU technique

APPLICATION OF ETHICS

A fellow student in your public speaking class gives a speech on the dangers to freedom of speech posed by renewing The Patriot Act. After listening to the speech, you realize that your classmate has made inaccurate claims based on inadequate research. Apparently the rest of your classmates are enthusiastic about her speech. You also know that she has stage fright and just getting through the speech has been a victory for her. There is a question and answer period where you could point out her inaccuracies. Should you remain silent, hoping that no harm will come to the class from hearing the speech? Or should you approach her privately and tell her that her claims are inaccurate and her research is inadequate? Or should you inform the instructor about the inaccuracies and research shortcomings?

QUESTIONS FOR FURTHER THOUGHT

1. What demographic clusters can you identify for the people in your class? In your dorm? In a club? Elsewhere?

2. What is a task-oriented message? Give examples from ads in which persuaders used this technique effectively. Give other examples from ads in which they failed.

3. What are the forms of organization? How do they differ from the forms of support? What might be other ways to organize a message?

4. What is AIDA, and how does it differ from the motivated sequence?

5. What are Rank's desire-building tactics? How do they work?

6. What are the factors that make up a speaker's credibility? Give examples of people who have them. Find ads that rely on each factor.

7. Where does humor fit into the persuasion process? Give examples of sources that use humor. Does it relate to the audience? How?

8. How can a persuader get his or her audience more involved? What are some examples you have seen or heard recently?

9. What is the difference between the forms of proof discussed here and those discussed in Chapter 8?

10. How does "planting" work? What about "getting an IOU"?

 For online activities, go to the *Persuasion* book companion website at http://communication.wadsworth.com/larson11.

References

Chapter 1

All Things Considered, April 11, 2005.

Alter, J. (2002). "The Body": So Jesse's act is suddenly very old. We've learned that wrestlers can govern until government has to wrestle with something truly important. *Newsweek*, July 1, p. 37.

Beckett, J. (1989). Ad pitches popping up in unusual places. *San Francisco Examiner*, July 17.

Berger, A. A. (2000). *Ads, fads, and consumer culture: Advertising's impact on American character and culture.* Oxford: Rowan & Littlefield.

Berkowitz, L. (Ed.). *Advances in experimental social psychology* (*Vol. 19*, pp. 123–205). Orlando, FL: Academic Press.

Brembeck, W., & Howell, W. S. (1952). *Persuasion: A means of social control.* Englewood Cliffs, NJ: Prentice-Hall.

Brembeck, W., & Howell, W. S. (1976). *Persuasion: A means of social control* (2nd ed.). Englewood Cliffs, NJ: Prentice-Hall.

Burke, K. (1970). *A grammar of motives.* Berkeley: University of California Press.

Fotheringham, W. (1966). *Perspectives on persuasion.* Boston: Allyn & Bacon.

Gearhart, S. M. (1979). The womanization of rhetoric. *Women's Studies International Quarterly, 2,* 195–201.

Hall Jamieson, K. (1992). *Dirty politics: Deception, distraction and democracy.* New York: Oxford University Press.

Marwell, G., & Schmitt, D. R. (1990). An introduction. In J. P. Dillard (Ed.), *Seeking compliance: The production of interpersonal influence messages* (pp. 3–5). Scottsdale, AZ: Gorsuch Scarisbrick.

McLuhan, M. (1964). *Understanding media: The extensions of man.* New York: Signet.

News Record, Gillette, Wyoming, May 10, 2005.

Petty, R. E., & Cacioppo, J. T. (1986). The elaboration likelihood model of persuasion. In L. Berkowitz (Ed.), *Advances in experimental social psychology* (Vol. 19, pp. 123–205).

Postman, N. (1981). Interview. *U.S. News & World Report*, Jan. 19, p. 43.

Postman, N. (1985). *Amusing ourselves to death: Public discourse in the age of show business.* New York: Penguin Books.

Rank, H. (1976). Teaching about public persuasion. In D. Dieterich (Ed.), *Teaching and doublespeak.* Urbana, IL: National Council of Teachers of English.

Roberts, R. (1924). *The works of Aristotle.* Oxford: Clarendon.

Shannon, C. E., & Weaver, W. (1949). *The mathematical theory of communication.* Urbana: University of Illinois Press.

Simons, H. W. (1976). *Persuasion: Understanding, practice, and analysis.* Reading, MA: Addison-Wesley.

Sullivan, P. A. (1993). Signification and Afro-American rhetoric: A case study of Jesse Jackson's "Common ground and common sense" speech. *Communication Quarterly, 41,* 1–15.

Toffler, A. (1980). *The third wave.* New York: Bantam Books.

Chapter 2

Adam, A. (2005). *Gender, ethics, and information technology.* New York: Palgrave Macmillan.

Alter, J. (1987). The search for personal flaws. *Newsweek,* Oct. 19, p. 79.

Bailey, R. W. (1984). George Orwell and the English language. In E. J. Jensen (Ed.), *The future of nineteen eighty-four* (pp. 23–46). Ann Arbor: University of Michigan Press.

Baker, S., & Martinson, D. L. (2001). The TARES test: Five principles for ethical persuasion. *Journal of Mass Media Ethics, 16,* 148–175.

Bate, B. (1992). *Communication and the sexes.* (Reissue). Prospect Heights, IL: Waveland Press.

Beck, J. (1998). Clinton's character under siege once again. *Chicago Tribune,* Jan. 25, sec. 1, p. 19.

Berkman, R. I., & Shumway, C. A. (2003). *Digital dilemmas: Ethical issues for online media professionals.* Ames, IA: Blackwell Publishing.

Bennett, M. J. (1979). Overcoming the golden rule: Sympathy and empathy. In D. Nimmo (Ed.), *Communication yearbook 3* (pp. 407–422). New Brunswick, NJ: Transaction Books.

Booth, W. C. (2004). *The rhetoric of RHETORIC: The quest for effective communication.* Malden, MA: Blackwell Publishing.

Bosmajian, H. (1983). *The language of oppression* (rpt. ed.). Lanham, MD: University Press of America.

Bovee, W. G. (1991). The end can justify the means— but rarely. *Journal of Mass Media Ethics, 6,* 135–145.

Buursma, B. (1987). Do-or-die deadline rallies Roberts' flock. *Chicago Tribune,* Jan. 17, pp. 1, 10.

Callahan, D. (2004). *The cheating culture: Why more Americans are doing wrong to get ahead.* New York: Harcourt.

Christians, C., et al.(2005). *Media ethics* (7th ed.). Boston: Pearson/Allyn & Bacon.

Cooper, M. (2002). Covering tragedy: Media ethics and TWA flight 800. In R. L. Johannesen (Ed.), *Ethics in human communication* (5th ed.) (pp. 319–331). Prospect Heights, IL: Waveland Press.

Cooper, T. W. (1998). New technology inventory: Forty leading ethical issues. *Journal of Mass Media Ethics, 13,* 71–92.

Corn, D. (2003). *The lies of George W. Bush: Mastering the politics of deception.* New York: Crown.

Courtright, J. A., & Perse, E. M. (1998). *Communicating online: A guide to the Internet.* Mountain View, CA: Mayfield.

DeGeorge, R. (1999). *Business ethics* (5th ed.). New York: Prentice-Hall.

Dobel, J. P. (1999). *Public integrity.* Baltimore, MD: Johns Hopkins University Press.

Ermann, D. M., Williams, M. B., & Shauf, M. S. (1997). *Computers, ethics, and society* (2nd ed.). New York: Oxford University Press.

Foss, S. K., & Griffin, C. (1995). Beyond persuasion: A proposal for an invitational rhetoric. *Communication Monographs, 62,* 2–18.

Freund, L. (1960). Responsibility: Definitions, distinctions, and applications. In J. Friedrich (Ed.), *Nomos III: Responsibility* (pp. 28–42). New York: Liberal Arts Press.

Froman, L. A. (1966). A realistic approach to campaign strategies and tactics. In M. K. Jennings & L. H. Ziegler (Eds.), *The electoral process.* Englewood Cliffs, NJ: Prentice-Hall.

Goodwin, H. E. (1987). *Groping for ethics in journalism* (2nd ed.). Ames: Iowa State University Press.

Gorsevski, E. W. (2004). *Peaceful persuasion: The geopolitics of nonviolent rhetoric.* Albany: The State University of New York Press.

Green, M., & MacColl, G. (1987). *There he goes again: Ronald Reagan's reign of error* (rev. ed.). New York: Pantheon Books.

Griffin, E. A. (1976). *The mind changers: The art of Christian persuasion.* Wheaton, IL: Tyndale House.

Gunkel, D. J. (2001). *Hacking cyberspace.* Boulder, CO: Westview.

Hamelink, C. J. (2000). *The ethics of cyberspace.* London: Sage.

Hauerwas, S. (1977). *Truthfulness and tragedy.* Notre Dame, IN: University of Notre Dame Press.

Johannesen, R. L. (1971). The emerging concept of communication as dialogue. *Quarterly Journal of Speech, 57,* 373–382.

Johannesen, R. L. (1985). An ethical assessment of the Reagan rhetoric: 1981–1982. In K. R. Sanders, L. L. Kaid, & D. Nimmo (Eds.), *Political communication yearbook 1984* (pp. 226–241). Carbondale: Southern Illinois University Press.

Johannesen, R. L. (1991). Virtue, ethics, character, and political communication. In R. E. Denton, Jr. (Ed.), *Ethical dimensions of political communication* (pp. 69–90). New York: Praeger.

Johannesen, R. L. (1997). Diversity, freedom, and responsibility. In J. Makau & R. C. Arnett (Eds.), *Communication ethics in an age of diversity* (pp. 155–186). Champaign: University of Illinois Press.

Johannesen, R. L. (2000). Nel Noddings' uses of Martin Buber's philosophy of dialogue. *Southern Communication Journal, 65,* 151–160.

Johannesen, R. L. (2002). *Ethics in human communication* (5th ed.). Prospect Heights, IL: Waveland Press.

Johnson, D. G. (2001). *Computer ethics* (3rd ed.). Upper Saddle River, NJ: Prentice-Hall.

Kane, R. (1994). *Through the moral maze: Searching for absolute values in a pluralistic world.* New York: Paragon.

Kass, J. (1998). Blame for crisis lies not in the stars but in our apathy. *Chicago Tribune,* Jan. 16, sec. 1, p. 3.

Klaidman, S., & Beauchamp, T. L. (1987). *The virtuous journalist.* New York: Oxford University Press.

Kramer, J., & Kramerae, C. (1997). Gendered ethics on the Internet. In J. M. Makau and R. C. Arnett (Eds.), *Communication in an age of diversity* (pp. 226–243). Urbana: University of Illinois Press.

Lebacqz, K. (1985). *Professional ethics.* Nashville, TN: Abingdon.

Lester, P. M. (1991). *Photojournalism: An ethical approach.* Hillsdale, NJ: Erlbaum.

Lester, P. M. (2003). *Visual communication* (3rd ed.). Belmont, CA: Wadsworth.

Ludwig, A. (1965). *The importance of lying.* Springfield, IL: Thomas.

Maraniss, D. (1996). The comeback kid's last return. *Washington Post National Weekly Edition,* September 2–8, pp. 8–9.

McCammond, D. B. (2004). Critical incidents: The practical side of ethics. In D. Lattimore et al., *Public relations: The profession and the practice* (5th ed.) (pp. 84–85). New York: McGraw Hill.

Merrill, J. C., & Odell, S. J. (1983). *Philosophy and journalism.* New York: Longman.

Miller, C., & Swift, K. (1981). *The handbook of nonsexist writing.* New York: Barnes & Noble.

Niebuhr, H. R. (1963). *The responsible self.* New York: Harper & Row.

Opotow, S. (1990). Moral exclusion and injustice: An introduction. *Journal of Social Issues, 46,* 1–20.

Pennock, J. R. (1960). The problem of responsibility. In C. J. Friedrich (Ed.), *Nomos III: Responsibility* (pp. 3–27). New York: Liberal Arts Press.

Perelman, C., & Olbrechts-Tyteca, L. (1969). *The new rhetoric.* Notre Dame, IN: University of Notre Dame Press.

Pincoffs, E. L. (1975). On being responsible for what one says. Paper presented at Speech Communication Association convention, Houston, TX, Dec.

Primer: Blogs and blogging. (2005). *Media Ethics* (Spring), *16,* pp. 14–16.

Rakow, L. (1994). The future of the field: Finding our mission. Address presented at Ohio State University, May 13.

Ross, R. S., & Ross, M. G. (1982). *Relating and interacting.* Englewood Cliffs, NJ: Prentice-Hall.

Samovar, L. A, Porter, R. E., & Stefani, L. A. (1998). *Communication between cultures* (3rd ed.). Belmont, CA: Wadsworth.

Samuelson, R. (1998). Clinton's problems with the other L word. *Chicago Tribune,* Jan. 30, sec. 1, p. 17.

Schwartz, T. (1974). *The responsive chord.* Garden City, NY: Anchor.

Sellers, M. (2004). Ideals of public discourse. In C. T. Sistare (Ed.), *Civility and its discontents* (Ch. 1). Lawrence: University Press of Kansas.

Singer, J. B. (2002). The unforgiving truth in the unforgivable photo. *Media Ethics, 13,* 30–31.

Singer, M. G. (1963). The golden rule. *Philosophy, 38,* 293–314.

Singer, M. G. (1967). The golden rule. In P. Edwards (Ed.), *Encyclopedia of philosophy,* Vol. 3 (pp. 365–366). New York: MacMillan.

Spence, E. H., & Van Heekeren, B. (2005). *Advertising ethics.* Upper Saddle River, NJ: Pearson/Prentice-Hall.

Stewart, J., & Zediker, K. (2000). Dialogue as tensional, ethical practice. *Southern Communication Journal, 65,* 224–242.

Toulmin, S. (1950). *An examination of the place of reason in ethics.* Cambridge: Cambridge University Press.

Wellman, C. (1988). *Morals and ethics* (2nd ed.). Englewood Cliffs, NJ: Prentice-Hall.

Wheeler, T. H. (2002). *Phototruth or photofiction? Ethics and media imagery in the digital age.* Mahwah, NJ: Erlbaum.

Williams, H. M. (1974). What do we do now, boss? Marketing and advertising. *Vital Speeches of the Day, 40*, 285–288.

Wolf, M. J. P. (Ed.). (2003). *Virtual morality: Morals, ethics, and the new media.* New York: Peter Lang.

Wood, J. T. (1994). *Gendered lives: Communication, gender, and culture.* Belmont, CA: Wadsworth.

Chapter 3

Andrews, J. (1980). History and theory in the study of the rhetoric of social movements. *Central States Speech Journal, 31*, 274–281.

Aristotle. (1984). *Rhetoric.* (W. R. Roberts, Trans.). New York: Modern Library.

Bowers, J. W., & Ochs, D. J. (1971). *The rhetoric of agitation and control.* Reading, MA: Addison-Wesley.

Buckley, W. F., Jr. (2002). Burying Wellstone. *National Review Online,* Nov. 1. Accessed Dec. 19, 2002, at http://www.nationalreview.com/buckley/buckley110102.asp.

Burns, S. (1990). *Social movements of the 1960s: Searching for democracy.* Boston: Twayne.

Campbell, K. K. (1998). Inventing women: From Amaterasu to Virginia Woolf. *Women's Studies in Communication, 21*, 111–126.

Fairhurst, G. T., & Sarr, R. A. (1996). *The art of framing: Managing the language of leadership.* San Francisco: Jossey-Bass.

Fisher, W. R. (1978). Toward a logic of good reasons. *Quarterly Journal of Speech, 64*, 376–384.

Fisher, W. R. (1984). Narration as a human communication paradigm: The case of public moral argument.*Communication Monographs, 51*, 1–22.

Fisher, W. R. (1987). *Human communication as narration: Toward a philosophy of reason, value, and action.* Columbia: University of South Carolina Press.

Foss, K. A., Foss, S. K., & Griffin, C. L. (1999). *Feminist rhetorical theories.* Thousand Oaks, CA: Sage.

Foss, S. K., & Griffin, C. L. (1995). Beyond persuasion: A proposal for an invitational rhetoric. *Communication Monographs, 62*, 2–18.

Foss, S. K. (1996). *Rhetorical criticism: Exploration and practice* (2nd ed.). Prospect Heights, IL: Waveland Press.

Griffin, L. M. (1952). The rhetoric of historical movements. *The Quarterly Journal of Speech, 38*, 184–188.

Kilbourne, J. (1979). *Killing us softly.* Cambridge, MA: Cambridge Documentary Films.

Kilbourne, J. (2001). *Deadly persuasion: Why women and girls must fight the addictive power of advertising.* New York: Free Press.

McGee, M. C. (1980). The ideograph: A link between rhetoric and ideology. *Quarterly Journal of Speech, 66*, 1–16.

Plato. (1937). *The dialogues of Plato* (Vol. 1). (B. Jowett, Trans.). New York: Random House.

Rowland, R. C. (1989). On limiting the narrative paradigm: Three case studies. *Communication Monographs, 56*, 39–54.

Scott, R. L. (1993). Rhetoric is epistemic: What difference does that make? In T. Enos & S. C. Brown (Eds.), *Defining the new rhetoric* (pp. 120–136). Mahwah, NJ: Erlbaum.

Warnick, Barbara (1987). The narrative paradigm: Another story. *Quarterly Journal of Speech, 73*, 172–182.

Chapter 4

Ajzen, I. (1991). The theory of planned behavior. *Organizational Behavior and Human Decision Processes, 50*, 179–211.

Ajzen, I. (2001). Nature and operation of attitudes. *Annual Review of Psychology, 52*, 27–58.

Allen, M. (1998). Comparing the persuasive effectiveness of one- and two-sided messages. In M. Allen & R. W. Preiss (Eds.), *Persuasion: Advances through meta-analysis* (pp. 87–98). Cresskill, NJ: Hampton Press.

Allen, M., & Stiff, J. (1998). The sleeper effect. In M. Allen & R. W. Preiss (Eds.), *Persuasion: Advances through meta-analysis* (pp. 175–188). Cresskill, NJ: Hampton Press.

Armitage, C. J., & Christian, J. (2003). From attitudes to behavior: Basic and applied research on the theory of planned behavior. *Current Psychology, 22*, 187–195.

Bless, H., & Schwarz, N. (1999). Sufficient and necessary conditions in dual-process models. In

S. Chaiken & Y. Trope (Eds.), *Dual-process theories in social psychology* (pp. 423–440). New York: Guilford Press.

Bornstein, R. F. (1989). Exposure and affect: Overview and meta-analysis of research, 1968–1987. *Psychological Bulletin, 106*, 265–289.

Chaiken, S., & Eagly, A. H. (1976). Communication modality as a determinant of message persuasiveness and message comprehensibility. *Journal of Personality and Social Psychology, 34*, 605–614.

Chaiken, S., Giner-Sorolla, R., & Chen, S. (1996). Beyond accuracy: Defense and impression motives in heuristic and systematic information processing. In P. M. Gollwitzer & J. A. Bargh (Eds.), *The psychology of action: Linking cognitions and motivation to behavior* (pp. 553–578). New York: Guilford Press.

Chaiken, S., & Trope, Y. (Eds.). (1999). *Dual process theories in social psychology*. New York: Guilford Press.

Cody, M. J., Canary, D., & Smith, S. (1987). Compliance-gaining strategy selection: Episodes and goals. In J. Daly & J. Wiemann (Eds.), *Communicating strategically*. Hillsdale, NJ: Erlbaum.

Dahl, D. W., Frankenberger, K. D., & Manchanda, R. V. (2003). Does it pay to shock? Reactions to shocking and nonshocking advertising content among university students. *Journal of Advertising Research*, 268–280.

DeSteno, D., Petty, R. E., Rucker, D. D., Wegener, D. T., & Braverman, J. (2004). Discrete emotions and persuasion: The role of emotion-induced expectancies. *Journal of Personality and Social Psychology, 86*, 43–56.

Dillard, J. P. (Ed.). (1990). *Seeking compliance: The production of interpersonal influence messages*. Scottsdale, AZ: Gorsuch Scarisbrick.

Eagly, A. H., & Chaiken, S. (1993). *The psychology of attitudes*. Fort Worth, TX: Harcourt Brace Jovanovich.

Falk, E., & Mills, J. (1996). Why sexist language affects persuasion: The role of homophily, intended audience, and offense. *Women and Language, 19*, 36–43.

Fazio, R. H. (1989). On the power and functionality of attitudes: The role of attitude accessibility. In A. R. Pratkanis, S. J. Breckler, & A. G. Greenwald (Eds.), Attitude structure and function (pp. 153–179). Hillsdale, NJ: Erlbaum.

Fazio, R. H., & Towles-Schwen (1999). The MODE model of attitude-behavior processes. In S. Chaiken & Y. Trope (Eds.), *Dual-process theories in social psychology* (pp. 97–116). New York: Guilford Press.

Festinger, L. (1956). *A theory of cognitive dissonance*. Stanford, CA: Stanford University Press.

Festinger, L. (1962). *A theory of cognitive dissonance*. Stanford, CA: Stanford University Press.

Fishbein, M., & Ajzen, I. (1975). Belief, attitude, intention, and behavior. Reading, MA: Addison-Wesley.

Fishbein, M., & Ajzen, I. (1981). Acceptance, yielding and impact: Cognitive processes in persuasion. In R. E. Petty, T. M. Ostrom, & T. C. Brock (Eds.), *Cognitive responses in persuasion* (pp. 339–359). Hillsdale, NJ: Erlbaum.

Frey, K. P., & Eagly, A. (1993). Vividness can undermine the persuasiveness of messages. *Journal of Personality & Social Psychology, 65*, 32–44.

FUD-Counter. (2001). How does FUD relate to Linux? Nov. 1. Accessed Dec. 17, 2002, at http://fud-counter.nl.linux.org/rationale.html.

Giner-Sorolla, R. (1999). Affect in attitude. In S. Chaiken & Y. Trope (Eds.), *Dual-process theories in social psychology* (pp. 441–461). New York: Guilford Press.

Grush, J. E., McKeough, K. L., & Ahlering, R. F. (1978). Extrapolating laboratory exposure research to actual political elections. *Journal of Personality and Social Psychology, 36*, 257–270.

Heider, F. (1946). Attitudes and cognitive organization. *Journal of Psychology, 21*, 107–112.

Heider, F. (1958). *The psychology of interpersonal relations*. New York: Wiley.

Hovland, C. I. (1957). *The order of presentation in persuasion*. New Haven, CT: Yale University Press.

Hovland, C. I., Janis, I. L., & Kelley, H. H. (1953). *Communication and persuasion*. New Haven, CT: Yale University Press.

Janis, I. L. (1967). Effects of fear arousal on attitude change: Recent developments in theory and experimental research. In L. Berkowitz (Ed.), *Advances in experimental social psychology* (Vol. 3, pp. 166–224). New York: Academic Press.

Janis, I. R., & Feshbach, S. (1953). Effects of fear arousing communications. *Journal of Abnormal Social Psychology, 48*, 78–92.

Kellermann, K. (2004). A goal-directed approach to gaining compliance. *Communication Research, 31,* 397–446.

Kellermann, K., & Cole, T. (1994). Classifying compliance-gaining messages: Taxonomic disorder and strategic confusion. *Communication Theory, 4,* 3–60.

Kipnis, D., Schmidt, S. M., & Wilkinson, I. (1980). Intraorganizational influence tactics: Explorations in getting one's way. *Journal of Applied Psychology, 65,* 440–452.

Kumkale, G. T., & Albarracin, D. (2004). The sleeper effect in persuasion: A meta-analytic review. *Psychological Bulletin, 130,* 143–171.

Lavine, H., Thomsen, C. J., Zanna, M. P., & Borgida, E. (1998). On the primacy of affect in the determination of attitudes and behavior: The moderating role of affective-cognitive ambivalence. *Journal of Experimental Social Psychology, 34,* 398–421.

Leventhal, H. (1970). Findings and theory in the study of fear communications. In L. Berkowitz (Ed.), *Advances in experimental social psychology* (Vol. 5, pp. 119–186). New York: Academic Press.

Lund, F. H. (1925). The psychology of belief, IV: The law of primacy in persuasion. *Journal of Abnormal Social Psychology, 20,* 183–191.

Mackie, D. L., & Worth, L. T. (1989). Cognitive deficits and the mediation of positive affect in persuasion. *Journal of Personality and Social Psychology, 57,* 27–40.

Martin, P. Y., Laing, J., Martin, R., & Mitchell, M. (2005). Caffeine, cognition, and persuasion: Evidence for caffeine increasing the systematic process of persuasive messages. *Journal of Applied Social Psychology, 35,* 160–183.

Marwell, G., & Schmitt, D. R. (1967). Dimensions of compliance-gaining behavior: An empirical analysis. *Sociometry, 30,* 350–364.

Miller, G. R., Boster, F. J., Roloff, M. E., & Seibold, D. R. (1977). Compliance-gaining message strategies: A typology and some findings concerning effects of situational differences. *Communication Monographs, 44,* 37–51.

Mitchell, M. M. (2000). Able but not motivated? The relative effects of happy and sad mood on persuasive message processing. *Communication Monographs, 67,* 215–226.

Mitchell, M. M., Brown, K. M., Morris-Villagran, M., & Villagran, P. D. (2001). The effects of anger, sadness, and happiness on persuasive message processing: A test of the negative state relief model. *Communication Monographs, 68,* 347–359.

Mongeau, P. A. (1998). Another look at fear arousing persuasive appeals. In M. Allen & R. W. Preiss (Eds.), *Persuasion: Advances through meta-analysis* (pp. 53–68). Cresskill, NJ: Hampton Press.

Nabi, R. L. (1998). The effect of disgust-eliciting visuals on attitudes toward animal experimentation. *Communication Quarterly, 46,* 472–484.

Nabi, R. L. (2002). Anger, fear, uncertainty, and attitudes: A test of the cognitive-functional model. *Communication Monographs, 69,* 204–216.

Nabi, R. L. (2003). Exploring the framing effects of emotion. *Communication Research, 30,* 224–247.

Petty, R. E., & Cacioppo, J. T. (1979). Effects of forewarning of persuasive intent and involvement on cognitive responses and persuasion. *Journal of Personality and Social Psychology, 37,* 1915–1926.

Petty, R. E., & Cacioppo, J. T. (1986). *Communication and persuasion: Central and peripheral routes to attitude change.* New York: Springer-Verlag.

Petty, R. E., Wegener, D. T., & Fabrigar, L. R. (1997). Attitudes and attitude change. *Annual Review of Psychology, 48,* 609–647.

Petty, R. E., & Wegener, D .T. (1999). The elaboration likelihood model: Current status and controversies. In S. Chaiken & Y. Trope (Eds.), *Dual-process theories in social psychology* (pp. 41–72). New York: Guilford Press.

Pfau, M., Szabo, E. A., Anderson, J., Norrill, J., Zubric, J. C., & Wan, H. (2001). The role and impact of affect in the process of resistance to persuasion. *Human Communication Research, 27,* 216–252.

Pornpitakpan, C. (2004). The persuasiveness of source credibility: A critical review of five decades' evidence. *Journal of Applied Social Psychology, 34,* 243–281.

Prislin, R., & Pool, G. L. (1996). Behavior, consequences, and the self: Is all well that ends well? *Personality and Social Psychology Bulletin, 22,* 933–948.

Rogers, R. W. (1975). A protection motivation theory of fear appeals and attitude change. *Journal of Psychology, 91,* 93–114.

Roskos-Ewoldsen, D. R. (2004). Fear appeal messages affect accessibility of attitudes toward the threat and adaptive behaviors. *Communication Monographs, 71,* 49–69.

Rule, B. G., Bisanz, G. L., & Kohn, M. (1985). Anatomy of a persuasion schema: Targets, goals, and strategies. *Journal of Personality and Social Psychology*, *48*, 1127–1140.

Shaw, M. E., & Costanzo, P. R. (1970). *Theories of social psychology*. New York: McGraw-Hill.

Sherif, M., & Hovland, C. I. (1961). *Social judgment: Assimilation and contrast effects in communication and attitude change*. New Haven, CT: Yale University Press.

Smith, S. M., & Petty, R. E. (1996). Message framing and persuasion: A message processing analysis. *Personality and Social Psychology Bulletin*, *22*, 257–268.

Stone, J., Wiegand, A.W., Cooper, J., & Aronson, E. (1997). When exemplification fails: Hypocrisy and the motive for self-integrity. *Journal of Personality and Social Psychology*, *72*, 54–65.

Wegener, D. T., Petty, R. E., & Smith, S. M. (1995). Positive mood can increase or decrease message scrutiny: The hedonic contingency view of mood and message processing. *Journal of Personality and Social Psychology*, *69*, 5–15.

Wilson, S. R. (2000) Identity implications of influence goals. *Journal of Language & Social Psychology*, *19*, 195–222.

Wilson, S. R. (2002). *Seeking and resisting compliance: Why people say what they do when trying to influence others*. Thousand Oaks, CA: Sage.

Wiseman, R. L., & Schenk-Hamlin, W. (1981). A multidimensional scaling validation of an inductively-derived set of compliance-gaining strategies. *Communication Monographs*, *48*, 251–270.

Witte, K. (1992). Putting the fear back into fear appeals: The extended parallel process model. *Communication Monographs*, *59*, 329–349.

Witte, K., & Allen, M. (2000). A meta-analysis of fear appeals: Implications for effective public health campaigns. *Health Education & Behavior*, *27*, 591–615.

Wood, W. (2000). Attitude change. Persuasion and social influence. *Annual Review of Psychology*, *51*, 539–570.

Zajonc, R. B. (1968). Attitudinal effects of mere exposure. *Journal of Personality and Social Psychology*, *9*, 1–27.

Chapter 5

American Heritage Dictionary. (1985). Boston: Houghton Mifflin.

Berger, A. A. (1989). *Signs in contemporary society: An introduction to semiotics*. Salem, WI: Sheffield.

Burke, K. (1950). *A rhetoric of motives*. Berkeley: University of California Press.

Burke, K. (1966). *Language as symbolic action: Essays on life, literature, and method*. Berkeley: University of California Press.

Burke, K. (1986). *Language as symbolic action*. Berkeley: University of California Press.

Feig, B. (1997). *Marketing straight to the heart: From product to positioning to advertising*. Chicago: American Management Association.

Hahn, D. (1998). *Political communication: Rhetoric, government and citizens*. State College, PA: Strata.

Korzybski, A. (1947). *Science and sanity*. Lakeville, CT: Non-Aristotelian Library.

Langer, S. K. (1951). *Philosophy in a new key*. New York: New American Library.

Lederer, R. (1991). *The miracle of language*. New York: Pocket Books.

National Public Radio. (1999). *Morning Edition*, Feb. 3.

Postman, N. (1992). *Technopoly: The surrender of culture to technology*. New York: Vintage Books.

Suplee, K. (1987). Semiotics: In search of more perfect persuasion. *Washington Post*, Jan. 18, Outposts sec., pp. 1–3.

Sopory, P., & Dillard, J. (2002). Figurative language and persuasion. In Dillard and Pfau (Eds.), *The persuasion handbook: Developments in theory and practice*. Thousand Oaks, CA: Sage.

Chapter 6

American Heritage Dictionary. (1985). Boston: Houghton Mifflin.

Andrews, L. A. (1984). Exhibit A: Language. *Psychology Today*, Feb., p. 30.

Barol, B. (1988). The 80s are over. *Newsweek*, Jan. 4, pp. 40–48.

Berger, A. (1984). *Signs in contemporary culture*. New York: Longman.

Black Elk. (1971). *Touch the earth*. New York: Outerbridge & Dienstfrey.

Broder, D. (1984). The great American values test. *Psychology Today*, Nov., p. 41.

Buissac, P. (1976). *Circus and culture: A semiotic approach*. Bloomington: Indiana University Press.

Burke, K. (1960). *A grammar of motives*. Berkeley: University of California Press.

Chicago Daily News. November 24, 1972. "Fed up? It may lead to an ulcer."

Cialdini, R. (2001). *Influence: Science and practice*. Boston: Allyn & Bacon.

Democracy Project (1999). www.ipa.udel.edu/democracy.

Dillard, J. P., & Pfau, M. (2002). *The persuasion handbook: Developments in theory and practice*. Thousand Oaks, CA: Sage.

Domzal, T., & Kernan, J. (1993). Mirror, mirror: Some postmodern reflections on global marketing. *Journal of Advertising*, Dec., p. 20.

Eco, U. (1979). *The role of the reader*. Bloomington: Indiana University Press.

Eco, U. (1984). *Semiotics and the philosophy of language*. London: Macmillan.

Eisenberg, E. M. (1984). Ambiguity as a strategy in organizational communication. *Communication monographs*, *51*, 227–242.

Farrell, W. (1974). *The liberated male*. New York: Random House.

Hahn, D. (1998). *Political communication: Rhetoric, government and citizens*. State College, PA: Strata.

Hosman, L. H. (2002). Language and persuasion. In J. P. Dillard & M. Pfau (Eds.), *The persuasion handbook: Developments in theory and practice*. Thousand Oaks, CA: Sage.

Kallend, J. S. (2002). Skydiving responsibility lies solely with jumper. *Chicago Tribune*, Aug. 11, sec. 2, p 8.

Kittredge, W. (1996). The war for Montana's soul. *Newsweek*, April 15, p. 43.

Koenig, P. (1972). Death doth defer. *Psychology Today*, Nov., p. 83.

Lederer, R. (1991). *The miracle of language*. New York: Pocket Books.

Lewis, C. (1999). The athletes are the games. *Newsweek*, Feb. 15, p. 56.

Lewis, H., & Lewis, M. (1972). *Psychosomatics: How your emotions can damage your health*. New York: Viking Press.

Marshall, D. (1999). An Olympic-size problem. *Newsweek*, Feb. 15, p. 20.

Messner, M. R. (1998). *Politics and masculinity: Men in movements*. Thousand Oaks, CA: Sage.

Nimmo, D., & Combs, J. (1984). *Mediated political realities*. New York: Longman.

Osborn, M. (1967). Archetypal metaphors in rhetoric: The light-dark family. *Quarterly Journal of Speech*, April, 115–126.

Seigel, B. (1989). *The healing power of communicating with your body*. New York: Weider.

Swanson, S. L. (1981). Sensory language in the courtroom. *Trial Diplomacy Journal*, Winter, pp. 37–43.

Tannen, D. (1990). *You just don't understand: Men and women in conversation*. New York: Morrow.

Weaver, R. (1953). *The ethics of rhetoric*. Chicago: Regnery.

Yates, S. J. (2001). Gender, language and CMC for education. *Learning and instruction*, *11*, 23–34.

Chapter 7

Austin, N. (2002). The power of the pyramid: The foundation of human psychology, and thereby motivation; Maslow's hierarchy is one powerful pyramid. *Incentive*, July, p. 10.

Bellah, R. N., Madsen, R., Sullivan, W. M., Swoder, A., & Tipton, S. M. (1985). *Habits of the heart: Individualism and commitment in American life*. New York: Harper & Row.

Booth, E. (1999). Getting inside a shopper's mind: Direct marketers are working out how and why consumers arrive at decisions, in order to satisfy their needs. *Marketing*, June 3, p. 32.

Booth-Butterfield, S., & Welbourne, J. (2002). The elaboration likelihood model: Its impact on persuasion theory and research. In J. P. Dillard & M. Pfau (Eds.), *The persuasion handbook: Developments in theory and practice* (pp. 155–173). Thousand Oaks, CA: Sage.

Borchers, T. A. (2005). *Persuasion in the media age*. (2nd ed.). Boston: McGraw-Hill.

Burke, K. (1961). *The rhetoric of religion: Studies in logology*. Boston: Beacon Press.

Carnegie, D. (1952). *How to win friends and influence people*. New York: Simon & Schuster.

Colley, R. H. (1961). *Defining advertising goals for measured attitude results*. New York: Association of National Advertisers.

De Bono, K. G., & Harnish, R. (1988). Source expertise, source attractiveness, and the processing of persuasive information. *Journal of Personality and Social Psychology*, *55*, 541–546.

Egley, A. H., & Chaiken, S. (1993). *The psychology of attitudes*. New York: Harcourt Brace Jovanovich.

Eiser, R. J. (1987). *The expression of attitude*. New York: Springer-Verlag.

Feig, B. (1997). *Marketing straight to the heart: From product to positioning to advertising—how smart companies use the power of emotion to win loyal customers.* New York: American Marketing Association.

Festinger, L. (1962). *A theory of cognitive dissonance.* Stanford, CA: Stanford University Press.

Fishbein, M., & Ajzen, I. (1975). *Belief, attitude, intention, and behavior: An introduction to theory and research.* Reading, MA: Addison-Wesley.

Fonda, J. (2005). *My life so far.* New York: Random House.

Frankl, V. (1962). *Man's search for meaning: An introduction to logotherapy.* New York: Washington Square.

Freedman, D. H. (1988). Why you watch some commercials—whether you want to or not. *TV Guide,* Feb. 20.

Friedman, J. L., & Dagnoli, J. (1988). Brand name spreading: Line extensions are marketers' lifeline. *Advertising Age,* Feb. 22.

Lafavore, R. (1995). From here to eternity: Men's desire for immortality. *Men's Health,* Nov., p. 74.

Lane, W. R., King, K. W., & Russell, J. T. (2005), *Kleppner's advertising procedure* (16th ed.). Upper Saddle River, NJ: Pearson Education.

Larson, C. U., & Sanders, R. (1975). Faith, mystery, and data: An analysis of "scientific" studies of persuasion. *Quarterly Journal of Speech, 61,* 178–194.

Lears, T. J. J. (1983). From salvation to self realization: Advertising and the therapeutic roots of the consumer culture. In *The culture of consumption: Critical essays in American culture, 1880–1980.* New York: Pantheon Books.

Levitt, S., & Dubner, S. (2005). *Freakonomics: A rogue economist explores the hidden side of everything.* New York: Harper Collins.

Maslow, A. (1954). *Motivation and personality.* New York: Harper & Row.

Nabi, R.L. (2002). Discrete emotions and persuasion. In J. P. Dillard & M. Pfau (Eds.), *The persuasion handbook: Developments in theory and practice.* (pp. 289–309). Thousand Oaks, CA: Sage.

National Public Radio. (2002). *All things considered,* Aug. 30.

Naughton, R. (2002). More headwind for Martha: As investigators run out of patience, the diva of domesticity may be ordered to testify in Washington. *Newsweek,* Sept. 2, p. 45.

Nelson, R. (2001). On the shape of verbal networks in organizations. *Organization Studies,* Sept.–Oct., 797.

Osgood, C. E., & Tannenbaum, P. H. (1955). The principle of congruity in the prediction of attitude change. *Psychological Review, 62,* 43.

Packard, V. (1964). *The hidden persuaders.* New York: Pocket Books.

Petty, R., & Cacioppo, J. (1986). *Communication and persuasion.* New York: Springer-Verlag.

Petty, R. E., & Wegener, D. T. (1998). Attitude change: Multiple roles for persuasion variables. In D. T. Gilbert, S. T. Fiske, & G. Lindsay (Eds.), *Handbook of social psychology.* Boston: McGraw-Hill.

Pinsky, M. S. (2002). Houston minister views Gospel according to the Sopranos. *Orlando Sentinel,* Sept. 4, 2000.

Porter, R., & Samovar, L. (1998). *Intercultural communication: A reader.* Belmont, CA: Wadsworth Publishing Co.

Putnam, R. (1995). Bowling alone: America's declining social capital. *Journal of Democracy 6,* 65–68.

Putnam, R. D. (2000). *Bowling alone: The collapse and revival of American community.* New York: Simon & Schuster.

Rokeach, M. (1968). *Beliefs, attitudes, and values: A theory of organization and change.* San Francisco: Jossey-Bass.

Rowan, J. (1998). Maslow amended. *The Journal of Humanistic Psychology,* Winter, 84.

Rowell, R. (2002). Martha's taste, not her ethics lures fans. Knight Rider/*Business News,* Oct. 2.

Schiffman, L., & Kanuk, L. (1997). *Consumer behavior.* Upper Saddle River, NJ: Prentice Hall.

Schrader, D. C. (1999). Goal complexity and the perceived competence of interpersonal influence messages. *Communication Studies,* Fall, 188.

Shavitt, S. (1990). The role of attitude objects in attitude functions. *Journal of Experimental Psychology, 26,* 124–148.

Sibley, K. (1997). The e-mail dilemma: To spy or not to spy. *Computing Canada,* March 31, p. 14.

Staal, S. (2001). Warning: living together may ruin your relationship. *Cosmopolitan,* Sept., p. 286.

Williams, M.A. (2001). *The ten lenses: Your guide to living and working in a multicultural world.* Herndon, VA: Capitol Books.

Wood, W. (2000). Attitude change: Persuasion and social influence. *Annual Review of Psychology*, 539.

Zemke, R. (1998). Maslow for a new millennium. *Training*, Dec., 54.

Zimbardo, P. G., Ebbesen, E. E., & Maslach, C. (1976). *Influencing attitudes and changing behavior*. Reading, MA: Addison-Wesley.

Zimbardo, P. G., & Leippe, M. R. (1991). *The psychology of attitude change and social influence*. New York: McGraw-Hill.

Chapter 8

American Heritage Dictionary. (1985). Boston: Houghton Mifflin.

Burke, K. (1985). Dramatism and logology. *Communication Quarterly*, *33*, 89–93.

Butler, L. D., Koopman, C., and Zimbardo, P. (1995). The psychological impact of watching the film *JFK*: Emotions, beliefs and political intensions. *Political Psychology*, *16*, 237–257.

Clark, H. H. (1969). Linguistic processes in deductive reasoning. *Psychological Review, 76*, 387–404.

Consider the facts. (2002). *Pine County Courier*, July 25, p. 10.

Dahl, S. (2000) *Communications and cultural transformation: Cultural diversity, globalization, and cultural convergence*. London: E.C.E.

Deardorf, J., & Finan, E. (1999). Barton wins $29.6 million. *Chicago Tribune*, March 2, p. 1.

Fishbein, M., & Ajzen, I. (1975). *Beliefs, attitude, intention and behavior: An introduction to theory and research*. Reading, MA: Addison-Wesley.

Fishbein, M., & Ajzen, I. (1980). Predicting and understanding consumer behavior: Attitude behavior correspondence. In I. Ajzen & M. Fishbein (Eds.), *Understanding attitudes and predicting social behavior*. Englewood Cliffs, NJ: Prentice-Hall.

Fisher, W. R. (1987). *Human communication as narration: Toward a philosophy of reason, value, and action*. Colombia: University of South Carolina Press.

Garfield, B. (1988). Ad review: Good commercials finally outnumber the bad ones on TV. *Advertising Age*, March 14, p. 86.

Guttmacher, A. (1993). Social science and the citizen. *Society*, July–Aug., p. 2.

Huglen, M, & Clark, N. (2004). *Argument strategies from Aristotle*. Belmont: Thomson Learning.

Jensen, J. V. (1981). *Argumentation: Reasoning in communication*. New York: Van Nostrand.

Kahane, H. (1992). *Logic and contemporary rhetoric: The use of reason in everyday life*. Belmont, CA: Wadsworth.

Loftus, E. F. (1980). *Eyewitness testimony*. Cambridge, MA: Harvard University Press.

Loftus, E. F. (1984). Eyewitness testimony. *Psychology Today*, Feb., p. 25.

Lunsford, A., & Ruszkiewicz, J. (2004). *Everything's an argument*. Boston: Bedford/St. Martins Press.

Moore, C. (1909). *A short life of Abraham Lincoln*. Chicago: Houghton Mifflin.

The payoffs for preschooling. 1984, *Chicago Tribune*, Dec. 25, p. 25.

Peck, M. S. (1983). *People of the lie: The hope for healing human evil*. New York: Simon & Schuster.

Reinard, J. C. (1988). The empirical study of evidence: The status after fifty years of research. *Human Communication Research*, Fall, pp. 25–36.

Reynolds, R., & Burgoon, M. (1983). Belief processing, reasoning and evidence. *Communication Yearbook*, 7, 83–104.

Reynolds, R., & Reynolds, J. L. (2002). Evidence. In J. P. Dillard & M. Pfau (Eds.), *The persuasion handbook: Developments in theory and practice* (pp. 427–444). Thousand Oaks, CA: Sage.

Santos, M. (1961). *These were the Souix*. New York: Dell books, p. 148.

Scott, B. (1989). *Rockford Register Star*, Nov. 8, editorial page.

Thompson, W. N. (1971). *Modern argumentation and debate: Principles and practices*. New York: Harper & Row.

Toulmin, S. (1964). *The uses of argument*. Cambridge: Cambridge University Press.

Zorn, E. (2002). Season to kill enriches some, repulses many. *Chicago Tribune*, Nov. 11, sec. 2.

Chapter 9

American Heritage Dictionary. (1985). Boston: Houghton Mifflin.

America's abortion dilemma. (1985). *Newsweek*, Jan. 14, pp. 20–23.

Baudhin, S., & Davis, M. (1972). Scales for the measurement of ethos: Another attempt. *Speech Monographs, 39,* 296–301.

Beane, W. C., & Doty, W. G. (1975). *Myths, rites, and symbols: A Mercia Eliade reader.* New York: Harper Colophon.

Bellah, R. N., Madsen, R., Sullivan, W. M., Swidler, A., & Tipton, S. M. (1985). *Habits of the heart: Individualism and commitment in American life.* New York: Harper & Row.

Berlo, D., Lemmert, J., & Davis, M. (1969). Dimensions for evaluating the acceptability of message sources. *Public Opinion Quarterly, 33,* 563–576.

Cialdini, R. (2001). *Influence: Science and practice* (4th ed.). Needham Heights, MA: Allyn & Bacon.

Edelman, M. (1967). Myths, metaphors and political conformity. *Psychiatry, 30,* 217–228.

Eliade, M. (1971). *The myth of the eternal return: Of cosmos and history.* Princeton, NJ: Princeton University Press.

Hahn, D. (1998). *Political communication: Rhetoric, government, and citizens.* State College, PA: Strata.

Hofstadter, R. (1963). *Anti-intellectualism in America.* New York: Knopf.

Hofstadter, R. (1967). *The paranoid style in American politics and other essays.* New York: Vintage Books.

Hovland, C., Janis, I., & Kelley, H. (1953). *Communication and persuasion.* New Haven, CT: Yale University Press.

Kelman, H., & Hovland, C. (1953). Reinstatement of the communicator: Delayed measurement of opinion changes. *Journal of Abnormal and Social Psychology, 48,* 327–335.

Kosicki, G. M. (2002). The media priming effect: News media and considerations affecting political judgments. In J. P. Dillard & M. Pfau (Eds.), *The persuasion handbook: Developments in theory and practice* (pp. 63–82). Thousand Oaks, CA: Sage.

Parenti, M. (1994). *Land of idols: Political mythology in America.* New York: St. Martin's Press.

Reich, R. (1987). *Tales of a new America.* New York: Times Books.

Santos, M. (1961). *These were the Sioux.* New York: Dell.

Steele, E. D., & Redding, W. C. (1962). The American value system: Premises for persuasion. *Western Speech, 26,* 83–91.

Tocqueville, A. de. (1965). *Democracy in America.* New York: Mentor.

Chapter 10

Andersen, P. A. (1985). Nonverbal immediacy in interpersonal communication. In A. W. Seligman & S. Feldstein (Eds.), *Multichannel integrations of nonverbal behavior* (pp. 1–36). Hillsdale NJ: Erlbaum.

Andersen, P. A. (1999). *Nonverbal communication: Forms and functions.* Mountain View, CA: Mayfield.

Burgoon, J., Bufler, D., & Woodall, W. (1996). *Nonverbal communication: The unspoken dialog* (2nd ed.). New York: McGraw Hill.

Burgoon, J. K., Dunbar, N. E., & Segrin, C. (2002). Nonverbal influences. In J. P. Dillard & M. Pfau (Eds.) *The persuasion handbook: Developments in theory and practice* (pp. 445–473). Thousand Oaks, CA: Sage.

Ekman, P. (1999). A few can catch a liar. *Psychological Science, 10,* 3.

Ekman, P. (2004). *Emotions revealed.* New York: Times Books.

Ekman, P., & Friesen, W. V. (1975). *Unmasking the face: A guide to recognizing emotions from facial expression.* Englewood Cliffs, NJ: Prentice-Hall.

Ellyson, S., Dovidio, J., & Fehr, B. J. (1984). Visual behavior and dominance in men and women. In C. Mayo & N. Henley (Eds.), *Gender and nonverbal behavior.* New York: Springer-Verlag.

Fornoff, S. (2005). Money talks, so builders listen to the experts. *The San Francisco Chronicle.* June 4, 2005.

Fromme, D., Jaynes, W., Taylor, D., Hanhold, E., Daniell, J., Rountree, R., & Fromme, M. (1989). Nonverbal behavior and attitude toward touch. *Journal of Nonverbal Behavior, 13,* 3–13.

Giles, H., Coupland, N., & Coupland, J. (1991). Accommodation theory: Communication, context, and consequence. In H. Giles, J. Coupland, & N. Coupland (Eds.), *Contexts of accommodation: Developments in applied sociolinguistics* (pp. 1–68). Cambridge: Cambridge University Press.

Goffman, E. (1959). *The presentation of self in everyday life*. New York: Doubleday.

Guerrero, L., DeVito, J., & Hecht, M. (1999). *The nonverbal communication reader: Classic and contemporary readings*. Mt. Prospect, IL: Waveland Press.

Hall, E. T. (1959). *The silent language*. Garden City, NY: Doubleday.

Hall, J. A. (1984). *Nonverbal sexual differences: Communication accuracy and expressive style*. Baltimore, MD: Johns Hopkins University Press.

Knapp, M. L., & Comendena, M. E. (1985). Telling it like it isn't: A review of theory and research on deceptive communication. *Human Communication Research*, *5*, 270–285.

Knapp, M. L., & Hall, J. (2002). *Nonverbal communication in human interaction* (5th ed.). Belmont, CA: Wadsworth.

Kotulak, R. (1985). Researchers decipher a powerful "language." *Chicago Tribune*, April 7, sec. 6.

Leathers, D. (1986). *Successful nonverbal communication: Principles and applications*. New York: Macmillan.

Major, B. (1984). Gender patterns in touching behavior. In C. Mayo & N. Henley (Eds.), *Gender and nonverbal behavior*. New York: Springer-Verlag.

Mehrabian, A. (1971). *Silent messages*. Belmont, CA: Wadsworth.

Murray, J. (1989). *The power of dress*. Minneapolis, MN: Semiotics.

Orban, D. K. (1999). The integrative nature of argument and non-verbal communication in different communication contexts. Unpublished paper delivered to Midwest Basic Course Directors Conference, Feb. 4–6.

Packard, V. (1964). *The hidden persuaders*. New York: Pocket Books.

Porter, N., & Geis, F. (1984). Women and nonverbal leadership cues: When seeing is not believing. In C. Mayo & N. Henley (Eds.), *Gender and nonverbal behavior*. New York: Springer-Verlag.

Scheflen, A. (1973). *Communicational structure: Analysis of a psychotherapy session*. Bloomington: Indiana University Press.

Siennicki, J. (2000). Gender Differences in Nonverbal Communication. www.colostate.edu/Depts/Speech/recs/theory20.

Umiker-Sebeok, J. (1984). The seven ages of women: A view from American magazine advertisements. In C. Mayo & N. Henley (Eds.), *Gender and nonverbal behavior*. New York: Springer-Verlag.

Chapter 11

Ahuja, B. (2005). *Buzz marketing: Honest deception*. www.commercialfreechildhood.org/articles/4thsummit/ahuja.

Bales, R. F. (1970). *Personality and interpersonal behavior*. New York: Holt, Rinehart & Winston.

Binder, L. (1971). *Crisis and sequence in political development*. Princeton, NJ: Princeton University Press.

Borchers, T. A. (2005). *Persuasion in the media age* (2nd ed.). Boston: McGraw-Hill.

Bormann, E. G. (1985). *The force of fantasy*. Carbondale and Edwardsville: Southern Illinois University Press.

Bowers, J. W., Ochs, D. J., & Jensen, R. J. (1993). *The rhetoric of agitation and control*. Prospect Heights, IL: Waveland Press.

Cragan, J. F., & Shields, D. C. (1994). *Applied communication research: A dramatistic approach*. Annandale, VA: Speech Communication Association and Creskill, NJ: Hampton Press.

Cragan, J. F., & Shields, D. C. (1995). *Symbolic theories in applied communication research: Bormann, Burke, and Fisher*. Cresskill, NJ: Hampton Press.

Denton, R., & Woodward, D. (1998). *Political communication in America* (3rd ed.). Westport, CT: Praeger.

Faucheux, R. (1998). Strategies that win! *Campaigns and Elections*, Jan., pp. 24–32.

Fortini-Campbell, K. (1992). *The consumer insight book*. Chicago: Copy Workshop.

Garcia, G. (2005). *American mainstream: How the multicultural consumer is transforming American business*. New York: Harper Collins/Rayo.

Lavidge, R. J., & Steiner, G. A. (1961). A model for predictive measurements of advertising effectiveness. *Journal of Marketing*, *24*, 59–62.

Metter, B. (1990). Advertising in the age of spin. *Advertising Age*, Sept. 17, p. 36.

Morrissey, B. (2005). Mitsubishi issues web "Thrill ride challenge." *Adweek*, June 8, 2005.

National Public Radio. (1999). *All things considered*, April 2.

Rogers, E. (1962). *The diffusion of innovation*. New York: Free Press.

Schultz, D. E., & Barnes, B. (1999). *Strategic advertising campaigns* (4th ed.). Lincolnwood, IL: N.T.C. Business Books.

Schwartz, T. (1973). *The responsive chord*. New York: Anchor/Doubleday.

Stewart, C. J., Smith, C. A., & Denton, R. E., Jr. (2001). *Persuasion and social movements* (4th ed.). Prospect Heights, IL: Waveland Press.

Trent, J. S., & Friedenberg, R. V. (2000). *Political campaign communication* (4th ed.). New York and London: Praeger.

Trout, J. (1995). *The new positioning: The latest on the world's # 1 business strategy*. New York: McGraw Hill.

Trout, J. & Ries, A. (1986). *Positioning: The battle for your mind*. New York: Harper & Row.

Valdivia, A. N. (1997). The secret of my desire: Gender, class, and sexuality in lingerie catalogs. In K. T. Frith (Ed.), *Undressing the ad: Reading culture in advertising*. New York: Peter Lang.

Chapter 12

Cantola, S. J., Syme, G. I., & Campbell, N. A. (1985). Creating conflict to conserve energy. *Psychology Today*, Feb., p. 14.

Carnegie, D. (1952). *How to win friends and influence people*. New York: Simon & Schuster.

Cialdini, R. (2001). *Influence: Science and practice*. Boston: Allyn & Bacon.

German, K. Gronbeck, B, Ehninger, D., & Monroe, A. (2004). *Principles of public speaking*. New York: Allyn & Bacon.

Howell, W. S., & Bormann, E. G. (1988). *The process of presentational speaking*. New York: Harper & Row.

Molloy, J. T. (1977). *The dress for success book*. Chicago: Reardon & Walsh.

Monroe, A., Ehninger, D., & Gronbeck, B. (1982). *Principles and types of speech communication*. Chicago: Scott, Foresman.

Rank, H. (1982). *The pitch*. Park Forest, IL: Counter Propaganda Press.

Russell, J. T., & Lane, W. R. (2005). *Kleppner's advertising procedure* (16th ed.). Upper Saddle River, NJ: Prentice-Hall.

Scheflen, A. E. (1964). The significance of posture in communication systems. *Psychiatry*, 27, 316–331.

Schwartz, T. (1973). *The responsive chord*. Garden City, NY: Anchor.

Selby, P. (1902). *Lincoln's life story and speeches*. Chicago: Thompson & Thomas.

Simons, H. (2001). *Persuasion in society*. Thousand Oaks, CA: Sage.

Woods, M. (1993). Toothbrush tips for wellness. *Chicago Tribune*, Sept. 12, sec. 5, p. 3.

Chapter 13

Blumler, J. (1979). The role of theory in uses and gratifications studies. *Communicationo Studies*, 6, pp. 9–34.

Boorstin, D. (1961). *The image: A guide to pseudo-events in America*. New York: Harper & Row.

Brand, S. (1987). *The media lab: Inventing the future at M.I.T*. New York: Viking Penguin Books.

Chicago Tribune. (2005). Time to explode the Internet? July 4, 2005, editorial page.

Cirino, R. (1971). *Don't blame the people*. Los Angeles: Diversity.

Gumpert, G., & Drucker, S. J. (2002). From locomotion to telecommunication, or paths of safety, streets of gore. In L. Strate, R. Jacobson, & S. J. Gibson (Eds.), *Communication in cyberspace: Social interaction in an electronic environment* (2nd ed.). Cresskill, NJ: Hampton Press.

Hall Jamieson, K., & Kohrs-Campbell, K. (1996). *The interplay of influence* (4th ed.). Belmont, CA: Wadsworth.

Kaiser Family Foundation. (1999). *Kids and media at the new millennium*. Menlo Park, CA: Author.

Kaplan, D., Wingert, P., & Chideya, F. (1993). Dumber than we thought. *Newsweek*, Sept. 20, pp. 44–45.

Larson, C. U. (2002). Dramatism and virtual reality: Implications and predictions. In L. Strate,

R. Jacobson, & S. J. Gibson (Eds.), *Communication and cyberspace: Social interaction in an electronic environment* (2nd ed.). Cresskill, NJ: Hampton Press.

Lederer, R. (1991). *The miracle of language.* New York: Pocket Books.

Levin, D. (1998). *Remote control childhood?* Washington, DC: National Association for the Education of Young Children.

Madigan, C. M. (1993). Going with the flow. *Chicago Tribune Magazine,* May 2, pp. 14–26.

Matusow, B. (1983). *The evening stars: The making of a network news anchor.* New York: Ballantine Books.

McCombs, M., & Shaw, D. (1972). The agenda setting function of the media. *Public Opinion Quarterly, 36,* 176–187.

McLuhan, M. (1963). *Understanding media: The extensions of man.* New York: Signet.

Meyrowitz, J. (1985). *No sense of place: The impact of electronic media on social behavior.* New York: Oxford University Press.

Ong, W. S. (1967). *The presence of the word.* New Haven, CT: Yale University Press.

Ong, W. S. (1977). *Interfaces of the word.* Ithaca, NY: Cornell University Press.

Ong, W. S. (1982). *Orality and literacy: The technologizing of the word.* London: Metheun.

Postman, N. (1996). Cyberspace, schmyberspace. In L. Strate, R. Jacobson, & S. J. Gibson (Eds.), *Communication and cyberspace: Social interaction in an electronic environment.* Cresskill, NJ: Hampton Press.

Powers, R. (1978). *The newscasters: The news business as show business.* New York: St. Martin's Press.

Ramhoff, R. (1990). Bart's not as bad as he seems: Simpsons as positive as other family. *Rockford Register Star,* Oct. 18, sec. 2, p. 1.

Rubin, A. (2002). The uses and gratifications perspective of media effects. In J. Bryant & D. Zillman (Eds.), *Media effects: Advances in theory and research.* Mahwah, NJ: Erlbaum.

Schwartz, T. (1973). *The responsive chord.* Garden City, NY: Anchor/Doubleday.

Theall, D. (2002). *The Virtual McLuhan.* Toronto: McGill-Queens University Press.

Victory, V. B. (1988). Pocket veto. *Advertising Age,* April 25, p. 20.

Zettl, H. (1996). Back to Plato's cave: Virtual reality. In L. Strate, R. Jacobson, & S. J. Gibson (Eds.), *Communication and cyberspace: Social interaction in an electronic environment.* Cresskill, NJ: Hampton Press.

Chapter 14

Ajmone, T. (2004). *The Age of Subliminal Communication.* www.subliminal-message.info/age_of_subliminal_communication/html.

Alexander, A., & Hanson, J. (2003). *Taking sides: Clashing views on controversial issues in mass media and society.* Burr Ridge, IL: McGraw-Hill/Dushkin.

Amft, J. (2004). Psychographics: A Primer. www.psychographics.net.

Baker, R. (1997). The squeeze. *Columbia Journalism Review,* Sept.–Oct.

Becker, H., & Glanzer, N. (1978). *Subliminal communication: Advances in audiovisual engineering applications. Proceedings of the 1978 Institute of Electronical and Electronics Engineers: Region 3.* Atlanta: Institute of Electronical and Electronics Engineers.

Berger, A. (2000). *Ads, fads, and consumer culture: Advertising's impact on American character and society.* Lanham, MD: Rowan & Littlefield.

Borchers, T. (2002). *Persuasion in the media age.* Burr Ridge, IL: McGraw-Hill.

Chaffee, J. (1998). How advertising informs to our benefit. *Consumers' Research,* April.

Chicago Tribune (2005). Time to explode the Internet? July 12, p. 12.

Cuneo, A. (2002). Creative execs stress the importance of the Internet. Accessed Nov. 13, 2002, at www.adage.com using QuickFind Id: AAO20F.

Diamond, E., & Bates, S. (1984). *The spot: The rise of political advertising on television.* Cambridge, MA: M.I.T. Press.

Dollas, C. (1986). Butterball turkeys: An examination of advertising theory and practice. Unpublished starred paper, Department of Journalism, Northern Illinois University, De Kalb.

Engel, J., Blackwell, D., & Miniard, P. (1993). *Consumer behavior.* Chicago: Dryden.

Espejo, E., & Romano, C. (2005). Children and media policy brief. *Children Now,* Spring, pp. 1–8.

Gallonoy, T. (1970). *Down the tube: Or making television commercials is such a dog-eat-dog business, it's no wonder they're called spots.* Chicago: Regenery.

Global marketers spend $71 billion. (2002). *Advertising Age*, Nov. 11, pp. 1–18.

Goodkin, O., & Phillips, M. (1983). The subconscious taken captive. *Southern California Law Review, 54*, 1077–1140.

Happy 65th birthday to 5,500 Americans—daily. (1988). *Chicago Tribune*, April 20, sec. 8, p. 10.

Hogan, K. (2005) Covert subliminal persuasion: 7 facts that will change the way you influence forever. *The Science of Influence Library*. Eagan MN: Network 3000 Publishing, Forthcoming.

Honomichl, J. (1984). *Marketing research people: Their behind-the-scenes-stories*. Chicago: Crain Books.

Key, W. B. (1973). *Subliminal seduction: Ad media's manipulation of a not so innocent America*. New York: Signet.

Lander, A. (1981). In through the out door. *OMNI*, Feb., p. 45.

Larson, C. (2001). *Persuasion: Reception and responsibility* (9th ed.). Belmont, CA: Wadsworth Publishing Company.

Mitchell, A. (1983). *Nine American lifestyles: Who we are and where we are going*. New York: Macmillan.

National Public Radio. (2006). *All things considered.* January 3.

O' Guinn, T., Allen, C., & Semenik, R. (2006). *Advertising and integrated brand promotion*. Mason, OH: Thomson-Southwestern.

O'Toole, J. (1985). *The trouble with advertising*. New York: Times Books/Random House.

Parente, M. (2004). *Advertising Campaign Strategy* (4th ed.). Mason, OH: Thomson-Southwestern.

Phillips, M., & Goodkin, O. (1983). The subconscious taken captive: A social, ethical, and legal analysis of subliminal communication technology. *Southern California Law Review, 54*, 1077–1140.

Postman, N. (1987). *Amusing ourselves to death: Public discourse in the age of show business*. New York: Penguin Books.

Rank, H. (1991). *The pitch*. Park Forest, IL: Counter Propaganda Press.

Reis, A. (1996). *Focus: The future of your company depends on it*. New York: Harper Collins.

Ries, A., & Trout, J. (1986). *Positioning: The battle for your mind*. New York: McGraw-Hill.

Rogers, S. (1992). How a publicity blitz created the myth of subliminal advertising. *Public Relations Quarterly*, Winter, pp. 12–18.

Rothschild, M. (1987). *Advertising: From fundamentals to strategies*. Lexington, MA: Health.

Schudson, M. (1984). *Advertising, the uneasy persuasion: Its dubious impact on American society*. New York: Basic Books.

Schwartz, T. (1973). *The responsive chord*. New York: Anchor Doubleday.

Segmentation and targeting. (2004). At www. kellog.northwestern.edu/sterntha/htm/module2/1. Evanston, IL: Kellog School of Business.

Storch, C. (1988). Humble grocery cart now a video ad vehicle. *Chicago Tribune*, May 1, Tempo sec., pp. 1, 5.

Subliminals used to fight smoking. (1987). *De Kalb Daily Chronicle*, Nov. 18.

Thompson, S. (2002). Frito-Lay reports Doritos online ad success. Accessed Nov. 18, 2002, at www. adage.com using QuickFind Id: AAO21A.

Trout, J. (1995). *The new positioning: The latest on the world's # 1 business strategy*. New York: McGraw Hill.

Valdivia, A. H. (1997). The secret of my desire: Gender, class, and sexuality in lingerie catalogs. In K. T. Frith (Ed.), *Undressing the ad: Reading culture in advertising*. New York: Peter Lang.

Vestergaard, T., & Schroeder, K. (1985). *The language of advertising*. London: Basil Blackwell.

Weiss, M. J. (1989). *The clustering of America: A vivid portrait of the nation's 40 neighborhood types —Their values, lifestyles, and eccentricities*. New York: Harper & Row.

Wentz, L., & Cuneo, A. (2002). Double-digit Hispanic ad growth continues. Accessed Sept. 16, 2002, at www.adage.com using QuickFind Id: AAN95S.

Williamson, J. (1977). *Decoding advertising: Meaning and ideology in advertising*. London: Marion Boyers.

Winkelman, P. (2004). *Emotion and consciousness*. Eagan, MN: Network 3000 Publishing, Forthcoming.

Wrighter, C. (1972). *I can sell you anything*. New York: Ballantine Books.

Epilogue

Hart, R. P. (1999). Teaching the undergraduate persuasion course: Why? In A. Vangelesti, A. Daly, & G. Friedrich (Eds.), *Teaching communication: Theory, research, and methods* (2nd ed.). Hillsdale, NJ: Erlbaum.

Index